Standard Catalog of U.S.

MILITARY VEHICLES

★ ★ ★ ★ ★ ★ ★ ★ ★ ★ ★ ★ ★ ★ **1940-1965**

by Thomas Berndt

Published by

**krause
publications**

700 East State St., Iola, WI 54990-0001

**Library of Congress Catalog Number: 92-72123
ISBN: 0-87341-223-0
Printed in the United States of America**

ACKNOWLEDGEMENTS

I would like to thank the following individuals for their friendship, hospitality, and generous sharing of their expertise over the last 20 years. Their love of the military vehicle hobby has made a great deal of this book possible.

Tommy Hunt	Don Smith
Jack Tomlin	Ralph Doubek
Arliss Gandy	Dave Butler
Thomas Phair	Lee Atchison
Roy Hamilton	Jon Bircheff
Reg Hodgson	Chet Krause
Jim Fitzgerald	Mark Dodd
George Rabuse	Jacques Littlefield
Fred Ropkey	Joe Hudak
Dennis Spence	Bob Anderson
Stan Poole	Tony Roca
Brian Asbury	David Wright
Paul Chilek	Royce Anderson
James Welty	Shirley Laird
Bill Barker	Duane Johnston
Louis Larson	Lou Bircheff
Carl Tong	Chuck Barnett
George Hilton	Frank Donnelly
Dana Zwang	

I would also like to thank all the other authors who have written books on this subject, which I have read over the years. The people who let me photograph their vehicles and collections deserve special credit as well. Thanks and gratitude go to all the individuals and businesses that let me look at their yards and salvage collections behind sheds or out in the back row. Thank you to all.

CONTENTS

INTRODUCTION

This book covers vehicles from 1940 to 1965, with the majority of coverage on World War II vehicles. My goal was to introduce the military vehicle hobby to automotive collectors and restorers in the United States and other countries around the world. It is truly an international hobby.

I have personally owned many of these vehicles, some from almost every group or type. They are often misunderstood. I felt it was time to clarify many things, and I hope this guide will do that. It is a fun and very affordable hobby.

This book is an excellent reference guide, providing information needed to identify military vehicles. It has been a fascinating task to compile all this information. I have been involved in the hobby for 20 years, and it never ceases to amaze me. Treasures are constantly being found. The hobby of collecting military vehicles is basically an automotive interest with restorations being done to the same standards as collectible automobiles.

Collecting, parts sourcing, buying, selling, and restoring military vehicles follow the same principles as the collector car hobby. Shows, rallies and swap meets are held by local and national organizations all over the United States on a year-round basis. However, there are some differences that should be explained.

Military vehicles can often be in worse condition than cars because they were often used for commercial purposes. Consequently, they were always modified or changed in some way. Most World War II vehicles were never built after 1943. Our production facilities were so vast that most needs were met by then.

Another difference is demilitarization. The government usually cut or dismembered tanks, half-tracks, armored cars, scout cars -- really almost anything with armor -- or some type of gun mount was incapacitated from its original form. This could mean many things. Gun mounts and armor were literally cut with a torch. Large guns were cut off or welded shut to the point of none-use. Often, the rear bodies on armored vehicles were cut off or cut down, sometimes completely cut to pieces. The process varied from base to base. The people who performed the work had different interpretations of how it was to be done.

Tens of thousands of vehicles were left overseas. Very few were brought back to the United States because they were literally not worth the freight. Many were given to other governments as foreign aid. The majority of the vehicles seen in collectors' hands in the United States were the ones left here during the war.

Several areas are covered in the book. First, it serves as an identification source. Often, high speed tractors are mistaken as tanks. They are completely different from each other. I've even heard people refer to Dodge trucks as jeeps. The photos will help identification immensely. Vehicles can look similar, but in reality be completely different.

Second, physical characteristics are listed in this book. This enables a purchaser to see what logistics are needed to move and or store vehicles. Mechanical and technical specifications are provided for parts sourcing and book access. This can aid hobbyists in their search to find people who can help them locate parts. It is not uncommon to find people who have even worked on the actual vehicles.

Third, I've provided values according to six different states of condition. However, the six different condition grades in this book have different explanations than in Krause Publications' other Standard Catalog series. The prices are based on actual sales by collectors and dealers.

I have tried to put information in this book for all types of people: beginners; people who have a vehicle and know very little about it; collectors; experienced restorers. It can be a handy reference guide for anyone.

* * *

Two additional items should be mentioned. First, there was a great deal of standardization in U.S. military vehicles. This greatly helped our vehicle manufacturers with the war effort. Speed and quantity of production were essential. This made many of the models hard to write about at times.

Second, the accessories on the vehicles -- spare parts, weapons, ammunition, personal stowage, and countless other items added to or carried on the vehicles -- are a hobby in themselves. Vehicles in no. 1 or 2 condition have most or all of their basic issue items. These accessories add a tremendous amount of character and value to the vehicles. But the basic restored vehicle must first be appreciated. It's very easy to put several accessories on a mediocre unit and call it restored. A restored unit must encompass all aspects of the vehicle: mechanical, body and all the other areas of the vehicles.

There are approximately 254 million people in the United States. Many have or have had military vehicles or have wanted one. Tens of thousands of these vehicles have been sold to the public. A definitive work such as this should help dispel many of the myths and misunderstandings of the wonderful old vehicles that played such a great role in keeping our country free.

Tremendous respect is due to people who designed them and helped in their construction, and to the veterans who fought with them. This book will give beginners, collectors, restorers and dealers a great opportunity to share their interests with each other.

CONDITION CODES

Military trucks and vehicles were functional, utilitarian and designed for rugged off-road use, usually under the most strenuous conditions. All-wheel drive or all-terrain vehicles produced before World War II were never made in large quantities, were never sold at low prices to the public, and were not available in large quantities as their counterparts were after World War II. The reason for this was because the vehicles used during World War II had to be designed and built quickly for specific jobs. The production facilities in the United States were quite capable of this fast-paced schedule, and many vehicles were supplied to the military by the end of 1943, a year-and-a-half before the end of the war.

After their military duties were over, large numbers of vehicles were released to the public and consumed very quickly. Before these vehicles could be sold, however, the U.S. Armed Forces were required to demilitarize armored vehicles by cutting or damaging the armor so it could not be used. This also included weapons. At the very least, gun mounts were removed or torched beyond repair.

Once sold, these vehicles were often modified by the people who bought them. In many instances, the purchaser would take off the rear body or armor and install whatever type of equipment was needed for the vehicle to perform civilian work. Many of the vehicle's original parts were discarded. And they were just simply "used up."

M series vehicles — designed in the early 1950s and 1960s — were much more sophisticated and had a longer service life than their predecessors, but even these vehicles suffered the same fate as the World War II units. As a result, vehicles in original condition are very valuable. The most challenging aspect of the military vehicle hobby is to find a completely original vehicle.

1) Excellent

A completely restored vehicle, done to current professional standards in every area, with all factory equipment, basic accessories and canvas; or an original vehicle with all components operating and appearing as new. Not driven.

2) Fine

Well restored or combination of superior restoration and excellent original. An extremely well maintained original showing minimal wear. A restored vehicle in excellent condition, used for regular transportation or pleasure. Having all factory equipment, basic accessories and canvas. Driven little; parades or shows only.

3) Very Good

Completely operable original or older restoration showing wear, or amateur restoration. All presentable and serviceable inside and out. Also well-done restoration and good operable components, or partly restored vehicle with all parts to complete and/or valuable NOS items. Armored vehicles being uncut with correct demilitarized weapons and mounts. Driven regularly.

4) Good

A driveable vehicle needing no or only minor work to be functional. A deteriorated restoration. All components may need restoration, but mostly usable as is. Good running condition with all basic body or armor parts and mechanical components. Some usable accessories or canvas. Uncut armor.

5) Restorable

Needs complete restoration of body, chassis, interior, etc. May or may not run. Complete vehicle with possible minor parts missing, but is restorable under normal circumstances. A clean restorable running chassis with rear body or armor missing or damaged. Repairable armored vehicle with possible damaged armor. No accessories or canvas.

6) Salvage

Poor condition with major body, chassis or armor damage or missing parts from use, weather or demilitarization. Usable major components for rebuilding or restoration. Heavily damaged, modified, demilitarized or cut armored vehicles. Beyond restoration under normal conditions.

THIN-SKINNED VEHICLES

Trucks

M274A1 4X4 half-ton Mechanical Mule by Willys. (Jon Bircheff, Fontana, California)

Model M274: — The M274 "mechanical mule" vehicle was a small half-ton platform truck. This lightweight utility unit was used by the infantry for transporting personnel, ammunition, weapons, and general cargo over all types of terrain. It was air transportable and had a very low silhouette. Very slow speeds were used to keep pace with the troops it accompanied. The M274 through M274A4 had magnesium platforms and wheels. The M274A5 had aluminum wheels and platform.

A four-wheel drive power train, made up of steel axle housings and a small tubular frame, was bolted to the bottom of the platform. There was no suspension and shock was absorbed by the large low pressure tires. Aluminum shims were used between the steel parts and magnesium or aluminum parts. The flat opposed four-cylinder air-cooled gasoline engine was at the rear of the unit.

With driving controls at the front, a single adjustable seat was provided for the driver and could be removed and stowed under the right side of the vehicle when necessary. Early models had side rails that were bolted to the platform, later ones had removable side rails. These were used for tying down cargo. Hand holds were provided in later models for loading and unloading the vehicles when shipped. Steering controls could be swung off to the side, and the operator could walk alongside the unit and control it. The vehicle could carry about as much as it weighed, approximately 1,000 pounds. A litter kit was available for carrying wounded personnel. Provisions were built into all the models for mounting a

106mm recoiless rifle, ammunition racks, barrel travel lock, gun tripod and stowage box.

These vehicles had no electrical or lighting system. Starting the engine was accomplished by pulling a rope at the front, which engaged the recoil starter. In later years, the M274A5 did have electric starter kits and capacitive discharge ignitions. An hour meter was on the engine, so service and maintenance could be recorded.

The fuel tank was located on the left side. Engine guards were used and varied from model to model. Two- or four-wheel steering was used. A manual pedal-operated single drum brake was mounted on the front differential.

The vehicle could be operated with one front wheel missing if cargo was shifted in the rear to retain balance. The transmission was directly attached to the rear differential housing, along with the engine and clutch. The M274 had dual mufflers, oil bath air cleaner, solid cargo rails and no mesh under the driver's feet. The ends of the axle housings had drop gears or planetary drives, which were increased in size for reinforcement in later model units.

Model M274A1: — This was the same basic vehicle as the M274. The four-cylinder engine was retained, and an improved brake system was used. Cargo rails were removable, hand holds were added, the hour meter location was moved, and the engine guard was modified. There were engine improvements also.

M274A5 4X4 half-ton Mechanical Mule by Brunswick Corporation. (James Welty, Ohio Military Museum Inc., Fairborn, Ohio)

Model M274A2: — This model had the same characteristics as the previous ones. In addition, the drop gear housings were increased in size, and the transmission had some minor bearing and spring changes. The engine guard was the same as the M274A5.

Model M274A3: — These were converted M274s. The steering gear was updated, and an improved brake system was installed. They were converted to the two-cylinder engine with a different engine guard, and the publications bag on the back of the seat was eliminated.

Model M274A4: — These also were converted units, using the M274A1 trucks. The four-cylinder engine was exchanged for the two-cylinder model. Larger drop gear housings were added. An improved transmission was installed.

Model M274A5: — This was a new model built with even more changes. The platform was all aluminum with aluminum wheels. Two-wheel steering was the only one used. Terra tires with extended fenders were added when needed. A TOW missile kit was designed. Only four identification plates were used on the side of the platform. Electric starter, alternator, and capacitive discharge ignition were also available.

I.D. Data: — The serial number was located on the identification data plate on the side of the platform, just above the left front wheel.

Model No.	Body Type	Weight	GVW	Prod. Total
M274	Platform	900	2075	2452
M274A1	Platform	900	2075	1905
M274A2	Platform	900	2075	3609
M274A3	Platform	900	2075	—
M274A4	Platform	900	2075	—
M274A5	Platform	900	2075	3274

Front view of M274A5 Mechanical Mule. (James Welty, Ohio Military Museum Inc., Fairborn, Ohio)

Engine: — Willys A053, M274, A053-1, M274A1. Four-cylinder, horizontally opposed, air-cooled, OHV, four-cycle. Cast iron block, aluminum heads cylinders. Displacement: 53 cubic inches. Bore and stroke: 2.75x2.25 inches. Compression ratio: 6.5:1. Brake horsepower: 17 at 3200 rpm. Three main bearings. Carburetor: military design.

Continental A042, two-cylinder, horizontally opposed, air cooled, OHV, four-cycle. Cast iron block, aluminum heads and cylinders. Displacement: 42 cubic inches. Bore and stroke: 3.00 x 3.00 inches. Compression ratio: 6.8:1. Brake horsepower: 13 at 3,000 rpm. Two main bearings. Mechanical valve lifters. Carburetor: military design.

Rear view of M274A5 Mechanical Mule. (James Welty, Ohio Military Museum Inc., Fairborn, Ohio)

Chassis and Body: — Wheelbase: 57 inches. Overall length: 119 inches. Height: 49 inches. Width: 49 inches. Tread: center to center, 40.5 inches. Tires: 7.50 x 10 4-ply military non-directional.

Technical: — Manual transmission, synchromesh. Speeds: 3F/1R. Two-speed-transfer case. Single dry disc clutch. Solid suspension. Military design banjo differentials with planetary final drives. Gear ratio: 4.11:1. Mechanical brakes. Manual two- or four- speed steering. Early models had no electrical system, late models had the 24-volt electrical system. Top speed: 25 mph. Fuel capacity: Eight gallons. Cruising range: 108 miles.

Standard Accessories: — Hand and vehicle tools, spare parts, tow bar, lug wrench, manuals, hand crank.

Historical: — Designed and built by Willys, M274. Kaiser Jeep, M274A1. Bowen McLaughlin, M274A2. The U.S. Army rebuilt M274s and M274A1s into the M274A3 and M274A4. Baifield Company, Brunswick Corporation and Automatic Sprinkler Corporation built the M274A5. Built from the late 1950s to the early 1970s.

PRICE

Model	6	5	4	3	2	1
M274	500	1000	1500	2500	3500	5000
M274A1	500	1000	1500	2500	3500	5000
M274A2	750	1250	1750	2800	4000	5500
M274A3	750	1250	1750	2800	4000	5500
M274A4	750	1250	1750	2800	4000	5500
M274A5	750	1250	1750	2800	4000	5500

1941 Bantam BRC jeep.

Model BRC: — The BRC was Bantam's prototype for the government's research and development program in 1940-'41.

This vehicle was completely different from the Willys MA and the Ford GP. The body of the BRC was the only one of the three prototypes that really used extensive flat sheet metal for its construction. The rear corners of the body were square whereas the other vehicles' corners were rounded. The only curves on the BRC were the cowl and the front fenders.

The earlier bodies in the order had corrugated steel floors; later units had smooth steel used on the bottom side with hat channel reinforcements. The windshield frame was made of square steel tubing, and the grille used round steel bar stock for the vertical pieces. The headlights actually sat down in the front fenders in a recess provided for them. Each entry area by the front seats had a distinct curve to it, and the top lip of the body had a rounded metal lip around it. The rear of the body had a center panel welded in it. The rear spare tire carrier was made of flat plate with bolts through small tubes holding onto the body. Foot rests were welded to the floor of the body, just behind the front seats.

The small stowage compartments in the rear corners of the body had a smaller lid, and the release button lock was on the top panel near the lid. A lockable tool compartment was under the passenger seat. The fire extinguisher was fastened to the seat frame on the front passenger's side. The front inner wheel wells had louvers cut into them. The windshield stop brackets were used as a mount for the rearview mirror and a place for the safety strap to be fastened to.

The brake and clutch pedals were round and covered with rubber pads. The dimmer switch was mounted directly under the steering column on the floor. The seats were made of angle steel on the bottom and sheet metal on the back rest. Removable cushions were provided for them. The transfer case shift levers were mounted on the left side of the transmission shift tower. The accelerator pedal was a very small round metal unit and almost looked like a starter pedal on later military trucks. The rear seat had a wooden back and bottom under the cushions. The bottom could also fold up when needed.

Oval civilian gauges were used on the instrument panel, common only to the Bantam unit. The chassis was also interesting and unique. The frame was an inverted U-shaped steel channel, sometimes referred to as

hat channel, with a flat plate welded to the bottom, thus closing it for increased strength. The rear bumperettes were smaller than later military vehicles and had a small octagon plate riveted to them. The rear pintle hitch had a protrusion on the bottom half that came out a little farther than the top half.

The leaf springs were tapered like an automobile's. The front and rear differentials were offset to the driver's side of the vehicle. A honeycombed radiator was used. All three prototypes used Spicer axles, but the Bantam's brakes were slightly different. Tubular hydraulic shock absorbers were mounted vertically in front and angled in the rear. Combat wheels were not used on the prototype vehicles, and the Bantam's wheels were a little narrower than the other trucks. The skid plate under the transmission had four strips of steel fastened to two cross members, one of which was the transmission mount. The engine was a Continental automotive unit, L-head in design, and used a disposable oil filter that was mounted on the fire wall.

A few four-wheel steer units were built experimentally, possibly 30 to 50 vehicles. These had a much larger steering wheel and a different rear axle assembly with steering knuckles. But it did not interchange with the front axle. Shock absorber mounts were modified, and a different steering sector was used. The rear of the frame was changed to allow for the movement of the rear wheels when turning. These vehicles are incredibly rare, but a few are in collectors' hands.

I.D. Data: — The serial number was located on the identification data plate on the instrument panel; none on the frame.

Model No.	Body Type	Weight	GVW	Prod. Total
BRC	Personnel	2100	2600	2642

Engine: — Continental BY 4112; four-cylinder, in-line, L-head, four-cycle. Cast iron block and head. Displacement: 112 cubic inches. Bore and Stroke: 3-3/16 x 3-1/2 inches. Compression ratio: 6.83:1. Brake horsepower: 45 at 3500 rpm. Three main bearings. Mechanical valve lifters. Carburetor: Stromberg BXV downdraft.

Chassis: — Wheelbase: 79.5 inches. Overall length: 126 inches. Width: 54 inches. Height: 72 inches. Tread center to center front: 47.5 inches. Tires: 5.50 x 16 6-ply military non-directional.

Left rear view of Bantam BRC jeep.

Driver's compartment of Bantam BRC jeep.

Seats in Bantam BRC jeep.

Technical: — Manual synchromesh transmission. Speeds: 3F/1R. Two-speed transfer case. Single dry disc clutch. Semi-elliptic tapered leaf spring suspension front and rear. Spicer Model 40 front and rear differentials with hypoid gears. Gear ratio: 4.88:1. Hydraulic brakes. Manual steering. Top speed: 55 mph. Fuel capacity: 10 gallons. Cruising range: 165 miles.

Standard Accessories: — Hand, vehicle tools; tire chains, jack, lug wrench, fire extinguisher; canvas top with bows, small side curtains on entry areas.

Historical: — The BRC was built by the Bantam Car Company of Butler, Pennsylvania in 1941. It is an extremely rare vehicle, completely different from the Willys MA or Ford GP.

	PRICE					
Model No.	6	5	4	3	2	1
BRC	3000	8000	12,000	19,000	23,000	28,000

Left rear view of Ford GP jeep.

Model Ford GP: The GP was Ford Motor Company's entry in the U.S. Government's quest for a small quarter-ton four-wheel-drive vehicle. GP stood for "general purpose" and is thought to be the origination of the word "jeep."

The Ford GP was a completely different vehicle from the Bantam model. Although the goal was to use existing automotive parts, many modifications had to be made. Eventually, the production models of the GPW used hardly any car parts.

The grille was quite different from the Bantam's. The headlights were actually behind the grille and under the hood, which was made of flat stock. Small early-design blackout lights were directly beneath the headlights. The hood latches protruded through the fenders and latched the hood in place.

The Ford body was much smoother in appearance than those of its competitors. Extensive use of rounded openings and curves in the sheet metal made it more appealing to the eye. The Bantam was made from almost all flat sheet metal. Ford's stamping facilities were much more sophisticated. The windshield frame on the GP was made of round tubular steel. Most of the spot-welded body parts were stamped. A rounded lip went around the top of the body with a hat channel-type metal reinforcement just below it and on the inside. A small rearview mirror for the driver slid into the bottom tube of the windshield frame.

The one-piece rear body panel had the Ford name stamped in script in the lower left corner. A stamped one-piece spare tire carrier was on the right upper corner of the rear panel. The rear inside corners of the body had small stowage compartments built into them. A button release was located on the side of the wheelwell just below the lid. The lid had ribbing stamped in it, with the appearance of an "A."

The all-metal rear seat folded up and down when needed. Tubular steel footrests were mounted on the floor just behind the front seats. The tube was bent on the outside ends near the wheelwells. Both ends were threaded for bolts. One end was bolted to the wheelwell, and the other was bolted to a bracket on the floor panel.

The gas tank was under the driver's seat, and the seat cushion had to be

1941 Ford GP jeep.

removed to fill the tank. Windshield hold-downs were mounted on the hood. The body mounts on the frame had springs on them for twisting when offroad. Bar stock grab handles were on the side of the body. This truck had a conventional C channel frame, rather than the boxed hat channel one used on the Bantam.

Mechanically, the GP had many interesting items as well. The radiator had a lower opening in the front, and it curved around to the back where the lower hose could be attached. The radiator was a fin and tube type rather than the honeycomb type used in the Bantam. The GP's engine was from a Ford tractor and sat offset to the right in the frame. The battery was in front of the driver's side of the engine compartment. The ignition coil was on the fire wall, and the voltage regulator was under the instrument panel. A push-button starter was used. The steering sector

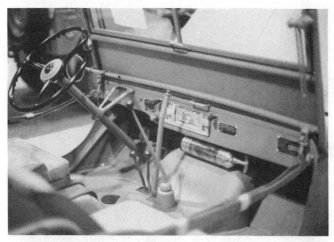

Interior of Ford GP jeep.

Seats in Ford GP jeep.

was mounted on the outside of the frame rail, and the differentials were offset to the driver's side of the vehicle. The foot pedals were round and covered with rubber pads. A tall rectangular accelerator pedal was used. The oil filter was mounted on the engine with a gauge unit in the top of it.

A modified Model A transmission, with a skid plate under the oil pan and transfer case, was fitted to the vehicle. Leaf spring suspension was used front and rear with the ends of the spring leaves sheared rather than tapered like the Bantam. Model A knee action-type shocks were fitted as well. The engine used a different distributor and fuel intake system than the tractor. The engine was also recessed into the fire wall. All parts on the engine were identified with a GP somewhere on them.

Transfer case and emergency brake levers were located on the left side of the transmission shift lever. The GP and Bantam used the same pintle hitches, but the GP used solid disc wheels. The seats had small sides near the hip area, a round lip or bead around the edge, and three horizontal ribs stamped in the top of the backrest.

I.D. Data: The serial number was located on the top of the frame rails near the bottom corners of the radiator and on the instrument panel.

Model No.	Body Type	Weight	GVW	Prod. Total
GP	Personnel	2100	2800	3700

Engine: Ford GP, four-cylinder, in-line, L-head, four-cycle. Cast iron head and block. Displacement: 119 cubic inches. Bore and Stroke: 3-3/16 x 3-3/4 inches. Compression ratio: 6.9:1. Brake horsepower: 45 at 3600 rpm. Three main bearings. Mechanical valve lifters. Carburetor: Holley GP-9510.

Chassis: Wheelbase: 80 inches. Overall length: 129 inches. Width: 62 inches. Height: 71 inches. Tread center to center front: 47.5 inches. Tires: 5.50 or 6.00 x 16 four-ply non-directional.

Technical: Manual nonsynchromesh transmission. Speeds: 3F/1R. Two-speed transfer case. Single dry disc clutch. Semi-elliptic leaf spring suspension front and rear. Spicer hypoid gear differentials. Gear ratio: 4.88:1. Hydraulic brakes. Manual steering. Top speed: 55 mph. Fuel capacity: 10 gallons. Cruising range: 165 miles.

Standard Accessories: Hand, vehicle tools; tire chains, jack, lug wrench; fire extinguisher; canvas top with bows, small side curtains on the side openings.

Historical: Built by Ford Motor Company in Dearborn, Michigan in 1941. Extremely rare vehicle. A completely different vehicle compared to the Bantam BRC or the Willys MA.

Model	6	5	4	3	2	1
GP	3000	8000	12,000	19,000	23,000	28,000

1945 Willys MB jeep.

Model MB/GPW: — The Willys MB and Ford GPW were the original production models of the famous jeep. Production began in late 1941 to early 1942, and proceeded with many small variations in appearance and function until mid-1945 when the war was ending.

After the three prototypes were built in 1941 — the Bantam BRC, Ford GP and Willys MA — Willys was chosen as the prime contractor, and Ford was asked by the government to help produce the vehicle shortly after. No license fees were paid to Willys.

Although there were differences between the two vehicles, all parts could be interchanged. Most of the major assemblies and large components, such as the frame, body, axles, transfer case and transmission, steering gear, electrical system, etc., were built by outside manufacturers. Willys and Ford built items for the vehicles, but the majority of these were castings as each company had its own foundry.

The original vehicle's design and requirements were provided by the

Left rear view of Willys MB jeep.

U.S. military in the very late 1930s. Bantam Car Company built a small quantity of test vehicles, and they were so well received that Bantam, Willys, and Ford were asked to produce 1500 per company. A very small quantity of Bantams and Fords were built with four-wheel steering. The Willys may have been also, but none have been found to date. The Bantam was called the BRC, the Ford was called the GP, and the Willys was called the MA. Willys was chosen because of its stronger engine.

The jeep was really a simple vehicle mechanically. It was designed to carry four personnel or a small payload cross-country, and pull a quarter-ton trailer when required. The uses and modifications by using units were endless, as it was such a handy vehicle. The engine was a four-cylinder, in-line, L-head with a three-speed transmission and two-speed transfer case. Solid tube front and rear automotive axles were used with conventional leaf spring suspension. The bodies were sheet steel panels that were stamped and welded together on a steel channel frame.

Right rear view of Willys MB jeep.

Front view of Willys MB jeep.

Rear bench seat in Willys MB jeep.

Standard military items were fitted to the jeep: blackout drive and marker lights, rear pintle hitch, bumperettes, gas can with carrier, pioneer tools on the left and right sides of the body, and trailer electrical receptacle at the rear. The windshield was a folding unit with manual or vacuum wipers, or a combination of both. The unit was provided with a canvas top, side curtains and doors mounted on collapsible bows. Military style gauges and canvas-covered seats were standard.

Early production vehicles had some distinct differences. Both Willys and Ford had their names embossed in the left rear panel of the body. The grille was also noticeably different. It was built of flat steel stock with the headlights behind. These were called "slat grilles" on the Willys. The most visible difference between the Willys and the Ford was the front cross member. The Willys had a round or tubular one, and the Ford had an inverted U-shaped one, often referred to as a "hat channel" type. Small stowage compartments with lids were located at the rear of the

body at the back corners of the wheel housings. The Willys lid was smooth with a round-shaped recess for the release button. The Ford lid had ribbing stamped in it with a rectangular recess for the release button.

Many small components on the Ford vehicle had the script F stamped onto or cast into them. The most noticeable was the F on the pintle hitch. The early trucks with names embossed in the rear had no spare gas cans or carriers. The floor in the Ford body had different reinforcements in the pan, but the bodies were interchangeable. Both vehicles had a torque stabilizing spring under the left front spring, but there were differences in the clamps holding the spring leaves together in each vehicle. The upper shock brackets on the Ford were slightly different also.

Later production vehicles had a rifle rack on the windshield. Early trucks had plastic steering wheels; later ones had metal spoke steering wheels. Some early Fords used a much narrower neck and cap on the gas tank. The engine of each vehicle had a pad cast in it which contained the

Driver's compartment of Willys MB jeep.

World War II Willys MB jeep.

World War II Willys MB jeep. (Chet Krause, Iola, Wisconsin)

Rear view of Willys MB jeep. (Chet Krause, Iola, Wisconsin)

World War II Ford GPW with machine gun mount.

World War II Ford GPW jeep.

engine serial number. Willys had an MB stamped into the pad, and Ford had GPW stamped into the pad. Some vehicles were equipped with a capstan-type winch in front with power off the transfer case. Jeeps carrying radio equipment were fitted with 12-volt electrical systems. Radio suppression was incorporated into the vehicles with filters, condensors, shielding and suppressors.

I.D. Data: — The serial numbers on these vehicles was located on the data plate on the instrument panel, and on the top of the front frame rails near the radiator on the GPW, and on a small plate inside the front left frame rail just behind the front bumper on the MB.

Model No.	Body Type	Weight	GVW	Prod. Total
MB	Personnel	2450	3650	350,349
GPW	Personnel	2450	3650	281,578

Engine: — Willys MB or Ford GPW. Four-cylinder, in-line, L-head, four-cycle. Cast iron block and bead. Displacement: 134 cubic inches. Bore and Stroke: 3.125 x 4. 375 inches. Compression ratio: 6.48:1. Brake horsepower: 54 at 4000 rpm. Three main bearings. Mechanical valve lifters.

Chassis: — Wheelbase: 80 inches. Overall length: 132 inches. Width: 62 inches. Height: 72 inches. Tread center to center front: 49 inches. Tires 6.00 x 16 6-ply military non-directional.

Technical: — Manual synchromesh transmission. Speeds: 3F/1R. Two-speed transfer case. Single dry disc clutch. Semi-elliptic leaf spring suspension front and rear. Dana model 25 front axle and model 23 rear axle with hypoid gear differentials. Gear ratio: 4.88:1. Hydraulic brakes. Manual steering. Six- or 12-volt electrical system, 12-volt on radio-equipped models. Top speed: 65 mph. Fuel capacity: 15 gallons. Cruising range: 285 miles.

Standard Accessories: — Hand, vehicle, pioneer tools; spare parts, fire extinguisher; canvas top, side curtains, doors, top bows; spare gas can with carrier.

Historical: — Built by Willys and Ford from late 1941 to mid-1945 in several facilities. They were the most numerous and the most popular vehicle built in World War II. These vehicles are the most practical to restore and own. They are owned by more collectors than any other model military vehicle. They are also fun to drive. Most jeeps that went overseas during the war were never sent back to the United States. The auto manufacturers didn't want the market flooded with these vehicles as they would compete with the retooling for civilian car production.

Model No.	PRICE					
	6	5	4	3	2	1
MB	500	3000	7000	10,000	12,000	15,000
GPW	500	3000	7000	10,000	12,000	15,000

World War II Ford GPW jeep. (George Rabuse, St. Paul, Minnesota)

World War II half-ton Ford GPW jeep with trailer. (George Hilton, North Bangor, New York)

Early 1950s M38 jeep with winch.

Model M38: — This was the second model in the quarter-ton truck or jeep series of vehicles begun in World War II. This particular model used some of the World War II jeep components but had many new improvements.

The M38 was basically a militarized version of the CJ3A civilian model. It was a taller, heavier truck with larger tires and one-piece wheels rather than the combat wheels of the World War II jeeps. A heavier frame and springs with improved shackles were used. The same basic model 25 Dana front axle was used with slight improvements. However, the rear axle was upgraded to the heavier Model 44 series. A heavier front bumper was used with new lifting shackles front and rear. The rear of the body had a tailgate that was bolted in place rather than one that folded down. The spare tire and gas can with holder were mounted on the rear body panel, in the same basic positions as the World War II models. Pintle hitch, bumperettes, and electrical receptacle for the trailer were new models.

The wiring and electrical system were completely different. The new waterproof sealed ignition system that was standardized on all the M series vehicles in the early 1950s was used on this model also. A new exhaust system was built and designed for use with the fording kits now available. The muffler was now at the rear of the body, with the exhaust coming out the right rear corner, rather than on the side. The fuel system, gas tank, air intake system, cooling system and radiator were all new. All new M series controls and instruments appeared on the instrument panel. A much more detailed and thorough set of data plates were also on the instrument panel. The windshield was still the folding type of one-piece glass with a vent under the center of the glass. Many small body changes were made; headlight guards, grab handles, reflectors, hood blocks for the windshield, larger headlights, and an all new grille were just a few. The passenger seat folded forward, and the rear seat folded up when needed.

A toolbox was located under the passenger seat, and heavier, thicker seat cushions were used. The emergency brake was moved to the left side of the instrument panel. The batteries were moved to two different locations. One was under the hood, the other was in the cowl just below the windshield. The voltage regulator was mounted on the frame. A fender-mounted slave receptacle was located on the right side of the hood.

The engine was still the same basic unit as the World War II jeep but with improved carburetion and ignition. A new clutch, heavier transmission, and some updates were made in the transfer case. From a distance, the vehicle looked very similar to the World War II models but was really quite a different unit with many changes in the components. The foot starter was still retained. The vehicle was built for the Marine Corps. It had limited slip differentials and a reinforced cross member in the rear. The fuel pump had a vacuum pump added to the top of it. A front-mounted Ramsey 5,000-pound winch was used on some models. This was driven off a power take-off on the transfer case. When a command radio set was installed on the right rear fender of the vehicle, a 100-amp generator kit was used with an air-cooled rectifier. Gasoline-fired heater kits were used on these vehicles.

The pioneer tools were mounted on the opposite side as the World War II jeeps. The toolboxes in the rear wheel housings were eliminated; top bows and top rear body items were all different. There was no interchangeability with the MB models. A larger fuel tank was used with an outside filler neck. This truck was quite a bit heavier than the World War II jeeps.

I.D. Data: — The serial number was located on the identification data plate on the instrument panel.

Model No.	Body Type	Weight	GVW	Prod. Total
M38	Personnel	2750	3950	45,473

Early 1950s Willys M38 jeep.

Engine: — Willys MC. Four-cylinder, in-line, L head, four-cycle. Cast iron block and head. Displacement: 134 cubic inches. Bore and Stroke: 3.125 X 4.375 inches. Compression ratio: 6.48:1. Brake horsepower: 60 at 4000 rpm. Three main bearings. Mechanical valve lifters. Carburetor: Carter YS637S.

Chassis: — Wheelbase: 80 inches. Overall length: 133 inches. Width: 62 inches. Height: 74 inches. Tread center to center front: 49 inches. Tires 7.00 x 16 6 ply military non-directional.

Technical: — Manual synchromesh transmission. Speeds: 3F/1R. Two-speed transfer case. Single dry disc clutch. Semi-elliptic leaf spring suspension front and rear. Dana model 25 front axle, model 44 rear axle, hypoid gear differentials. Gear ratio: 5.38:1. Hydraulic brakes. Manual steering. Twenty-four-volt electrical system. Top speed: 55 mph. Fuel capacity: 13 gallons. Cruising range: 225 miles.

Standard Accessories: Hand, vehicle, pioneer tools; spare parts, fire extinguisher; canvas top, side curtains, bows, doors; gas can and carrier.

Historical: — The M38 was designed from the CJ3A civilian model and built by Willys from 1950 to 1952. It represented the lowest number of jeeps built. Additional units were built for export in 1953 and 1955.

			PRICE			
Model No.	6	5	4	3	2	1
M38	1000	3000	5000	7000	10,000	13,000

Early 1950s Willys M38 jeep with M100 trailer. (George Rabuse, St. Paul, Minnesota)

Early 1950s M38A1 jeep. (Duane Johnston, Del Ray Beach, Florida)

Model M38A1: — The M38A1 was a four-wheel drive quarter-ton truck made by Willys and Kaiser Jeep International.

This was the last actual jeep made by Willys and Kaiser International for the U.S. military. Other models built later were produced by different companies with different components, resulting in completely different vehicles, but incorrectly still referred to as jeeps.

This vehicle was designed in 1952 and was so well liked that three years later it was introduced to the civilian market as the CJ5, which endured for many years as a very successful vehicle. The body was much more refined than the previous flat-fendered jeep vehicles, with smoother lines and the distinctly curved front fenders. The mission of the M38A1 was the same as its predecessors and successors — to carry four personnel or a light payload of cargo, as well as tow a quarter-ton trailer when required.

The mechanical components were the same basic ones used in the earlier M38, however, this vehicle was much heavier because of the larger body. The engine was the improved F-head design with the intake valves in the head and the exhaust valves in the block. Carburetion and ignition were the sealed waterproof design. The T-90 transmission, transfer case and axles were the same units used in the M38 and CJ3A trucks. The batteries were mounted in the cowl in front of the passenger. The frame was the simple, rugged channel style with front and rear leaf spring suspension. Solid tubular Dana axles were used; model 25 in front, model 44 in the rear — the same units as in the M38.

Improved metal frame canvas-covered seats were used. The windshield was changed to a two-piece glass unit that folded down. Collapsible top bows, canvas top with side curtains and doors were available. The glove compartment was relocated to the driver's side of the instrument panel.

Front fender-mounted blackout drive lights, front and rear towing and lifting shackles, rear pintle hitch and bumperettes, and trailer electrical receptacle were all standard. The gas tank was again under the seat, and the radio antenna was located on the left rear corner of the body. Spare gas can, carrier, and spare tire with carrier were on the back panel of the body. The removable center-mounted instrument panel was the standard M series unit. Most data plates were mounted on the right side of the instrument panel.

A series of footman loops for fastening the side curtains were located around the top of the body. The hood was a stamped one-piece unit. A left rearview mirror was provided. The lower half of the rear seat could fold up when needed. Most of the floor panels had ribbing stamped in them.

The mechanical fuel pump also had a vacuum pump on it. The muffler was under the rear of the body near the pintle hitch. The round indentation in the right front of the body was a slave receptacle. A Ramsey 5,000-pound winch was provided for some vehicles. Fording kits were available, also. The M38A1 did not have a tailgate in the rear of the body. Radios were mounted on the right rear wheel housing. Some vehicles with command radio sets used an optional 100-amp generator with a rectifier mounted in front of the radiator.

A hand fuel primer was used to cold start the engine. The M38A1 had a larger carburetor than the M38, had a different radiator and emergency brake, and had heavier steering components. Gasoline fired or hot water heater kits were available. Defroster ducts were built into the windshield frame of the M38A1. The Marine Corps vehicles had limited slip differentials.

One model that carried a 106mm recoiless rifle was built. The gun was mounted on the frame and the top of the rear fender wells. Ammunition racks were bolted to the floor. The windshield was a split design for the gun tube to rest in when traveling.

I.D. Data: — The serial number was located on the identification data plate on the instrument panel.

Model No.	Body Type	Weight	GVW	Prod. Total
M38A1	Personnel	2665	3865	80,290

Engine: — Willys Hurricane F4-134. Four-cylinder, in-line, F-head, four-cycle. Cast iron block and head. Displacement: 134 cubic inches. Bore and Stroke: 3.125 x 4.375 inches. Compression ratio: 7.4:1. Brake horsepower: 72 at 4000 rpm. Three main bearings. Mechanical valve lifters. Carburetor: Carter YS950S.

Left side view of M38A1 jeep. (Duane Johnston, Del Ray Beach, Florida)

Driver's compartment of M38A1 jeep. (Duane Johnston, Del Ray Beach, Florida)

Mid-1950s M38A1 jeep with recoiless rifle mount.

Early 1950s Willys M38A1 jeep with recoiless rifle ammunition racks and split windshield.

Early 1950s M38A1 jeep with PTO-driven welder. (Royce Anderson, Ponderosa Ranch, Incline Village, Nevada)

Chassis: — Wheelbase: 81 inches. Overall length: 139 inches. Width: 61 inches. Height: 74 inches. Tread center to center front: 49 inches. Tires: 7.00 x 16 6-ply military non-directional.

Technical: — Manual synchromesh transmission. Speeds: 3F/1R. Two-speed transfer case. Single dry disc clutch. Semi-elliptic leaf spring suspension front and rear. Dana Spicer hypoid gear axles; model 25 front, model 44 rear. Gear ratio: 5.38:1. Hydraulic brakes. Manual steering. Twenty-four-volt electrical system. Top speed: 55 mph. Fuel capacity: 17 gallons. Cruising range: 280 miles.

Standard Accessories: — Canvas top and bows; side curtains, doors; hand, vehicle, pioneer tools; spare parts, fire extinguisher; gas can.

Historical: — Designed in 1952 for military use, the M38A1 was built by Willys and Kaiser Jeep International from 1952 to 1957 for the U.S. military forces and from 1958 to 1971 for export to foreign services. It was so well liked it was released as the civilian model CJ5 in 1955. It was the last of the actual jeeps used and built for the U.S. services.

			PRICE			
Model No.	6	5	4	3	2	1
M38A1	500	2000	5000	7000	9000	10,000

Early 1960s M151 4X4 quarter-ton truck.

Model M151A1: — The M151 series of vehicles was the last family of tactical quarter-ton trucks used by the U.S. military. Everything manufactured since has been slightly larger in actual size and higher in payload capacity, usually half- to 1-1/4-ton cargo capacity.

The M151 was a small four-wheel drive truck. It was often referred to as a jeep but in reality was not. It was a completely different unit built by a completely different manufacturer. The truck was a military ordnance design that was built by Ford first, and later by AM General, to the military's specifications. Its design was quite a departure from its predecessors. The all-steel body was a unitized unit with the tube frame, front fenders and bumper built as one. The hood, grille, radiator and windshield were the removable sheet metals components.

The M151's power train layout was similiar to its predecessors, but many major changes were made. The engine was a military design with all new accessories on it. None of the parts were interchangeable with the earlier jeeps. It was a four-cylinder, cast iron, liquid-cooled engine with conventional carburetion and ignition, a manual transmission with clutch and a four-speed with a single-speed transfer case attached to it. The front axle was engaged by a small lever on the driver's side of the transmission tunnel. Conventional propeller shafts went to the front and rear differentials; these were bolted solidly to the unitized body.

This vehicle used independent front and rear suspension. A single A-frame with coil spring was used on all four wheel positions. This provided a very comfortable ride and excellent off-road performance, but was very unstable when taking fast turns. The suspension pivoted on the inside near the differential, but there was no pivot out near the drum. The pivot points were redesigned in the M151A2.

The front of the vehicle was noticeably different: The grille was horizontal rather than vertical on the jeep units. The lighting system was the standardized military system with blackout drive and marker lights. The fuel tank was under the driver's seat.

The entire vehicle had a lower silhouette and was slightly wider than the

M151A1 4X4 quarter-ton truck. (David Wright, Shrewsbury, Massachusetts)

earlier jeep models. The vehicle seated four personnel. A folding canvas top and bow assembly was provided. Double batteries were located under the passenger's seat. The seats folded forward for easier entrance to the rear seat area. Pintle hitch, bumperettes, gas can and carrier, and spare tire were on the rear body panel. Pioneer tools were carried on both sides of the body. Radio racks were mounted on the right rear

Mid-1960s M151A1 quarter-ton truck with hard top.

Rear view of M151A1 quarter-ton truck with hard top.

Mid-1960s M151A2 quarter-ton utility truck by Ford. (James Welty, Ohio Military Museum Inc., Fairborn, Ohio)

fender, with the antenna on the left rear of the body. The power plant compartment was very easy to service and featured many quick disconnect items, thus making engine switches very easy and fast. These trucks were not equipped with winches.

Several kits were provided for the vehicle: winterization kit for -65 degree F. temperatures, aluminum hard top enclosure kit, hot water heater kit, deep water fording kit, and 100-amp generator kit for improved radio performance.

Model M151A2: — This was the same basic vehicle as the M151A1 but had the larger style taillights and turn signals and used different front fenders. The windshield was changed to a one-piece unit. Rear lifting shackles were repositioned to the outside corners of the body. The rear suspension was redesigned with different lower A arms that pivoted from front to rear, rather than from side to side like the M151A1. This helped the truck's stability around corners although it did not eliminate the problem completely.

Model No.	Body Type	Weight	GVW	Prod. Total
M151A1	Personnel	2320	3570	—
M151A2	Personnel	2385	3625	—

I.D. Data: — The serial number was located on the identification data plate on the instrument panel.

Engine: — Military design four-cylinder, in-line, overhead valve, four-cycle. Cast iron block and head. Displacement: 141 cubic inches. Bore and Stroke: 3.875 x 3.00 inches. Compression ratio: 7.5:1. Brake horsepower: 71 at 4000 rpm. Five main bearings. Mechanical valve lifters. Carburetor: Military side draft.

Front view of M151A2 truck. (James Welty, Ohio Military Museum, Inc., Fairborn, Ohio)

Chassis: — Wheelbase: 85 inches. Overall length: 133 inches. Width: 64 inches. Height: 71 inches. Tread center to center front: 53 inches. Tires: 7.00 x 16 4-ply military non-directional.

Technical: — Manual synchromesh transmission. Speeds: 4F/1R. Single-speed transfer case. Single dry disc clutch. Independent coil spring suspension on all four wheels. Military split-case hypoid gear differentials. Gear ratio: 4.86:1. Hydraulic brakes. Manual steering. Twenty-four-volt electrical system. Top speed: 66 mph. Fuel capacity: 17 gallons. Cruising range: 288 miles.

Standard Accessories: — Hand, vehicle, pioneer tools; canvas top, bows, side curtains, doors; gas can, fire extinguisher.

Historical: — The M151A1 was developed from the late 1950s to the early 1960s and then built from 1961 to 1969 by Ford and AM General. This vehicle was the replacement for the M38 and M38A1 jeeps.

PRICE

Model No.	6	5	4	3	2	1
M151A1	500	2000	4000	6000	8000	10,000
M151A2	500	2000	4000	6000	8000	10,000

Rear view of M151A2 truck. (James Welty, Ohio Military Museum, Fairborn, Ohio)

Right side view of M151A2 truck. (James Welty, Ohio Military Museum, Fairborn, Ohio)

M422 "Mighty Mite" quarter-ton truck. (Ralph Doubek, Wild Rose, Wisconsin)

Model M422: — The M422 "Mighty Mite" was a very small quarter-ton four- wheel drive truck built for the U.S. Marine Corps. Its design had many features that were different from other quarter-ton trucks.

The Marine Corps requested many special items, and it got them in this vehicle. The unit was shorter, narrower and lighter than its predecessors. The body as well as the engine were made of aluminum. The engine was a V-4 air-cooled model, eliminating the need for a cooling system. The engine also used twin carburetion. A three-speed transmission with a two-speed transfer case was used.

The frame was unusual because it was made of tubular steel, quite the departure from the conventional steel channel previously used for years. The differentials were bolted solidly to the frame with the inspection covers facing upward. A very unique four-wheel independent suspension was used; it had cantilevered leaf springs that were quarter-elliptic in design. This suspension was mounted on the side of the frame between the front and rear wheels. Large arms went from the frame pivot point to the wheel hubs. The front faced forward, and the rear faced rearward. The quarter-elliptic springs were attached to each arm suspending the body and frame. Gear boxes and differentials were aluminum cased, and inboard brakes were attached to the differentials. Each differential was a limited slip design, greatly improving traction. The steering was exceptionally responsive because the steering sector was mounted ahead of the front wheels and the king pins were centered inside the front hubs. This is called center pivot steering when the center of the front tires were in line with the king pins. This greatly reduces steering effort and shortens the turning radius.

With the combination of the suspension system and a unique center of gravity, which was at the center of diagonal lines drawn from the opposite wheels front to rear, the handling was superb. The vehicle could be driven with one wheel off in the rear.

Batteries were located in the cowl in front of the passenger. The fuel tank was located under the body behind the front seats, and the filler tube was at the right rear corner of the body. The seats were one-piece units, and passengers sat on the rear wheel well housings. The fire extinguisher was mounted on the instrument panel, and a hand pull starter was mounted under the dash just above the driver's right foot. A deep water fording kit with air intake and exhaust pipe extension was available. A gasoline fired heater kit could be fitted to the vehicle. Canvas top, side curtains, bows and doors also could be used when needed.

Model M422A1: — This was the same basic vehicle as the M422, but it had a six-inch longer body and wheelbase.

I.D. Data: — The serial number was located on the identification data plate on the instrument panel.

Model No.	Body Type	Weight	GVW	Prod. Total
M422	Personnel	1700	2700	1250
M422A1	Personnel	1780	2780	2672

Engine: — AMC AV-108-4 V-4 cylinder air-cooled, overhead valve, four-cycle. Aluminum block and heads, steel sleeved. Displacement: 108 cubic inches. Bore and Stroke: 3.25 x 3.25 inches. Compression ratio: 7.5:1. Brake horsepower: 55 at 3600 rpm. Five main bearings. Mechanical valve lifters. Carburetor: Holly R1931A.

Chassis: — Wheelbase: 65 or 71 inches. Overall length: 107 or 113 inches. Width: 61 inches. Height: 60 inches. Tires: 6.00 x 16 4-ply military non-directional. Tread center to center front: 52 inches.

Left front view of M422 "Mighty Mite." (Ralph Doubek, Wild Rose, Wisconsin)

Right rear view of M422 "Mighty Mite." (Ralph Doubek, Wild Rose, Wisconsin)

Technical: — Manual synchromesh transmission. Speeds: 4F/1R. Two-speed transfer case combined with the transmission. Single dry disc clutch. Cantilever leaf spring independent suspension, using quarter-elliptic leaf springs. Military design hypoid gear limited slip differentials. Gear ratio: 5.375:1. Hydraulic sealed brakes. Manual center pivot steering. Twenty-four-volt electrical system. Top speed: 62 mph. Fuel capacity: 13 gallons. Cruising range: 225 miles.

Standard Accessories: — Fire extinguisher with bracket; double screw jack with lug wrench.

Historical: — The M422 was built by American Motors Corporation from January 1960 to January 1963 for the U.S. Marine Corps.

			PRICE			
Model No.	6	5	4	3	2	1
M422	2000	4000	7000	9000	10,000	11,000
M422A1	2000	4000	7000	9000	10,000	11,000

Early 1940s World War II Dodge WC40 closed cab pickup.

Model WC 1, 5, 12, 14, 20, 40, 41: — This WC series closed-cab pickup with the express body was the beginning of the production model half-ton four-wheel drive vehicles built by Dodge during World War II.

The first Dodge production four-wheel drive trucks were built for the Army in 1934; they were 1-1/2 ton models. These were the first trucks built using the rear differential components in the front drive axle. This simplified parts availability and interchangeability greatly. The transfer case was designed so the driven front axle could be disengaged when not needed. Eight different body configurations of the half-ton were built, some with winches. The series was built over a two-year period.

As production contracts were finished, each new group of models was slightly improved and modified. The closed-cab pickups had begun as an earlier VC series truck that used civilian front sheet metal. Several thousand of these were built in 1940. In 1941 the body was redesigned for added strength and ease of manufacture. The hood and grille were changed completely, and the brush guard was eliminated. The grille was made of steel round stock with reinforcements. This allowed it to be sturdy enough to act as radiator protection. The hood on the half-ton opened from the sides and had a very distinct slope upward to the rear towards the cowl. All the other military models built by Dodge after the half-tons had flat hoods on open cab models. This upward slope gave the truck a very unique appearance. The grille was also different because it was curved across the front. Later models had very similar grilles in appearance and construction, but were flat or straight across from left to right.

A small metal plate on each side of the hood had the Dodge name stamped on it. All the half-tons had this emblem. Tow hooks were mounted on the tops of the frame rails, and a narrow steel channel bumper with a center hole for the engine hand crank completed the front of the truck. Small brush guards covered the headlights and blackout drive lights. The half-ton trucks also had a "honeycomb"-type radiator,

World War II Dodge WC40 half-ton closed cab weapons carrier.

World War II Dodge WC12 quarter-ton closed cab weapons carrier.

World War II Dodge WC12 half-ton open cab weapons carrier.

Left rear view of Dodge WC12 weapons carrier.

which again was unique to the vehicle. The later model three-quarter-ton trucks went to the fin and tube radiators.

The engines in the trucks were Dodge's own L-head six-cylinder, which was used in future models as well. The early production half-tons used a 217 cubic inch engine, and later production trucks used the 230 cubic inch model that was installed in the three-quarter-tons and M37s. The engine was built well into the 1960s and was used in civilian power wagon trucks.

The cowl and hard cab were pretty much civilian components with military gauges, wiring, seats and other small changes. The crank-out windshield was retained. Some early trucks had civilian gauges instead of the later round standardized military units. Four-wheel drive controls were floor-mounted on the right side of the shift lever for the transmission. The trucks used running boards, which were mounted between the flat military design fenders; they had Dodge's own diamond shape stampings in them.

The rear body was referred to as the pickup or express box. The front, rear and sides of the box were civilian panels with flat, redesigned fenders. Troop seats, racks and top bows for the canvas cargo tarp were fitted into the stake pockets in the box. Unique reflectors containing round glass balls like marbles were used on the box and tailgate. This box was discontinued on the three-quarter-ton trucks because it was very narrow and had limited storage space. The rear bumperettes were larger than those on other Dodge military trucks. The standard pintle hitch, blackout lights, taillights and electrical trailer receptacle outfitted the rear of the frame.

The truck rode on front and rear leaf spring suspension with double-acting knee-action hydraulic shock absorbers. Dodge's own banjo axles and differentials carried the vehicle. The front axle used Bendix or Rzeppa knuckle joints for turning. Five-hole Budd-type sixteen wheels were used, and some models were fitted with dual rear wheels. The half-ton rims were not combat wheels and had a slightly different offset than the wheels on the future models, but they did interchange. Rim width was a little narrower on the half-ton units. A New Process single-speed transfer case with front axle engagement provided power to both axles. The half-ton models did not have low range in the transfer case. Later, single- and two-speed transfer cases would interchange. A civilian

pickup four-speed was behind the engine. The transmission was built by New Process. A power take-off on the left side of the transmission was used for the winch, which was front mounted.

The frames used in these trucks was almost straight. The larger frame in the three-quarter-ton trucks was double dropped, meaning that the center in between the axles was lowered so the body height could be reduced, making a much lower profile. Additional frame material was included in the winch model frames. Postwar trucks had bolt-on extensions when winches were mounted. The grille was shortened, and the bumper was split into two halves. The spare tire was mounted on the right corner of the box behind the passenger's door. The WC designation did not correspond with the term "weapons carrier." It was a sales symbol given to the truck by the Chrysler Corporation.

Model WC 3, 4, 13, 21, 22: — These trucks were the same basic models as the closed cab units. Mechanically they were identical, and the front sheet metal and rear body were the same. The difference was the cab itself. The cowl or fire wall was the same, but the top was modified for a folding windshield. The instrument layout was more militarized. The floor pan was altered to accept mounting two metal bucket seats with cloth upholstery. There was no cab sheet metal behind the seats. Doors, roof, cab back and windshield pillars were eliminated. The canvas cab was fastened to the top of the windshield and the front top bow and canvas of the cargo compartment.

Model WC 10, 17, 26: — This was the carryall-bodied truck, again with the same power train and front sheet metal. The body of the truck had the appearance of a station wagon and was built from the body of a late 1930s panel truck with windows in the sides. The windshield area, cowl, instrument panel, driving controls and doors were the same as the other trucks. The roof of the cab simply was extended to the rear, with side lines following the doors. The spare tire was carried on the right side, just behind the passenger's door. It was mounted on a large arm. A large indentation about the size of the tire was imprinted in the side of the body; this served as a recess in which the tire sat.

The side doors were almost the same as the closed cab pickup, but these had a square upper rear corner rather than the curved one on the pickup. Two large side windows were installed in the panels just behind the doors; the window next to the door could be rolled down. At the rear was

World War II Dodge WC17 half-ton carryall.

Right rear view of Dodge WC17 carryall.

Rear view of Dodge WC17 carryall.

a two-piece tailgate, the upper half of which had two fixed windows. This tailgate lifted upward with latches for the upright position. The lower half went down to a horizontal position and remained at the level of the floor in the interior. The rear interior floor was made of wooden planks on top of steel cross members. Steel skid strips covered the seams of the floor, similar to pickup bed floors of the period. One or two seats could be used in the rear of the body. The top of the rear body had a fabric roof over a wooden frame. It was a weather-tight area.

Model WC 11, 19, 42: — This was the same basic truck as the carryall but was called a panel truck. The interior was the same as the carryall,

but had no seats or side windows. The rear doors were different: They were side-by-side doors that opened to the left or right. Each door had a stationary window in the top; the handles were in the center.

Model WC 6, 7, 8, 15, 16, 23, 24, 25: — This was the command car. It had a unique body for a combat vehicle. The front sheet metal, cowl, power train, controls and other features were the standardized half-ton components. The body had front and rear bench seats covered in leather. Cutouts in the side panels allowed for entry and exit of passengers or driver. The spare tire was mounted above the running board on the left side next to the driver. This body also had an indentation for the tire.

A large 12-volt battery sat in a metal box on the right running board, and the radio antenna was mounted just above it on the body panel. A large folding tailgate was at the rear with chains on the inside to hold it in place when in the lowered position. Two handles were on the exterior with locks and reflectors. The taillights were on either side. Rear bumperettes, pintle hitch, and trailer electrical connections were standard. The side curtains were stored on the inside of the tailgate.

A map holder and a folding table were located on the back side of the front seat. On the radio-equipped vehicles, a mount for the radios was fastened to the floor and seat. This model was used mostly for high ranking officers with command responsibilities. A collapsible set of tubular steel top bows covered the entire passenger and driver's compartment. When folded, they sat on top of the rear trunk. The command cars were fitted with or without power take-off front-mounted winches. These were Braden 5,000-pound capacity models.

I.D. Data: — The serial number was located on the identification data plate on the glove compartment door, and on the left front frame rail above the left front spring.

Model No.	Body Type	Weight	GVW	Prod. Total
WC 1,5,12,14,20,40,41	Closed Cab	4640	5940	9585
WC 3,4,13,21,22	Open Cab	4440	5740	13,319
WC 10,17,26	Carryall	4850	6150	3717
WC 11,19,42	Panel	4470	5470	462
WC 6,7,8,15,16,23,24,25	Command Car	4975	6275	17,483

World War II Dodge WC19 half-ton panel truck.

Rear view of WC19 panel truck.

World War II Dodge WC23 command car. (Ralph Doubek, Wild Rose, Wisconsin)

Left side view of Dodge WC23 command car. (Ralph Doubek, Wild Rose, Wisconsin)

Rear tailgate of Dodge WC23 command car. (Ralph Doubek, Wild Rose, Wisconsin)

Engine: — Dodge T207 early, T215 late. Six-cylinder, in-line, L-head, four- cycle. Cast iron block and head. Displacement 217 cubic inches early, 230 cubic inches late. Bore and Stroke: 3.25 x 4.375 inches early, 3.25 x 4.625 inches late. Compression ratio: 6.5:1 early, 6.7:1 late. Brake horsepower: 78 at 3200 rpm early, 92 at 3200 rpm late. Four main bearings. Mechanical valve lifters. Carburetor: Carter DTA-1.

Chassis: — Wheelbase: 116 inches. Overall length: 181 to 191 inches. Width: 76 inches. Height: 83 to 89 inches. Tread center to center front: 59-3/8 inches. Tires: 7.50 x 16 military non-directional.

Technical: — Manual sliding gear transmission. Speeds: 4F/1R. Single-speed transfer case. Single dry disc clutch. Leaf spring suspension front and rear. Dodge banjo differentials. Gear ratio: 4.89:1. Hydraulic brakes. Manual steering. Six-volt electrical system. Top speed: 55 mph. Fuel capacity: 25 gallons. Cruising range: 300 miles.

Standard Accessories: — Hand, vehicle, pioneer tools; spare parts, fire extinguisher; canvas cab top, top bows, seats racks, cargo canvas.

Historical: — Designed and built by the Dodge Division of Chrysler Corporation in Mound Park, Michigan from 1941 to 1942.

			PRICE			
Model No.	6	5	4	3	2	1
WC 1,5,12,14,20, 40,41	2500	4000	6000	9000	12,000	15,000
WC 3,4,13,21,22	700	3000	5000	7000	10,000	12,000
WC 10,17,26	1500	4000	7000	9000	12,000	15,000
WC 11,19,42	2500	4000	6000	8000	—	—
WC 6,7,8,15,16,23, 24,25	3500	6000	10,000	15,000	20,000	25,000

World War II WC24 Dodge 4X4 half-ton command car with winch. (David Wright, Wright Museum, Shrewsbury, Massachusetts)

Right rear view of WC24 half-ton command car. (David Wright, Wright Museum, Shrewsbury, Massachusetts)

World War II Dodge WC24 half-ton command car.

World War II Dodge WC51 three-quarter-ton weapons carrier. (Chet Krause, Iola, Wisconsin)

Model WC 51: — The WC 51 was a three-quarter-ton four-wheel drive truck that was Dodge's successor to the earlier half-ton models. Although the half-ton was an excellent truck, it did have some deficiencies. The half-tons were made mostly of lighter civilian pickup components, and a rugged, more durable vehicle was needed with larger payload capacity. The box on the half-tons was quite narrow, limiting cargo space. The tall silhouette was somewhat undesirable as more and more combat was experienced.

With these items in mind, Dodge and the Army redesigned the entire truck. It was the first vehicle Dodge designed from the ground up for the military. The frame on the three-quarter-ton was made much stronger with heavier steel channel, and double dropped for more axle travel and a lower overall silhouette. The winch trucks had longer frame rails in the front. The winch was a Braden 5,000-pound model with the same basic configuration and installation as the half-ton. Most of the mounting components were increased in size.

The body of the three-quarter-ton was all new. The curved grille of the half-ton was dropped, and a simpler flat model made of the same bar stock was used. The radiator was a fin and tube type rather than the honeycomb style on the half-ton. The radiator cap protruded through the top cover just in front of the hood. Small brush guards were used over the headlights and blackout lighting system. The hood opened from the side but was flat on top rather than having the distinct slope of the half-tons. The Dodge nameplate was used on some of the earlier three-quarter-tons. The cowl was completely changed with a much lower profile. The base of the folding windshield was straight rather than curved like the half-ton which followed the shape of the modified civilian cowl it used.

All the three-quarter-ton weapons carriers were open cab trucks that used a canvas cargo tarp with top bows and a canvas cab top that attached to the windshield and the front of the rear tarp. The back of the cab was completely open.

All sheet metal on this truck was new. Running boards were used again with the civilian diamond pattern stamped in them. Front fenders were flat and curved downward to the running boards. The spare tire was carried on the driver's side, so the driver had to exit on the right side or else climb over the tire. The left running board had a dip in it for the tire as well as a cast arm to which the tire was bolted. This heavy steel bracket bolted directly to the frame of the truck.

World War II Dodge WC51 three-quarter-ton. (Ralph Doubek, Wild Rose, Wisconsin)

The rear body was much wider than the half-ton express model. Storage compartments were added in each corner under the troop seats. The troop seats and racks folded up and down, hinging near the top bow sockets. A small panel was at the front of the box, and a corresponding rear panel was used for a tailgate. The floor was made of oak boards with steel skid strips sitting on steel cross members. Some later model boxes used wooden wheel wells rather than all steel. The outside corners of the box were unique, having tie-down hooks that were recessed in a dish-like depression stamped in each corner of the box. The areas in the rear of the box had side reflectors as well as the hooks and were more oval shaped. The pioneer tool rack was bolted to the rear tailgate. Two gas can carriers were mounted on the right running board. The reflectors on the truck were a new one-piece design.

New combat wheels, with a different offset, were fitted to the truck. The lock ring bolted on the wheels and had a bead lock allowing the tire to be run a short distance as a flat.

World War II Dodge WC51 three-quarter-ton weapons carrier with postwar hard top.

World War II Dodge WC52 three-quarter-ton weapons carrier. (Ralph Doubek, Wild Rose, Wisconsin)

The engine was the same unit as in the late half-ton: Dodge's own L-head six-cylinder with improved carburetion. An improved New Process four-speed transmission and transfer case were used and could interchange with the half-tons. Heavier springs and axle housings with all new differentials were designed and installed. The three-quarter-ton truck was geared much lower than the half-ton model. The wheelbases of the vehicles changed. The weapons carriers and command cars were 116 inches in the half-tons and 98 inches in the three-quarter-tons. The carryall was almost the same with 116 inches in the half-tons and 114 inches in the three-quarter-tons. The ambulance was only one inch different at 122 inches for the half-ton and 121 inches for the three-quarter-ton. The width of the axle housings was quite a bit wider and gave a much better stance and stability in off-road conditions.

Model WC 52: — This was the same basic truck as the WC 51 and was equipped with a Braden 5,000-pound front-mounted power take-off driven winch.

Right rear view of Dodge WC56 command car. (David Wright, Wright Museum, Shrewsbury, Massachusetts)

Model WC 56: — This was the three-quarter-ton command car. Its design and function was the same as the half-ton model, but the truck actually had a different body, yet they looked the same. The front sheet metal power train, controls, cowl, wheels, etc. were the same as the other three-quarter-ton trucks. Standardization was an important goal.

The collapsible canvas top and frame assembly fastened to the top of the folding windshield and covered the entire driver's and passenger compartment. The body on this command car had a much lower profile than the half-tons. The cutouts in the sides were much larger and lower than the previous models. The leather-covered front and rear bench seats were built on tubular steel frames. The floor had a full-length rubber floor mat. A map board and compartment were on the back side of the front seat. Radios, when outfitted on a vehicle, sat in this same area but used a metal mount. The rear of the body had a large tailgate with two locking handles for release. The spare tire was carried on the standard cast steel arm on the driver's side. The driver's entry and exit was on the right side.

Body accessories and military equipment were the same as the other three-quarter-tons. The wheelbase was quite a bit shorter than the half-ton truck, reduced down to 98 inches. This made the vehicle more agile. These trucks had quite a bit more ground clearance due to the larger tires. A very large 12-volt battery with a metal cover was carried on the right running board. The increased capacity was for radio use.

Model WC 57: — This was the same truck as the WC 56, but was equipped with the Braden 5,000-pound power take-off driven front-mount winch.

Model WC 53: — The carryall model was a fully enclosed body similar to a station wagon. The body was a carryover from the late 1930s panel truck, but was redesigned to fit the three-quarter-ton chassis. This truck had a different hood than the open cab trucks. It sloped upward to the cowl, but was not quite as steep as the half-ton hood. The same hood was used on the ambulance. The cowl, crank-out windshield and instrument panel were from civilian trucks.

The wagon-type body was of steel construction except for the roof. This was made of a wooden lattice framework covered with a water-resistant

World War II Dodge WC53 three-quarter-ton carryall.

fabric, making a weather-tight enclosure for year-round use. The same principle was used on automobiles of the period. A very large die would have had to be used to stamp out the roof panel; this may have not been available. Nonetheless, this was barely visible from the side of the vehicle. Most carryalls found today have this feature replaced with a steel panel that someone has welded into place.

The rear floor was the familiar wood planks over steel cross members with steel skid strips bolted over the seams. One or two rear seats could be fitted in the rear compartment. The tailgate was in two pieces, one

World War II Dodge WC56 three-quarter-ton command car. (David Wright, Wright Museum, Shrewsbury, Massachusetts)

World War II Dodge WC56 three-quarter-ton command car. (George Hilton, North Bangor, New York)

going up, the other going down, and held in place with chains in a horizontal position. The top half had two fixed windows. Besides the door windows there were two windows in each side of the truck; the one closest to the door window could be rolled down. The chassis was the same as the other three-quarter-ton trucks. Extensive radio suppression equipment was employed in these trucks when they carried communications gear. Filters, resistors, suppressors, wire shielding, ground straps, and special lock washers on body bolts were used.

I.D. Data: — The serial number was located on the identification data plate on the glove compartment door and on the left front frame rail above the left front spring.

Model No.	Body Type	Weight	GVW	Prod.Total
WC 51	Weapons Carrier	5645	7445	123,541
WC 52	Weapons Carrier	5940	7740	59,124
WC 56	Command Car	5375	7175	21,156
WC 57	Command Car	5675	7475	6010
WC 53	Carryall	5750	7550	8400

Engine: — Dodge T214. six-cylinder, in-line, L-head, four-cycle. Cast iron block and head. Displacement: 230 cubic inches. Bore and Stroke: 3.25 x 4.625 inches. Compression ratio: 6.7:1. Brake horsepower: 92 at 3200 rpm. Four main bearings. Mechanical valve lifters. Carburetor: Zenith Model 29.

Chassis: — Wheelbase: 98 inches command car, weapons carrier; 114 inches carryall. Overall length: 166 to 186 inches. Width: 78 inches. Height: 81 to 86 inches. Tread center to center front: 64.75 inches. Tires: 9.00 x 16 8-ply military non-directional.

Technical: — Manual sliding gear transmission. Speeds: 4F/1R. Single-speed transfer case. Single dry disc clutch. Leaf spring suspension front and rear. Dodge banjo hypoid gear differentials. Gear ratio: 5.83:1. Hydraulic brakes. Manual steering. Six-volt electrical system, 12-volt on command cars and carryalls. Top speed: 54 miles per hour. Fuel capacity: 30 gallons. Cruising range: 240 miles.

Standard Accessories: — Hand, vehicle, pioneer tools. Spare parts, fire extinguisher. Canvas cargo and cab tops.

Historical: — Designed and built by Dodge Division of Chrysler Corporation from 1942 to 1945 in Mound Park, Michigan.

PRICE

Model No.	6	5	4	3	2	1
WC 51	1500	3000	6000	9000	12,000	15,000
WC 52	1500	3000	6000	9000	12,000	15,000
WC 56	5000	8000	10,000	15,000	20,000	25,000
WC 57	5000	8000	10,000	15,000	20,000	25,000
WC 53	3000	7000	10,000	15,000	20,000	25,000

Early 1950s Dodge M37 three-quarter-ton cargo truck.

Model M37: — The M37 three-quarter-ton trucks were an updated and improved vehicle, the basis of which was the simple, rugged WC series Dodge trucks of World War II. The body and box were larger and wider, and the all-new design improved personnel and cargo transport capabilities. Three people could sit in the cab, and six to eight could sit in the box. The spare tire was carried in the cargo box.

The same basic power train was used with improvements, such as two-speed transfer case, synchromesh transmission, and sealed electrical and fuel systems. Some basic components were interchangeable with older models. The steering sector was mounted on the outside of the frame, and a double drag link assembly went forward to a pivot and back to the front wheel for easier steering. The cargo box was of all-steel construction.

The truck was built with and without front-mounted PTO driven winches. Cargo capacity was 2,000 pounds. Factory steel hard cabs could be fitted. Fording, radio, and heater kits were available for the truck, which made it a very versatile vehicle used by all branches of service for many years. The vehicle had all the military requirements, such as blackout drive light system, brush guard type grille, and towing shackles front and rear. Rear-mounted pintle hitch was used for towing a one-ton cargo trailer, with appropriate electrical connections for lights. The familiar canvas cab top and folding windshield frame with fold-out windows were used. A slave receptacle was used for additional assistance in starting when needed.

Model M42: — This is the same truck as the M37, but it had a few extra items, and was referred to as a command and reconaissance model. The rear body was used as a command post and had side curtains with nonglare plastic windows. A different rear curtain was used, which went from the top bows all the way down to the bed floor and was split for easier entrance. These could be sealed for blackout use. A map light and folding table were furnished. A step in the tailgate was used for assistance in getting into the truck.

Model M37B1 and M43B1: — These trucks were manufactured in later years and had some minor differences from the M37 and M42. The wire harness for the electrical system had a different type of connector. The

Left rear view of Dodge M37 cargo truck.

transmission was updated with better synchromesh units. The spare tire was carried on a swinging rack mounted on the driver's door hinges. A volt meter, two rear stop lights, and turn signals were added as well. The M43B1 was the ambulance model.

I.D. Data: — The serial number was located on the identification data plate on the instrument panel and on the left front frame rail above the left front spring.

Model No.	Body Type	Weight	GVW	Prod.Total
M37	Cargo	5687	7687	47,404
M37B1	Cargo	5687	7687	43,975
M42	Command	6050	7550	8079

Dodge M37B1 three-quarter-ton with winch. (George Rabuse, St. Paul, Minnesota)

Right front view of Dodge M37B1 cargo truck. (Ralph Doubek, Wild Rose, Wisconsin)

Dodge M37B1 three-quarter-ton cargo truck. (Ralph Doubek, Wild Rose, Wisconsin)

Left rear view of Dodge M37B1 cargo truck. (Ralph Doubek, Wild Rose, Wisconsin)

Engine: — Dodge T245, six-cylinder, inline, L-head, four-cycle. Cast iron block and bead. Displacement: 230 cubic inches. Bore and Stroke: 3.25 x 4.625 inches. Compression ratio: 6.7:1. Brake horsepower: 78 at 3200 rpm. Four main bearings. Mechanical valve lifters. Carburetor Carter ETW-1.

Chassis and Body: — Wheelbase: 112 inches. Overall length: 185 inches. Height: 89.5 inches. Width: 73.5 inches. Tread center to center front: 62 inches. Tires: 9.00 x 16 8-ply military non-directional.

Technical: — Manual sychromesh transmission. Speeds 4F/1R. Two speed transfer case. Single dry disc clutch. Leaf spring suspension front and rear. Dodge hypoid full floating differentials. Gear ratio 5.83:1. Hydraulic brakes. Manual steering. 24-volt electrical system. Top speed: 55 mph. Fuel capacity: 24 gallons. Cruising range: 215 miles.

Standard Accessories: — Hand, vehicle, pioneer tools; spare parts; fire extinguisher; canvas cab top and cargo tarp; gas can.

Historical: — Designed and built by Dodge Division of Chrysler Corporation from 1950 to 1954 (M37, M42, M43), 1958 to 1968 (M37B1, M43BI) at Mound Road, Michigan.

Model No.	6	5	4	3	2	1
			PRICE			
M37	300	1200	2500	4000	6500	9500
M37B1	300	1200	2500	4000	6500	9500
M42	300	1200	2500	4000	6500	9500

Add $500 for winch model.

Early 1960s Dodge R2 crash truck. (Chuck Barnett, Upland, California)

Model R2: — The R2 crash truck was an airport type fire truck using the M37 series 4x4 chassis. The actual chassis model number was the M56.

This vehicle had a reinforced frame, heavier springs, and a 14-inch longer wheelbase. The M-series front sheet metal, cowl and instrument panel were used along with a special body that was constructed for the rear. It was built of aluminum and insulated for winter use with a variety of heater kits available for different climates.

The truck was designed to be used with other fire fighting trucks that would foam a path to crashed aircraft; it was also used to forcibly enter the plane and rescue the personnel, extinguishing small fires with its own extinguishers carried on board as it went along.

The rear body was literally filled with this type of equipment. Cabinets on the right of the truck held 150-foot hose reel for dispensing the unit's 22 gallons of pressurized foam, which was dispensed by a replaceable ni-trogen cylinder. A 150-foot electrical reel with cord was also located here. This was used to run an electric metal-cutting saw and floodlights. Hand tools were carried on the right side as well. The cabinets on the left side held more hand tools along with communication equipment and some of the chemical dispensing items.

A revolving red beacon was located on the top center of the roof. Two floodlights were located on the front roof corners. A gas-fired heater was mounted on one front fender, and a 24-volt siren was on the other front fender. The spare tire was carried in the center rear of the roof and was held down by straps.

The engine had a 60-amp alternator for vehicle use, and a 3.0 KW PTO-driven auxiliary generator was mounted inside the body. The power from the PTO was transferred upward by a chain-drive transfer case. An en-gine governor was used with the auxiliary generator.

The double doors at the rear of the vehicle gave access to the 20-foot aluminum ladder and pike pole stored in the raised part of the roof. Two large fire extinguishers were stored here as well as many more hand tools and equipment. A vehicle-mounted ladder was on the left side of the rear for access to the catwalk on the top left side of the truck. A front-mounted PTO-driven winch with a grapple hook was used to open

Rear view of Dodge R2 crash truck. (Chuck Barnett, Upland, California)

the aircraft. A hydraulic ram, hand pump and kit were also used for rescue when metal needed to be moved.

The front interior and controls were nearly identical to the M37 trucks. A switch panel for electrical equipment was just to the right of the instru-ment panel. The generator control gauges were mounted up and behind the driver's head.

Dodge R2 crash truck.

I.D. Data: — The serial number was located on the identification data plate on the right side of the instrument panel, and on the left front frame rail above the spring.

Model No.	Body Type	Weight	GVW	Prod. Total
R2	Fire	7690	7690	308

Engine: — Dodge T245, six-cylinder, in-line, L-head, four-cycle. Cast iron block and head. Displacement: 230 cubic inches. Bore and Stroke: 3.25 x 4.625 inches. Compression ratio: 6.7:1. Brake horsepower: 78 at 3200 rpm. Four main bearings. Mechanical valve lifters. Carburetor: Carter ETW-1.

Chassis and Body: — Wheelbase: 126 inches. Overall length: 206 inches. Width: 79 inches. Height: 105 inches. Tread center to center front: 62 inches. Tires: 9.00 x 16 8-ply military non-directional.

Technical: — Manual synchromesh transmission. Speeds: 4F/1R. Single dry disc clutch. Two-speed transfer case. Leaf spring suspension, front and rear. Dodge banjo hypoid gear full-floating differentials. Gear ratio: 5.83:1. Hydraulic brakes. Manual steering. Twenty-four-volt electrical system. Top speed: 55 mph. Fuel capacity: 24 gallons. Cruising range: 225 miles.

Standard Accessories: — Chemical agent dispensing system with nitrogen cylinder; fire extinguishers; auxiliary generator; hose and electrical cable reels; metal-cutting saw, floodlights, ram and pump kit, trouble lamp, siren; beacon light, rescue tools and belts, fire axe; ladder and pike pole; electric lanterns, felt pads; pioneer tools, wrecking bar, cable cutter; hand tools, grapple hook on front winch.

Historical: — Built by ACF Brill Motors Company of Philadelphia, Pennsylvania in the early 1960s.

Model	6	5	4	3	2	1
R2	900	1800	3500	5500	8500	—

World War II M-2-4 I.H.C. one-ton cargo truck. (Shirley Laird, North Bend, Oregon)

Model M-2-4: — The M-2-4 truck was a one-ton four-wheel-drive model built for the Navy and Marine Corps. It had many similarities to its Dodge three-quarter-ton counterpart, but being built by International Harvester Corporation, it was a completely different truck.

All were open cab models except for some early models that were equipped without winches and had hard cabs. Almost all trucks had a cargo box on the rear. The open cab and type of narrower box gave the trucks a similar appearance to the early World War II Dodge half-ton models. The rear body was longer and the fenders were mounted on the outside of the box. Top bows, racks, canvas, and troop seats were standard. The spare tire was mounted on the right of the rear body, and a tool box was on the left running board.

The open cab had two bucket seats with no provision for a top or doors. The gas tank was under the seats. The folding windshield was a one-piece unit with vacuum or electric wipers. The hood opened from the side and was unique because the radiator cap protruded through a hole in the right front of the hood and was quite visible above the brush guard. The brush guard was different also, as it was an upright model that bolted to the frame in front of the radiator and was not a grille. Most other trucks had a grille in front of the radiator that was heavy and acted as a brush guard. When this truck was without the brush guard, the radiator was completely exposed.

The truck had Tulsa or Braden front-mounted power take-off driven winches, and the frame was manufactured longer rather than having extensions riveted on the ends. Most vehicles for the Navy and Marine Corps had lifting rings for loading onto ships; this truck had them as well. They were in addition to and located near the towing hooks on the frame ends.

Some early models used civilian instruments and later used the standard round military gauges. Many subtle features of the civilian K model trucks of the period were evident in the design and appearance. The power train was conventional in its layout using International's own six-cylinder gas engine and transmission transfer case assemblies. The axles were Eaton banjo models, and had a lower ratio than those used on other trucks in its class. The five-hole Budd wheels with 9.00 x 16 tires were interchangeable with Dodge trucks. The frame was a simple chan-

nel unit with conventional leaf springs front and rear. Standard wheels with lock rings or combat wheels were used.

I.D. Data: — The serial number was located on the identification data plate on the instrument panel.

Model No.	Body Type	Weight	GVW	Prod. Total
M-2-4	Cargo	5820	8020	9100

Engine: — International Harvester Corporation GRD-233C. Six-cylinder, in-line, L-head, four-cycle. Cast iron head and block. Displacement: 233 cubic inches. Bore and Stroke: 3-5/16 x 4-1/2 inches. Compression ratio: 6.3:1. Brake horsepower: 93 at 3400 rpm. Four main bearings. Mechanical valve lifters. Carburetor: Zenith 63AW-11.

Chassis and Body: — Wheelbase: 125 inches. Overall length: 197 inches. Width: 84.5 inches. Height: 89 inches. Tread center to center: 63.5 inches. Tires: 9.00 x 16 8-ply military non-directional.

Technical: — Manual selective sliding gear transmission. Speeds: 4F/1R. Two-speed transfer case. Single dry disc clutch. Leaf spring suspension front and rear. Eaton spiral bevel banjo differentials. Gear ratio: 4.875:1. Hydraulic brakes. Manual steering. Six- or twelve-volt electrical system. Combat wheels on some units. Top speed: 45 mph. Fuel capacity: 35 gallons. Cruising range: 260 miles.

Standard Accessories: — Hand, vehicle, pioneer tools; spare parts; fire extinguisher; snatch block, jack; canvas cargo top, troop seats, bows and racks.

Historical: — Built by International Harvester Corporation for the U.S. Navy and the Marine Corps from 1942 to 1945.

PRICE

Model No.	6	5	4	3	2	1
M-2-4	1400	2500	3500	4500	6500	—

Right side of I.H.C. M-2-4 Marine Corps cargo truck. (Shirley Laird, North Bend, Oregon)

I.H.C. M-2-4 Marine Corps cargo truck.

Late 1970s Dodge M880 1-1/4-ton cargo truck.

Model M880: — The M880 was a 1-1/4-ton four-wheel-drive cargo truck and was used for all types of general cargo and troop transportation. It was a commercial vehicle used by the military as an alternative for the expensive tactical trucks.

The truck was a simple unit with some minor modifications for military use. The paints used on them were military colors. The standard civilian bench or bucket seats were used. The interior used all of Dodge's standard controls on the instrument panel, foot area, and power train functions as the civilian trucks. No civilian radios were in these trucks.

The lighting systems, front, rear and interior, were standard civilian, and no blackout night driving lights were used. The cargo box and tailgate were civilian issue. A folding top bow assembly with vinyl cover was available for covering the cargo area when needed. In its collapsed form, it was hinged at about the center of the box, and collapsed forward to lie right behind the rear window of the cab. Folding troop seats with racks could be used in the stake pockets of the bed. The rear step bumper was a civilian unit with a pintel hitch for towing military trailers.

Standard civilian Dana axles with front disc and rear drum brakes were power assisted. An on- and off-road radial tire was mounted on standard eight-hole truck wheels. Engine, transmission, and transfer case were also civilian. A Dodge 318-cubic inch commercial V-8, powered by a three-speed automatic transmission, and a full-time transfer case with high and low range powered the truck. The standard electrical system was 12-volt with a 60- or 100-amp 24-volt kit that could be installed for communications equipment use.

In this series of vehicles, slight differences in on-vehicle equipment designated a different model number for some reason. Two different grille and turn signal assemblies were used, an early and a late. Seven auxiliary equipment kits were available. Cargo cover, troop seats, 60- or 100-amp 24-volt generating kit, communications equipment kit, communications shelter, tie down kit, and arctic heating kits. These trucks were basically a W200 Dodge pickup.

Model M881: — Same vehicle as the M880, but had the additional 60-amp 24-volt generator kit.

Late 1970s Dodge M880 1-1/4-ton cargo truck.

Model M882: — Same vehicle as the M880, but had the additional 60-amp 24-volt generator kit and the communications kit.

Model M883: — Same vehicle as the M880, but had the additional 60-amp 24-volt generator kit and the slide in shelter kit.

Model M884: — Same vehicle as the M880, but had the additional 100-amp 24-volt generator kit and the slide in shelter kit with tie downs.

Model M885: — Same vehicle as the M880, but had the slide in shelter kit with tie downs.

Late 1970s Dodge M880 1-1/4-ton crew cab cargo truck.

Late 1970s Dodge M880 1-1/4-ton with ambulance body.

Rear view of M880 with ambulance body.

Model M886: — This vehicle was the ambulance model. The power train front sheet metal, cab and doors were the same as the M880 trucks. The larger body was attached to the rear and top of the cab.

Controls in the cab were the same as the other trucks, with the addition of some switches for the blackout lighting system and warning lights. A spotlight was on the roof along with a power ventilator. A sliding door behind the driver's seat allowed entry to the litter compartment. Litters were loaded from the rear through large double doors. A surgical ceiling light was provided, and a combination folding step and seat was at the rear for an attendant. Five litter patients or six ambulatory wounded could be carried.

The hot water heater was under the left rear bench seat. Blackout curtains were provided for all three windows. A door switch system was used for lights and could be controlled from the cab. The interior layout and function was similar to the M43, M725, and World War II half-ton and three-quarter ton Dodge ambulances. This body was also used for ordnance explosive demolition work.

Model M888: — Same vehicle as the M880, but had a telephone maintenance body on the rear with a roof-mounted spotlight. Two bows supported an aluminum ladder, 24 feet long and in two sections, above the box and cab. A combination double door used the tailgate as the lower half, enclosing the center section of the tool and equipment body.

Model M890: — Same vehicle as the M880, but was a two-wheel-drive model, with no transfer case case or front drive axle. Same engine, transmission and rear end were used. This was intended for mostly highway and secondary road use.

Model M891: — Same vehicle as the M890, but had the additional 60-amp 24-volt generator kit.

Model M892: — Same vehicle as the M890, but had the additional 60-amp 24-volt generator kit and communications kit.

Model M893: — Same vehicle as the M886 ambulance, but was the two-wheel-drive model without the transfer case or driven front axle.

I.D. Data: — The serial number was located on the identification data plate on the center of the instrument panel.

Model No.	Body Type	Weight	GVW	Prod.Total
M880	Cargo	4648	7748	—
M890	Cargo	4217	7317	—
M886	Ambulance	6116	7716	—
M893	Ambulance	5684	7284	—
M888	Maintenance	5168	7748	—

Engine: — Chrysler 318 V-8, OHV, eight-cylinder, four-cycle. Cast iron block and heads. Displacement: 318 cubic inches. Bore and Stroke: 3.91 x 3.31 inches. Compression ratio: 8.6:1. Brake horsepower: 150 at 4000 rpm. Five main bearings. Hydraulic valve lifters. Carburetor: Carter two-barrel.

Body and Chassis: — Wheelbase: 131 inches. Overall length: 219 inches, ambulance 216 inches. Width: 79.5 inches. Height: 71 to 101 inches. Tread center to center front: 65.25 (4x4), 63 inches (4x2). Tires: 9.50R16.5 civilian or all season or traction.

Technical: — Chrysler automatic transmission. Speeds: 3F/1R. Two-speed New Process 203 full-time transfer case. Leaf spring suspension front and rear, front coils on two wheel drive. Dana axles, front and rear. Gear ratio: 4.10:1. Hydraulic power-assisted brakes. Manual steering. 12-volt electrical system with 24-volt kits available. Top speed: 70 mph. Fuel capacity: 20 gallons. Cruising range: 160 miles.

Standard Accessories: — Jack with handle, lug wrench, fire extinguisher.

Historical: — Built by Dodge Division of Chrysler Corporation from 1976-1977 as a temporary replacement for the Gamma Goat, M715, and M37. Replaced by the CUCV 1-1/4-ton Chevrolet trucks in 1980 and the HMVEE.

Model	PRICE					
	6	5	4	3	2	1
M880	300	800	1500	2500	3500	4500
M890	300	600	1200	2000	2800	3200
M886	400	800	1500	2500	3500	4500
M893	400	600	1200	2000	2800	3200
M888	400	700	1100	2000	2500	3500

Mid-1980s Chevy M1008 CUCV 1-1/4-ton cargo truck. (John Bircheff, Fontana, California)

Model M1008: — The M1008 was a 1-1/4-ton four-wheel-drive truck that belongs to the CUCV series, which stands for Commercial Utility Cargo Vehicle. They were ordered and purchased in the mid-1980s for general transportation of troops and material in tactical and non-tactical situations.

The trucks could be used off-road, but did not have the waterproof fuel and electrical systems that the genuine tactical trucks did. Fording kits were not available for them either. They were basically a four-wheel-drive Chevrolet cargo truck that had quite a number of heavy-duty factory components added to them as well as additional items required by the military. The body was not altered a great deal, but a brush guard was attached to the front bumper with towing clevises on each side. These had a heavy bracket behind them and were attached directly to the frame.

Chevrolet's own commercial diesel engine and automatic were coupled to a standard New Process transfer case, which was manually engaged. The front drive axle was the Dana 60 model used in the one-ton trucks, and had lockout hubs, disc brakes, and standard civilian wheels. The rear axle was the General Motors corporate model used in three-quarter-ton trucks. Heavy duty brakes and a no spin differential were used to improve traction.

The cargo box was modified to accept several different kits, troop seats and racks, communications equipment, cargo and shelter tie down kits, and a collapsible cargo cover. A rear step bumper was used with towing clevises and a military pintle hitch. The rear of the frame had additional reinforcements for this heavier hitch. The front and rear bumpers were also modified for blackout marker lights.

The undercarriage of the truck also had fuel tank shields and a transfer case skid plate. The wiring harnesses are quite different as the truck was provided with a combination 12- and 28-volt electrical system, 12 for lights and instruments, 28 for charging and starting. Two large alternators were mounted on all the trucks.

A slave receptacle was provided for assistance when starting difficulties were encountered. Batteries were mounted on the right side of the engine compartment. Winterization kits were available with additional cab, battery, transmission, and engine coolant heaters. Another fuel burning heater could be installed in the cargo box for heating that area when

Rear view of Chevy M1008 CUCV. (John Bircheff, Fontana, California)

using the shelter or cover kit. Most models had rifle racks in the rear of the cab behind the seat. The cargo compartment cover was similar to the M880 vehicles — a series of folding tubular bows that collapsed forward on to the top sides of the box just behind the cab. The troop seat kits sat in the stake pockets in the box and could be removed in one piece. Shelter tie-down kits were heavy metal channels with rings welded to them, and there were four of them, one in each corner of the box.

Model M1008A1: — This was the same basic truck as the M1008, but had the communications kit consisting of the 100-amp 28-volt generator system, radio mounts in the box, fender- or body-mounted antennas, and modified wiring harness.

Model M1028: — This was the same basic truck as the M1008, but had the 100- amp 28-volt generator system, the S-250 shelter kit with tie downs, and the communications kit.

Mid-1980s Chevy M1009 CUCV utility vehicle.

Model M1028A1: — This was the same basic truck as the M1028, but had a different transfer case which could use a power take-off for operating additional equipment associated with the shelter kit.

Model M1031: — This was the same basic truck as the M1008, but had no rear body. This cab and chassis was used for special purpose bodies and equipment.

Model M1009: — This model used the Chevrolet Blazer body and chassis with the lighter half-ton axles. Factory bucket seats were used, and the truck was fitted with 100-amp 28-volt generator system, communications kit, or a folding rear seat when required. The rear seat was a factory model, which could be folded down or removed. The chassis used the same powertrain, electrical systems, engine, transmission, transfer case, bumpers, and other military items and equipment. The tires and wheels were also different in size and capacity, due to the fact that the half-ton axles had a different bolt pattern for the wheels and used 15-inch rims rather than the 16-inch on the three-quarter models.

Model M1010: — This truck was the ambulance model, which used the same chassis and power train as the M1008 vehicles. This ambulance had significant design changes and improvements over previous ambulance models. The basic function and layout of the interior was the same as earlier models but substantial improvements were made.

Four to eight patients could be carried. Four litter patients on racks mounted inside the compartment for the severely injured were used. Eight ambulatory patients as well as the attendant could sit on the seats in the rear body.

This unit had a 200-amp 28-volt electrical system, which provided power to the patient compartment air conditioning and heating systems and the very sophisticated air filtration unit which gave cab and patient compartment personnel protection from chemical and biological contaminants. A patient lifting device, an arm with block and tackle and sling assembly, was fastened to the upper right corner at the rear of the body. The rear compartment was ventilated and a spotlight was mounted on the cab roof with side flood lights installed on the left and right body panels. A sliding door was used to enter the cab from the rear compartment. An interior dome light, which was fluorescent, was in conjunction with side-mounted movable focus lights. This ambulance had a different attendant's seat which was mounted on a track inside the vehicle on the left side next to the lower litter rack and seat. The folding rear step raised up and slid under the body at the rear. The air filtration unit was mounted on the front of the rear body inside, along with the air conditioner and its controls.

I.D. Data: — The serial number was located on the identification data plate on the lower rear corner on the inside of the driver's door.

Model No.	Body Type	Weight	GVW	Prod.Total
M1008	Cargo	5900	8800	—
M1008A1	Cargo	5900	8800	—
M1028	Cargo	5800	9400	—
M1028A1	Cargo	5800	9400	—
M1031	Cab Chassis	5250	9200	—
M1009	Utility	5200	6400	—
M1010	Ambulance	7370	9450	—

Engine: — Chevrolet DDA 6.21 diesel V-8, overhead valve, four-cycle. Cast iron heads and block. Displacement: 379 cubic inches. Bore and stroke: 3.98 x 3.82 inches. Compression ratio: 22:1. Brake horsepower: 150 at 3600 rpm. Five main bearings. Hydraulic valve lifters. General Motors direct fuel injection.

Chassis and Body: — Wheelbase: 131.5 inches. Overall length: 192-227 inches. Width: 80-82 inches. Height: 75-107 inches. Tread center to center front: inches. Tires: 235/85R16 10-ply trucks or 10R15 utility 6-ply, civilian traction, all season, or highway tread.

Rear view of Chevy M1009 CUCV utility vehicle.

Technical: — General Motors Turbo Hydromatic 400 automatic transmission. Speeds: 3F/1R. Two-speed transfer case, New Process 208 or 205. Leaf spring suspension front and rear. Dana 60 front axle with lock out hubs. General Motors corporate rear axle with limited slip. Gear ratio: 4.10:1. Power assisted front disc and rear drum brakes. Power steering. 12- and 28-volt electrical system. Top speed: 55 mph. Fuel capacity: 20 gallons trucks, 27 gallons utility. Cruising range: 270 or 340 miles.

Standard Accessories: — Hand, vehicle, pioneer tools; fire extinguisher, first aid kit; chemical agent equipment for detection and decontamination; slave cable, tire chains.

Historical: — Built by Chevrolet Division of General Motors for the U.S. Army, Air Force, and Marine Corps from 1984 to 1987.

PRICE

Model No.	6	5	4	3	2	1
M1008	1000	2500	3500	5500	7500	9500
M1008A1	1000	2500	3500	5500	7500	9500
M1028	1000	2500	3500	5500	7500	9500
M1028A1	1000	2500	3500	5500	7500	9500
M1031	1000	2500	3500	5500	7500	9500
M1009	1500	3000	4000	6000	8000	9500
N1010	2500	3500	4500	6500	8500	10,000

1980s HUMVEE 1-1/4-ton cargo truck built by AM General.

Model M998: — This cargo truck is the 1-1/4 ton model called the "Hummer" or "Humvee." This name comes from the acronym HMMWV, which stands for High Mobility multipurpose Wheeled Vehicle.

This is the armed forces' most modern vehicle in its class. It is sophisticated compared to its predeccessors. The truck is still a front engine four-wheel drive layout built on a steel channel frame, but with much improved technology in all aspects. The body is made of aluminum and fiberglass with a fiberglass tilt hood. The folding windshield with a removable canvas top or a fiberglass hard top are used on the wide variety of models. The spare tire has been eliminated, and the new tires have a magnesium liner on the wheel inside the tire; this allows it to be run flat for about 30 miles. It's a modular design, so the body has panels that are easily removed or added and rearranged to perform the functions of the five different models: cargo troop carrier, TOW missile carrier, armament carrier, shelter carrier and ambulance. Each of these categories had several models as well, depending on armaments, winches, supplemental armor kits, or other equipment. All trucks have roll bars.

A General Motors V-8 diesel engine is used; it is the same basic model as in the CUCV trucks. The transmission is the same also. The New Process transfer case is offset to the driver's side and has an oil cooler. The engine actually sits a little to the right to clear the front differential. Both the front and rear differentials are bolted solidly to the frame with the four disc brakes, two mounted on the front and two on the rear. The suspension is four-wheel independent using modified A-frames. A small constant-velocity drive shaft goes to the gear reduction hub from the differential. Coil springs are used. The drive shafts are behind the front springs and ahead of the rear springs. This gives them quite a bit of protection as the entire suspension assembly on each corner of the vehicle protects the drive shaft.

Rear view of 1980s HUMVEE 1-1/4-ton cargo truck built by AM General.

The plastic fuel tank is mounted ahead of the rear differential and inside the right frame rail. Special radial tires and wheels were designed for the truck; the tires have a different tread pattern than conventional military tires. Batteries are located under the passenger's seat. Front-mounted winches are the electric 6000-pound models, which are behind the front cross member and are hardly visible. An electronic engine analysis system is provided for service when needed. Power steering and brakes are standard.

The vehicle is very wide and has a low profile. The engine sits back into the passenger's compartment with the seats actually alongside the power train. The cargo floor between the left and right passengers sits above the transmission transfer case assembly. The engine cover inside the front compartment is removable for service work. The fire extinguisher is carried on the front of the driver's seat.

Deep water fording kits are available. Removable canvas tops with bows cover the rear cargo area. Troop seats with side racks are an option. Along with standard headlights, this unit has turn signals, blackout drive light and marker system, reflectors, and side clearance lights. Towing clevises, lifting eyes, and pintle hitch are standard equipment. All units are equipped with water heaters and rifle racks. The hand-operated mechanical parking brake is a disc unit mounted on the rear differential. A retracting pioneer tool kit is mounted under the rear frame, just ahead of the pintle hitch. The cargo trucks came with seating for two or four men and had two or four doors.

Model M1038: — This is the same truck as the M998 cargo model but is equipped with the winch.

Model M966: — This has the same basic chassis as the other trucks, but it is a four-door model with a TOW missile mounted in the center of the fiberglass hard top. The rear compartment is covered with the hatchback style lid, where additional equipment and spare missiles are carried. The supplemental armor kit is fitted. This is a series of plates bolted to the body in different areas with different doors, glass and windshield. Electronic and radio equipment were carried in the center of the crew compartment. The missile launcher is mounted on a circular ring mount with 300-degree traverse and +20- or -10-degree elevation.

Model M1036: — This is the same truck as the M966 missile carrier but is equipped with winch.

Model M1045: — This is the same truck as the M966 missile carrier but has more armor applied in addition to the supplemental armor kit. This gives extra protection for the crew, missiles, ammunition, and systems components.

Model M1046: — This is the same truck as the M1045 missile carrier but has the winch.

Model M1025: — This truck uses the same basic chassis as the other units and is similar in appearance to the M966 missile carrier, but it is an armaments carrier for the Mk 19 grenade launcher, M2 .50 caliber heavy machine gun, or M60 7.62mm machine gun. These also are mounted on a circular ring mount in the center of the fiberglass hard top. This is a four-door model with enclosed rear.

Model M1026: — This is the same basic truck as the M1025 armaments carrier but is equipped with a front winch.

Model M1043: — This is the same basic truck as the M1025 and has the additional armor protection.

Model M1044: — This is the same basic truck as the M1043 but is equipped with the front winch.

Model M1037: — This is the same basic chassis as the M998 cargo truck but is used as a shelter carrier. The shelter slides into the cargo box and is secured with four turnbuckle-type tie downs, each mounted to one corner of the cargo area. The S-250 shelter is used.

Model M1042: — This is the same basic truck as the M1037 shelter carrier but is equipped with a front winch.

Model M996: — This is a two-door ambulance model with armor protection for the crew and patients. Two litters are carried under the low profile rear top, and it can be expanded to four litter capacity when needed. The low profile was for air transportability.

Model M997: — This is the large full-body ambulance with armor protection. This vehicle can carry four litter patients or eight ambulatory patients, or combinations of both. Air conditioning, heater, air filtration equipment and a patient lifting device are used. This body is equipped the same as the unit on the CUCV series ambulance, the M1010, although it is altered for the different chassis.

Model M1035: — This ambulance is a four-door model with two litter capacity. No armor protection is provided for the crew. This truck and the M996 are nearly the same and have two metal racks in the rear on which the litters sit. No sophisticated climate control systems are used.

I.D. Data: — The serial number is located on the identification data plate in the lower rear corner of the left driver's door jamb.

AM General HUMVEE 1-1/4-ton command and reconnaissance truck.

Rear view of HUMVEE command and reconnaissance truck.

Model No:	Body Type	Weight	GVW	Prod. Total
M966	TOW	6051	8200	—
M996	Ambulance	—	—	—
M997	Ambulance	7180	9100	—
M998	Cargo	5200	7700	—
M1025	Armament	5960	8200	—
M1026	Armament	6087	8327	—
M1035	Ambulance	—	—	—
M1036	TOW	6178	8327	—
M1037	Shelter	5424	8660	—
M1038	Cargo	5327	7827	—
M1042	Shelter	5551	8787	—
M1043	Armament	5960	8200	—
M1044	Armament	6087	8327	—
M1045	TOW	6051	8200	—
M1046	TOW	6178	8327	—

Engine: — General Motors DDA 6.21 Diesel. V-8, overhead valve, four-cycle. Cast iron block and head. Displacement: 379 cubic inches. Bore and Stroke: 3.98 x 3.82 inches. Compression ratio: 22:1. Brake horsepower: 150 at 3600 rpm. Five main bearings. Hydraulic valve lifters. General Motors direct fuel injection.

Chassis and Body: — Wheelbase: 130 inches. Overall length: 180-203 inches. Width: 85 inches. Height: 72-104 inches. Tread center to center front: 75 inches. Tires: Goodyear Wrangler radial all-terrain tread, 36x12.50R16.5.

Technical: — General Motors THM 400 automatic transmission. Speeds: 3F/1R. Two-speed transfer case, New Process 218. Independent coil spring suspension. Power-assisted steering and disc brakes. Twenty-four-volt electrical system. Top speed: 65 mph. Fuel capacity: 25 gallons. Cruising range: 300 miles.

Standard Accessories: — Hand, vehicle, pioneer tools; fire extinguisher, first aid kit; slave cable, tire and tow chains; chemical detection and decontamination equipment; chock blocks.

Historical: — Designed and built by AM General Corporation from 1984 to the present in South Bend, Indiana. A total of 103,000 are to be completed for the U.S. armed services by 1994. Several thousand have been sold to foreign governments to date. The "Hummer" is one of the most extensively tested vehicles ever bought by the Army. Civilian versions will possibly be available for public purchase in 1993.

PRICE

Model No.	6	5	4	3	2	1
M966	15,000	20,000	25,000	30,000	35,000	45,000
M996	15,000	20,000	25,000	30,000	35,000	45,000
M997	15,000	20,000	25,000	30,000	35,000	45,000
M998	15,000	20,000	25,000	30,000	33,000	40,000
M1025	15,000	20,000	25,000	30,000	35,000	45,000
M1026	15,000	20,000	25,000	30,000	35,000	45,000
M1035	15,000	20,000	25,000	30,000	35,000	45,000
M1036	15,000	20,000	25,000	30,000	35,000	45,000
M1037	15,000	20,000	25,000	30,000	33,000	40,000
M1038	15,000	20,000	25,000	30,000	33,000	40,000
M1042	15,000	20,000	25,000	30,000	33,000	40,000
M1043	15,000	20,000	25,000	30,000	35,000	45,000
M1044	15,000	20,000	25,000	30,000	35,000	45,000
M1045	15,000	20,000	25,000	30,000	35,000	45,000
M1046	15,000	20,000	25,000	30,000	35,000	45,000

M715 1-1/4-ton cargo truck with winch.

Model M715: — The M715 is a four-wheel drive cargo truck, used for general transportation requirements. It is rated in the 1-1/4 ton class, with a 3,000- pound capacity payload. The vehicle was an interim model in between the M37 and M880 Dodge trucks. It is a very rugged vehicle, using almost all commercial components, and being one of the first to do so as a tactical unit. The major changes from a civilian truck were extensive. The sheet metal had larger fender wells to allow for more suspension travel of the large tires, the cab was redesigned to military specifications, still using some civilian panels, and the cargo box was a military design on its own. These things gave it a very unique appearance.

The drivetrain was standard automotive in nature, but all of the components were stronger and larger for off-road use. The truck had particularly large brakes. The driver and one passenger sat in the cab, with the battery box between them. An additional eight men with equipment could be carried in the rear on folding troop seats in the box. The standard military equipment was incorporated into the truck: folding windshield, removable canvas top, front brush guard, tow hooks, pintle hitch, blackout lighting system, troop seats, top bows, rear cargo canvas, etc. The vehicle was supplied with or without power take-off driven front-mounted winches.

I.D. Data: — The serial number is located on the identification plate on the instrument panel inside the truck.

Model No.	Body Type	Weight	GVW	Prod. Total
M715	Cargo	5500	8500	22,000

Engine: — Jeep Tornado, six-cylinder, overhead camshaft, OHV, four-cycle, inline. Cast iron head and block. Displacement: 230 cubic inches. Bore and Stroke: 3.34 x 4.375 inches.Brake horsepower: 132 at 4,000 rpm. Four main bearings. Mechanical valve lifters. Carburetor: Holley R3615.

Chassis and Body: — Wheelbase: 126 inches. Overall length: 209 inches. Height: 95 inches. Width: 85 inches. Tread center to center: 67 inches. Tires 9.00 x 16 8-ply military non-directional.

Technical: — Manual transmission. Speeds 4F/1R. Two-speed transfer case. Single dry disc clutch. Leaf spring suspension. Dana 60 front dif-

Late 1960s M715 1-1/4-ton jeep cargo truck.

ferential, Dana 70 rear differential. Overall ratio: 5.87:1. Hydraulic brakes. Manual steering. Twenty-four-volt electrical system. Top speed: 60 mph. Fuel capacity: 28 gallons. Cruising range: 220 miles.

Standard Accessories: — Canvas cab and cargo top; racks and troop seats; hand, vehicle and pioneer tools; spare parts.

Historical: — Built by Kaiser Jeep from 1967 to 1969. This truck saw limited use in the Vietnam War.

PRICE

Model No.	6	5	4	3	2	1
M715	300	1200	2500	3500	5500	7000

Add $500 for winch model.

Late 1960s M715 1-1/4-ton cargo truck.

M726 jeep maintenance truck. (James Welty, Ohio Military Museum Inc., Fairborn, Ohio)

Right side view of Ford GTB cargo truck. (David Wright, Wright Museum, Shrewsbury, Massachusetts)

Model Ford GTB: — The GTB was a 1-1/2-ton four-wheel-drive cargo truck. Its origins came from a government low silhouette truck early in the war. It was the only truck of this kind that went into mass production and was used by the Army and the Navy in several different forms.

Cargo, bomb service, and wrecker were manufactured. It was the first all-military designed truck in World War II, consequently, all these units had open cabs, removable canvas tops and folding windshields.

The truck employed a cab-forward design where the driver and passenger sat alongside the engine but very low to the ground, and this actually made entrance and exit not too bad. The trucks were built with or without a front 10,000-pound winch. A nine-foot steel cargo body with troop seats was used.

The GTB's axles were the split housing type built by Timken. The transfer case was a separate unit with drive shafts going into and coming out of it.

The vehicle was very short, making it very maneuverable. The inside of the cab had an adjustable driver's seat, and the gearshift levers were to the rear behind the removable engine cover. The passenger seat was very unusual in that it sat facing the right side of the driver, with the passenger's back to the outside of the vehicle.

The engine was a militarized version of a standard Ford truck six-cylinder and had many changes. The short wheelbase and forward sitting position gave the driver good visibility and a very short turning radius.

The gas tank was unusual in shape compared to other trucks. It appeared to be soldered together with more stamped parts than others. The box was distinguished by the tiny wheel wells in the bottom lip.

A stowage box was on the driver's side of the grille. The front springs were mounted under the axle, thus giving the vehicle a lower silhouette. The unit was originally designed as a low-profile vehicle for possible air transport.

I.D. Data: — The serial number was located on the identification data plate on the engine cover in the cab, and on the left front frame rail of the truck above the front axle housing.

Seat and steering wheel of World War II Ford GTB bomb service truck. (Royce Anderson, Ponderosa Ranch, Incline Village, Nevada)

Model No.	Body Type	Weight	GVW	Prod. Total
GTB	Cargo	6900	10,250	6000

Engine: — Ford Military G8T, six-cylinder, inline, L-head, four-cycle, cast iron block and head. Displacement: 226 inches. Bore and Stroke: 3-1/3 x 4-2/5 inches. Brake horsepower: 90 at 3300 rpm. Four main bearings, mechanical valve lifters.

Chassis and Body: — Wheelbase: 115 inches. Overall length: 180 inches. Height: 100 inches. Width: 86 inches. Tread center to center front: 68 inches. Tires: 7.50 x 20 8-ply military non-directional.

GTB 4X4 1-1/2-ton cargo truck by Ford. (David Wright, Wright Museum, Shrewsbury, Massachusetts)

Left rear view of Ford GTB cargo truck. (David Wright, Wright Museum, Shrewsbury, Massachusetts)

World War II Fort GTB 1-1/2-ton bomb service truck.

World War II Ford GTB 1-1/2-ton bomb service truck.

Historical: — Designed and built by Ford Motor Co. from 1942 to 1944. Assembled at Ford's Edgewater, New Jersey factory.

	PRICE					
Model No.	6	5	4	3	2	1
GTB	800	1500	3000	7000	10,000	14,000

Technical: — Manual selective sliding transmission. Speeds: 4F/1R. Two-speed transfer case. Single dry disc clutch. Semi-elliptic leaf spring suspension. Timken front differential, Ford rear differential with split housings. Hydraulic brakes. Manual steering. Six-volt electrical system. Top speed: 45 mph. Fuel capacity: 49 gallons. Cruising range: 440 miles.

Standard Accessories: — Canvas cab top and side curtain; cargo bed canvas, troop seats, top bows; hand and vehicle tools; spare parts; fire extinguisher.

World War II Chevrolet 4X4 1-1/2-ton cargo truck. (Ralph Doubek, Wild Rose, Wisconsin)

Model G7107: — The Chevrolet G7107 was a 1-1/2-ton four-wheel-drive cargo truck with dual rear wheels. It was used for general personnel and cargo transportation by several branches of the services, mainly the Army and the Army Air Corps. It was a simple design by Chevrolet, using their standard 1-1/2 ton civilian truck that was used by the general public before the war. The well proven 235 cubic inch inline six-cylinder engine, with its four-speed transmission, was the power plant of the truck. The General Motors banjo axles were used in all of the trucks.

The nine-foot cargo box came in wood or steel, and was the standard military design. Five bows sat in stake pockets in the sides of the bed, along with the side racks. A cargo tarp was used with end curtains to completely enclose the cargo area. A tool box was under the rear tailgate.

The cab was the civilian model with minor modifications for military use. The data plates were on the roof inside the cab above the windshield. Early vehicles used the standard civilian gauges; later ones used the round military ones, with all military controls for lights, etc.

The front sheet metal was changed to accommodate the brush guard, and front fenders were changed for the extra wheel travel of the front driving axle. The other familiar military requirements were met with the rear pintle hitch and bumperettes, front tow hooks and blackout lighting system. The trucks were built with or without winches, and were very similar to the GMCs but were actually a different vehicle. They were built with the hard cab only, and usually did not have provisions for a ring mount above the cab. The crew was the driver and sometimes an assistant.

Model G7117: — Same truck as the G7107 but with a Garwood or Heil 10,000 pound PTO driven winch.

Model G7113: — This model was a cab and chassis with a stationary fifth wheel for towing small semi trailers. It came equipped with electric brake controls for the trailer.

Model G7106: — This was the dump truck model. A single-cylinder hydraulic scissors hoist and sub frame were mounted between the box and the frame of the truck. A hydraulic pump, PTO driven, was used to raise and lower the body. The box was the standard nine-foot cargo

Left rear view of Chevrolet 4X4 1-1/2-ton cargo truck. (Ralph Doubek, Wild Rose, Wisconsin)

model. The hoists were Perfection, Heil, or Hercules. The bodies had stake pockets, racks, bows and tarps so they could be used as general cargo trucks as well as dump trucks. A double-action tailgate at the rear allowed the box to be used in both ways as well.

Model G7116: — Same truck as the G7106, but with the 10,000 PTO driven winch.

Model G7105: — This was the van body truck. The body was one piece from the cab back with straight sides and no windows. Two rear doors were used with a window in each. Normally used for hauling radios or other equipment that needed extra care.

Model G7163: — This was the telephone earth borer. A special body housed a transfer case PTO-driven auger for setting telephone poles. A

Right side view of Chevrolet 4X4 1-1/2-ton cargo truck. (Ralph Doubek, Wild Rose, Wisconsin)

large winch was mounted behind the cab in the box, and the truck was equipped with a set of poles to raise the telephone poles when they were inserted into the hole dug by the auger. The winch was also driven off the transfer case PTO.

Model G7173: — This was the telephone maintenance truck. This had a different body than the auger truck, but was equipped with the same winch for raising and lowering telephone poles when constructing lines or repairing them. The winch also had extensions out the side of the body for wire reels, for playing out wire or recovering it.

Model G7123: — This was the cab-over-engine model. It used the same power train as the other trucks, but had a much longer wheelbase. The bed was a stake model with side racks and was 16 feet long. The civilian COE cab was used, and again with slight modifications for use by the military, blackout lighting, brush guard, different instruments, etc. Wheelbase was 175 inches.

Model G7127: — This was the same truck as the G7107 cargo truck but with a longer wheelbase, 175 inches.

Model M6: — This was the bomb service model with a very short wheelbase, 125 inches. It had an open body and a 4,000-pound hand-operated hoist for loading and unloading the bomb trailers it towed.

It had an open cab with a canvas top. There were two front seats and three rear seats. Electric trailer brakes were standard on this vehicle. This unit could be fitted with dual front or rear tires if needed. It was designed to have a low profile for working under planes.

I.D. Data: — The serial number was located on the identification data plate in the cab above the windshield on the driver's side and on the left front frame rail directly above the front axle housing.

Model No.	Body Type	Weight	GVW	Prod. Total
G7107	Cargo	7545	12,945	86,771
G7117	Cargo	8045	13,445	26,108
G7113	Tractor	6045	10,885	—
G7106	Dump	8300	11,300	5098
G7116	Dump	8700	11,800	9297
G7105	Van	6760	9760	3632
G7163	Auger	7200	10,200	1719
G7173	Maintenance	10,215	11,250	4328
G7123	Stake	8570	11,570	581
G7127	Cargo	8965	11,965	391
M6	Bomb	6325	8375	7857

World War II Chevrolet 1-1/2-ton bomb service truck. (Royce Anderson, Ponderosa Ranch, Incline Village, Nevada)

Left side view of Chevrolet bomb service truck. (Royce Anderson, Ponderosa Ranch, Incline Village, Nevada)

Winch on Chevrolet bomb service truck. (Royce Anderson, Ponderosa Ranch, Incline Village, Nevada)

Another view of winch on Chevrolet bomb service truck. (Royce Anderson, Ponderosa Ranch, Incline Village, Nevada)

Six-volt electrical system. Top speed: 48 mph. Fuel capacity: 30 gallons. Cruising range: 270 miles.

Standard Accessories: — Hand, vehicle, pioneer tools; spare parts; cargo canvas, troop seats.

Historical: — Designed and built by Chevrolet Division of General Motors from 1940 to 1945.

Engine: — Chevrolet BV1001UP, six-cylinder, inline, OHV, four-cycle, cast iron block and head. Displacement: 235 cubic inches Bore and Stroke: 3-9/16 x 3-15/16 inches. Compresssion ratio: 6.62:1. Brake horsepower: 83 at 3100 rpm. Five main bearings. Mechanical valve lifters.

Chassis and Body: — Wheelbase: 125, 145, 175 inches. Overall length: 221 to 296 inches. Width: 76 to 86 inches. Height: 91 to 106 inches. Tread center to center: 65.5 to 67.5 inches. Tires: 7.50 x 20 8-ply military non-directional.

Technical: — Manual selective sliding gear transmission. Speeds 4F/1R. Two-speed transfer case. Single dry disc clutch. Semi elliptic leaf spring suspension. General Motors banjo hypoid gear differentials. Overall ratio 6.67:1. Hydraulic vacuum assisted brakes. Manual steering.

	PRICE					
Model	6	5	4	3	2	1
G7107	400	1500	3000	5000	9000	14,000
G7117	700	1500	2300	5500	10,000	14,000
G7113	400	800	1200	—	—	—
G7106	1000	2000	3000	5500	9000	14,000
G7116	1500	2500	3500	5500	9000	14,000
G7105	1500	2500	3500	5500	9000	—
G7163	—	—	—	—	—	—
G7173	—	—	—	—	—	—
G7123	1500	2500	—	—	—	—
G7127	900	1500	3000	5000	9000	14,000
M6	—	—	—	—	—	—

World War II Dodge WC63 1-1/2-ton 6X6 cargo truck with winch.

Model Dodge WC62: —The WC62 Dodge truck was a six-wheel drive vehicle which was an improved and upgraded model. Its base design came from the WC51 Dodge weapons carrier, which was four-wheel drive. The trucks had many interchangeable parts. It was considered a substitute for the 2-1/2-ton trucks in many instances. The basic truck was the same as the 3/4-ton Dodge trucks of World War II, but it was longer and heavier, with an additional driving axle in the rear, and had a larger payload and towing capacity. It was a cargo truck with an open cab, and folding troop seats in the rear cargo area. There was a crew of two, driver and assistant, who sat in the front, and fifteen additional troops with equipment could be carried in the box.

The truck had the standard military equipment, such as tow hooks, steel brush guard, blackout lighting system, pintle hitch, folding windshield, canvas cab and cargo top with bows, etc. Some trucks were fitted with the machine gun, and circular ring mount above the passenger seat. The other driving axle in the rear required a two-speed transfer case to compensate for the additional weight. The ring and pinion gears in the differentials were larger, and the frame had side reinforcements beneath and behind the cab. Spare tire and bracket were carried above the running board on the driver's side of the truck. Cargo capacity was 5250 pounds.

The rear suspension was similar to the 2-1/2-ton trucks used during the war. Inverted leaf springs, with the six-link torque rod suspension, were used. The rear rear axle had equal length axle shafts, and the front rear axle had a longer shaft on the left side. The double drive shafts were attached to the back of the transfer case, and a pillow block was mounted on the front rear axle housing to support the drive shaft to the rear rear differential. The extra length in the body was added above the rear wheels. Nearly all the components in the vehicle were the same as the WC51 and WC52.

Model WC63: —This was the same basic truck as the WC62, but had a PTO-driven front-mounted winch of 7500-pound capacity.

I.D. Data: —Serial number was on the identification data plate on the instrument panel and on the left front frame rail above the front axle housing.

Model No.	Body Type	Weight	GVW	Prod. Total
WC62	Personnel	7250	12,450	23,092

Engine: — Dodge, inline six-cylinder, L-head, four-cycle, cast iron block. Displacement: 230 cubic inches. Bore and Stroke: $3\frac{1}{4}$ x $4\frac{5}{8}$ inches. Brake horsepower: 76 at 3200 rpm. Five main bearings. Mechanical valve lifters. Carburetor: Zenith cast iron.

Chassis and Body: — Wheelbase: 125 inches. Overall length: 224.5 inches. Height: 85.5 inches. Width: 82.75 inches. Tread center to center: 64.75 inches. Tires: 9.00 x 16 8-ply military non-directional.

Technical: — Manual selective sliding gear transmission. Speeds 4F/1R. Two-speed transfer case. Single dry disc clutch. Semi-elliptic leaf spring suspension. Dodge full-floating hypoid gear differentials. Gear ratio: 5.83:1. Hydraulic brakes. Steel combat wheels. Manual steering. Six-volt electrical system. Top speed: 50 mph. Fuel capacity: 30 gallons. Cruising range: 240 miles.

Standard Accessories: — Canvas top with bows, troop seats; .50 caliber machine gun with circular ring mount, if applicable; hand and vehicle tools; spare tire assembly; fire extinguisher.

Historical: — Designed in early 1942 at the request of the Ordnance Department. Built from 1942 to 1945 in the United States by Dodge Motor Company.

Model No.	6	5	4	3	2	1
			PRICE			
WC62	800	3000	7000	11,000	15,000	18,000
WC63	1000	3500	7500	12,000	16,000	19,000

World War II I.H.C. M3L4 1-1/2-ton crash tender.

Model M-3L-4: — The M-3L-4 was International Harvester's 1-1/2-ton four-wheel-drive model in World War II and was built almost entirely for use by the Navy and Marine Corps. This was a considerably heavier truck than the M-2-4 one-ton model. It was built as a hard cab, using the militarized version of the civilian K model body. The open cab was used as well, and was the same basic unit as the M-5H-6 model.

Metal doors and the folding canvas top were basically the same as the larger trucks. The brush guard on this truck was similar in design to the M-2-4, where it actually sat on the frame rails in front of the radiator. The radiator cap on this truck also protruded through the hood on the right side. The hood also opened from the side, as did all the International trucks.

Traditional military design and requirements were used throughout the truck. It was a simple unit with a steel channel ladder type frame using cross members. Leaf spring suspension was used front and rear. Banjo axles by Eaton put power to the ground. These had much heavier housings than the one-ton trucks, and were similar in size to the ones used in the M-5H-6 trucks. International's own six-cylinder overhead valve engine, with a five-speed overdrive transmission, were installed. This power plant was from the heavy-duty truck series, being larger and a sleeved model. A two-speed transfer case provided power to the axles. Six-hole Budd wheels with dual rear larger tires were used.

Tow hooks, lifting rings, rear pintle hitch, and bumperettes added towing and lifting capabilities. Rear beds were made of either wood or steel and were built by several manufacturers in design and assembly. Cargo models were made by Galion, Anthony, and Meteor Wood Co. Tank bodies were by Columbia; Dump bodies by Galion; wreckers and refuelers by Gar Wood; and crash trucks by Bean and American LaFrance.

Spare tires were mounted in different positions on these trucks. The rear bodies were slightly different in design and appearance than the other

Front view of Marine Corps I.H.C. M3L4 crash tender.

bodies used on trucks built for the Army. They were a little heavier, a little longer, had higher sides, larger tailgates, sometimes no cab shields, different cabinetry, and pioneer tools in different positions. Ribbing and reinforcements on the boxes were all different. Everything was just different enough to give them their own characters. Blackout lighting and driving lights were provided. The M-3L-4 was the short wheelbase model, and the M-3H-4 was the longer wheelbase model. Double gas tanks were used on these vehicles, one under the seats and the other mounted on the side of the frame.

I.D. Data: — The serial number was located on the identification data plate on the instrument panel.

World War II I.H.C. 4X4 1-1/2-ton crash tender with hard cab and winch. (George Kriewaldt, Iola, Wisconsin)

Rear view of I.H.C. crash tender. (George Kriewaldt, Iola, Wisconsin)

Engine: — International Harvester FAC-259B early, BLD-269-B late. Six-cylinder, inline, overhead valve, four-cycle. Cast iron block and head. Displacement: 259 and 269 cubic inches. Bore and Stroke: 3-1/2 or 3-9/16 x 4-1/2 inches. Compression ratio: 6.3:1. Brake horsepower: 88 at 2800 rpm. Four main bearings. Mechanical valve lifters. Carburetor Zenith 63AW-11.

Chassis and Body: — Wheelbase: 139 or 150 inches. Overall length: 240-251 inches. Width: 87 inches. Height: 91 inches. Tread center to center front: 62.5 inches. Tires: 8.25 x 20 8-ply military non-directional.

Technical: — Manual selective sliding gear transmission. Speeds: 5F/1R, with overdrive. Two-speed transfer case. Single dry disc clutch. Leaf spring suspension front and rear. Eaton spiral bevel banjo differentials. Gear ratio: 6.166:1 early, 7.166:1 late. Hydraulic vacuum assisted brakes. Manual steering. Six-volt electrical system. Fuel capacity: 36 gallons. Top speed: 46 mph. Cruising range: 300 miles.

Standard Accessories: — Hand, vehicle, pioneer tools; spare parts; fire extinguisher; tire chains, snatch block, jack; canvas cab and cargo top; bows, seats, racks.

Historical: — Built by International Harvester Corp. in Fort Wayne, Indiana from 1941 to 1944 for the Marine Corps and U.S. Navy.

Model No.	Body Type	Weight	GVW	Prod. Total
M-3L-4	Cargo	—	—	398
M-3L-4	Dump	—	—	20
M-3L-4	Tank	—	—	2
M-3L-4	Wrecker	—	—	122
M-3L-4	Refueler	—	—	2120
M-3L-4	Crash	—	—	1080
M-3H-4	Cargo	—	—	2220
M-3H-4	Crash	—	—	210
M-3H-4	Floodlight	—	—	260

	PRICE					
Model No.	6	5	4	3	2	1
M-3L-4 Cargo	700	1500	3000	5000	—	—
M-3L-4 Dump	—	—	—	—	—	—
M-3L-4 Tank	—	—	—	—	—	—
M-3L-4 Wrecker	—	—	—	—	—	—
M-3L-4 Refueler	—	—	—	—	—	—
M-3L-4 Crash	1000	2000	3000	—	—	—
M-3H-4 Cargo	1000	2000	3000	5000	—	—
M-3H-4 Crash	—	—	—	—	—	—
M-3H-4 Floodlight	—	—	—	—	—	—

Late 1960s M561 Gamma Goat with winch by Condec. (James Welty, Ohio Military Museum Inc., Fairborn, Ohio)

Model M561: — The M561 "Gamma Goat" was a six-wheel drive truck that was fully amphibious. The unique design gave it excellent cross-country performance and all terrain capabilities. The front and rear body assemblies were made of aluminum. It had two- or six-wheel drive available, selected by the driver as conditions warranted. All six wheels rode on A-frame-style independent suspension, with limited slip differentials in all three axles. The driver and assistant sat in the front tractor unit, with standard automotive controls. Behind them the diesel engine faced rearward, with transmission and transfer case attached. The front differential was attached directly to the transfer case with no drive shaft. A drive shaft from the transfer goes back to the rear differential, then through the double articulated universal joint to the rear-most axle. The tractor and rear body could be separated at the articulated joint for service. Steering was controlled by the front and rear-most axles.

The vehicles came equipped with or without front-mounted winches. Removable canvas tops were provided for the driver's compartment and the cargo compartment in the rear carrier. Propulsion in water was by the tires, and this was in "still-water" conditions, as the vehicle had very little freeboard, making in very easy to swamp the unit. The vehicle had waterproof hydraulic brakes, the drums were mounted outside the hubs, with the axle shafts and drums being one piece. A bilge pump was provided, and the truck could carry eight men.

I.D. Data: — The serial number was located on the identification data plate on the instrument panel in the driver's compartment.

Front view of M561 Gamma Goat. (James Welty, Ohio Military Museum Inc., Fairborn, Ohio)

Model No.	Body Type	Weight	GVW	Prod. Total
M561	Cargo	7330	10,200	14,000

Engine: — Detroit Diesel 3-53N Series, three-cylinder, in-line, OHV, two- cycle. Aluminum block and head. Displacement: 159 cubic inches. Bore and Stroke: 3.87 x 4.5 inches. Compression ratio: 22:1. Brake horsepower: 103 at 2800 rpm. Four main bearings. Mechanical valve lifters. Fuel injection.

Chassis and Body: — Wheelbase: 82 and 86 inches. Overall length: 226 inches. Height: 90 inches. Width: 83 inches. Tread center to center: 72 inches. Tires: 11.00 x 18 6-ply military non-directional.

Technical: — Manual synchromesh transmission. Speeds: 4F/1R. Two-speed transfer case. Single dry disc clutch. Independent coil spring suspension. Military design limited slip differentials. Gear ratio: 5.57:1. Sealed hydraulic brakes. Manual steering. 24-volt electrical system. Top speed: 50 mph. Fuel capacity: 40 gallons. Cruising range: 420 miles.

Rear view of M561 Gamma Goat. (James Welty, Ohio Military Museum Inc., Fairborn, Ohio)

Standard Accessories: — Canvas cab and cargo compartment tops; hand, vehicle, pioneer tools; spare parts; fire extinguisher.

Historical: — Designed in the late 1950s and early 1960s. Production began in 1969 to 1973. Built by Condec Corporation.

Model No.	6	5	4	3	2	1
			PRICE			
M561	1500	2500	4500	6000	8000	—

World War II GMC 6X6 2-1/2-ton cargo truck with winch and wood body. (Chet Krause, Iola, Wisconsin)

Model CCKW Cargo Truck: — The CCKW series of trucks was in the 2-1/2-ton class. It is a medium duty, six-wheel drive vehicle that was used for a large variety of work, with many different rear body configurations. Its more common name was GMC, "Jimmy," or "2-1/2." It is a relatively simple design, using standard automotive construction. It evolved from civilian trucks, with military requirements added, and was improved over its production run.

There were numerous small changes after the basic military design was standardized. The powertrain was modified for six-wheel drive by adding a two-speed transfer case, with shift levers in the cab for high and low range, and front axle engagement. The transfer case had provisions for a front driveshaft, and two driveshafts to the rear two axles. The driveshaft going to the rear rear axle used a pillow block mounted on the front rear axle housing to support its length and allow it to flex, when the suspension moved. Early trucks were built with closed cabs, and later models all had the military open top cabs with folding windshields and removable canvas tops and side curtains. A pintle hitch, bumperettes, and trailer electrical receptacle were at the rear of the frame.

Most models had dual rear wheel tandems, but could be equipped with the tire and wheel assemblies, and hub spacers from the DUKW, thus improving the off-road performance. The vehicles came equipped with or without 10,000-pound Garwood or Heil front-mounted, PTO-driven winches. One out of four trucks built was supposed to have the circular ring mount above the cab for the .50 caliber antiaircraft machine gun.

Short and long wheelbase models were built. The short wheelbase unit had the gas tank and spare tire mounted between the cab and box, on top of the frame, using a nine-foot body. The long wheelbase model had the gas tank and spare tire mounted on the sides of the frame, underneath the box, behind the running boards, and used a twelve-foot body. A tool box was under the tailgate, at the rear of the cargo body.

There were three types of cargo bodies: all wood, wood and steel, and all steel. The steel bodies were either all welded or bolted together. The engine blocks were cast iron, but due to a lack of hardness in the metal, the engine life was reduced. The original manufacturer used an outside vender, Timken, for the drivetrain assemblies. Due to increased demand, they were not able to supply the necessary parts. Consequently,

Close-up of wooden cargo body on GMC CCKW truck. (Chet Krause, Iola, Wisconsin)

the government contacted General Motors and they began to supply the "banjo" style axles, whereas the Timken axles were the split housing design. The axles both had their positive and negative aspects. The Timken had adjustable tapered roller bearings; the banjo had a stronger housing. The banjo used ball bearings, which had no adjustment. Approximately equal quantities of split or banjo axle trucks were built through the production run. A unique feature of the banjo axle vehicles was that the front and rear driveshafts turned in reverse rotation of each other when the all-wheel drive was engaged.

This, along with being manufactured by a different company, made the axles and transfer cases not interchangeable. The frames and driveshafts were also not interchangeable. Some trucks had "airborne" kits added to them which enabled them to be split in half. The frame had large brackets on it, so it could be bolted back together after being transported in

Tailgate on GMC CCKW. (Chet Krause, Iola, Wisconsin)

planes. The box was also split so it could be crated in two pieces. Cargo capacity of the CCKW truck series was approximately 10,000 pounds on roads; 5,000 pounds under off-road conditions. There were numerous other body styles and configurations used for many different purposes. The following is a list of the majority of them.

CCKW Dump Truck: — The dump truck used a Garwood or Heil single cylinder, PTO driven, hydraulic scissors-style hoist mounted on a subframe assembly that was bolted to the truck frame. The truck's appearance was very similar to the cargo, but the box was fitted with a removable partition about three feet to the rear of the front box panel. A cab shield was used to protect the driver from material being loaded into the box. The rear nine feet of the box was used for dumping purposes. These trucks were built with the airborne kits.

CCKW Water Tanker: — An all-metal 700-gallon, oval-shaped tank was used. There was a unit with one manhole cover in the top, and one with two manhole covers in the top. The model with two covers also had an equipment storage cabinet at the rear of the body, along with equipment racks on the sides. A heating system, using engine exhaust under the tank, warmed the water when needed. An auxiliary gasoline engine-driven pump was used to load or distribute water when needed. The truck could be camouflaged with a canvas top and bows to have the appearance of a cargo truck.

CCKW Gasoline Tanker: — This truck used two all-metal, oval-shaped tanks with manholes. Large valves were used at the rear for hoses to distribute gasoline by use of gravity. Each tank had a capacity of 375 gallons. Metal stowage boxes were on the rear corners of the bed with racks on the sides.

CCKW Air Compressor: — An engine driven LeRoi air compressor that was self-contained was mounted on the frame. This unit had its own fuel supply, air reservoir tank, hoses and reels, and carried a large variety of air powered tools. Jackhammers, with bits, were carried in two different sizes. Impact wrenches, drills, and an air-powered chain saw was used. The engine was a four-cylinder and the compressor would put out 210 cfm.

CCKW Wrecker Set No.7: — This truck used a trolley style chain hoist on a horizontal I beam, with a support leg at the front of the bed, and two support legs on each side of the bed at the rear. Used for general lifting and moving of cargo too heavy to be moved by personnel, and to lift and tow vehicles.

CCKW Van Body and Mobile Shops: — A large variety of these were used for mobile repair of many different items, and for service in rear echelon areas of combat zones. Some had collapsible tops. Later models height could be lowered, but the roofs had to be partially dismantled. The bodies were of all steel construction with their own heating and ventilation systems. Some had jackstands for stability.

Others even had dust control for working on fine instruments, with special benches designed for each type of repair. Some had their own generators in the truck, or they pulled a trailer with additional equipment

World War II GMC 6X6 2-1/2-ton cargo truck with metal body and winch. (Chet Krause, Iola, Wisconsin)

World War II GMC 6X6 2-1/2-ton cargo truck with winch, ring mount and steel box. (Chet Krause, Iola, Wisconsin)

World War II GMC CCKW 2-1/2-ton cargo truck with all-steel body. (Chet Krause, Iola, Wisconsin)

Left rear view of GMC CCKW dump truck. (Ralph Doubek, Wild Rose, Wisconsin)

and generator. Six windows were on each side with screens for light and ventilation. The rear doors were unequal size, and they had switches for a blackout lighting system. Artillery repair with specialized tools for maintenance and repair of heavy artillery weapons and related equipment. Automotive repair for maintenance of all types of auto repair, light testing and rebuilding. Electrical repair used to rebuild or repair automotive electrical components. Instrument bench repair for maintenance of artillery fire controls, anti-aircraft directors, range and height finders. Instrument repair for repair and maintenance of optical equipment for artillery. Mobile machine shop equipped with lathes, milling equipment, drill presses for any type of precision manufacturing or repair involving most types of metals. Signal Corps repair used for radio, radar, and wire equipment repair.

Small arms repair used for maintenance, rebuilding, and repair of all weapons used by the infantry. Tire repair truck used with steam and electrical tools for sectional tire repair and mold repair. Map reproduction truck using photographic equipment and laboratory for map printing and enlargement. These were called Ordnance Maintenance trucks. The following vehicles are more of a van body style with windows and doors. Medical trucks used as mobile surgical operating rooms, transporting of blood and plasma, dental workshops, eyeglass examination and workshops, first aid stations. Water purification with enclosed purification units that were driven by auxiliary engines. Signal Corps trucks used for transporting radio equipment. Tool and bench truck for general repair. Welding truck with gas and electric portable welding equipment.

CCKW Platform Hoist Truck: — A large scissors-style hoist lifted the entire truck bed vertically for loading and unloading aircraft. A special tailgate was used for a ramp into the aircraft. Garwood or Heil Companies furnished the equipment.

CCKW Bomb Transport: — A large PTO-driven winch behind the cab and a special box were used with cable and pulleys, running on a horizontal I beam with four I beam support legs to load and transport bombs.

CCKW Truck Tractor: — This unit was outfitted with a fifth-wheel assembly and trailer brake controls for pulling small semi-trailers.

Hoist mechanism of GMC CCKW dump truck. (Ralph Doubek, Wild Rose, Wisconsin)

CCKW Fire Truck: — This truck had a modified commercial fire truck body, with a distinguishing larger oval water tank inside the bed. Ladders, hoses, reels were carried. A 500 gpm pump was mounted on the front bumper and driven off the crankshaft. This vehicle was fitted with the 11.00x18 single combat wheels and tires.

CCKW Oil Field Equipment: — A McCabe Powers Auto Body oil field bed was fitted to this vehicle with a rear winch, gin poles, rolling tail board that was used for pipe line construction, repair and maintenance, and transporting related equipment.

CCKW Drill Rig: — An engine driven boring machine was used for soil testing, communication pole work, and general line repair and maintenance of electrical and communications systems.

CCKW Railroad Cars: — These were converted by the Ordnance Corps in Europe because of the shortage of steam locomotives. Used for mov-

World War II GMC CCKW 6X6 2-1/2-ton dump truck. (Ralph Doubek, Wild Rose, Wisconsin)

World War II GMC CCKW 6X6 2-1/2-ton air transportable cargo truck with split frame.

Split frame on GMC CCKW cargo truck.

Another view of split frame on GMC CCKW.

ing railroad cars in yards, and some general transport over the rail lines. They were fitted with special steel wheels for the gauge of the track.

CCKW Oil and Fuel Service: — This was used mainly by the Air Corps for fueling and lubrication of large aircraft. The Heil Company furnished the 750-gallon tank and pumping equipment.

CCKW Chemical Decontamination: — This was designed in the event that if chemical weapons were used, it would be available, but fortunately they were not used, and the trucks were used for fire fighting and portable showers. The engine-driven pump was used for spraying a combination chemical-and-water solution on affected areas, and could be used for disease control as well.

I.D. Data: — The serial number was located on the identification data page on the instrument panel, and on the left front frame rail above the front axle housing.

Model No.	Body Type	Weight	GVW	Prod. Total
CCKW	Cargo	11,000	16,000	412,385
CCKW	Dump	11,850	16,850	48,345
CCKW	Compressor	14,300	14,300	—
CCKW	Van	11,930	16,930	15,205

Engine: — GMC 270, six-cylinder, in-line, OHV, four-cycle, cast iron block and head. Displacement 270 cubic inches. Bore and Stroke: 3 25/32 x 4 inches. Compression ratio: 6.75:1. Brake horsepower: 91.5 at 2750 rpm. Four main bearings. Mechanical valve lifters. Carburetor

Chassis and Body: — Wheelbase: 145 inches and 164 inches. Overall length: 231 inches and 256 inches. Height: 93 inches. Width: 88 inches. Tread center to center front: 62.25 inches split. 60 inches banjo. Tires 7.50 x 20 8-ply or 11.00 x 18 12-ply military non-directional.

Technical: — Manual constant mesh overdrive transmission. Speeds: 5F/1R. Two-speed transfer case. Single dry disc clutch. Leaf spring suspension front and rear. Timken spiral bevel full-floating axles or General

World War II GMC CCKW 353 long wheelbase 6X6 2-1/2-ton airborne model truck with split frame and dump bed.

World War II GMC 6X6 2-1/2-ton cargo short wheelbase truck with closed cab and metal box.

World War II GMC 6X6 2-1/2-ton short wheelbase cargo truck with open cab, winch and metal bed. (George Hilton, North Bangor, New York)

World War II GMC CCKW 2-1/2-ton amphibious repair truck. (Royce Anderson, Ponderosa Ranch, Incline Village, Nevada)

Left rear view of GMC CCKW amphibious repair truck. (Royce Anderson, Ponderosa Ranch, Incline Village, Nevada)

World War II GMC CCKW 6X6 2-1/2-ton truck with compressor body. (Mark Dodd, Bowie, Texas)

Motors banjo style hypoid axles. Overall ratio: 6.6:1. Hydraulic vacuum-assisted power brakes. Manual steering. Combat wheels used with 11.00 x 18 tires. Six-volt electrical system. Top speed: 45 mph. Fuel capacity: 40 gallons. Cruising range: 300 miles.

Standard Accessories: — Canvas cab top, side curtains and cargo compartment canvas; hand, vehicle, pioneer tools; spare parts; fire extinguisher; rifle carriers on open cab models.

Historical: — Designed and built by GMC's Yellow Truck and Coach Division from 1941 to 1943, and by GMC from 1943 to 1945. Similar 2-1/2 ton trucks built by IHC, Studebaker and Reo. Over 800,000 of all makes built in World War II. The GMC was used on the famous "Red Ball Express" in late 1944. Probably the most numerous military vehicle built in World War II. Built in Detroit, Michigan and St. Louis, Missouri. U.S. Army stopped using them in 1956. A total of 527,104 were built in all body types.

Model No.	PRICE					
	6	5	4	3	2	1
CCKW Cargo	500	2000	4000	8000	11,000	14,000
CCKW Dump	500	2000	4000	8000	11,000	14,000
CCKW Compressor	500	2000	4000	7000	9000	—
CCKW Van	500	2000	4000	7000	9000	—

Model: GMC AFKWX: — The AFKWX was a medium duty cab-over-engine cargo truck. It was a long wheelbase model that was used to haul light bulky freight and cargo. Early models were civilian hard cabs modified to military specifications, and had 15-foot wood or metal cargo bodies. Later models were the familiar military open-style cabs with removable canvas tops and folding windshields. These had a longer 17-foot wooden cargo body. It was designed for maximum cargo capacity and minimum length. It worked well in difficult delivery areas, as it was very maneuverable due to its cab-over design.

The truck was based on the GMC CCKW design, and many parts were interchangeable. It used General Motors banjo axles and corresponding drive line. The major differences were related to the fact that the cab was much taller and sat farther forward. The major differences involved the steering gear, pedal assemblies, transmission and transfer case linkages, taller and much larger radiator, and different intake and exhaust manifolds with an updraft carburetor. Maintenance was extremely difficult because the cab did not tilt forward, and it often had to be removed for major engine work. Winches were not provided on these trucks.

These trucks were used in the United States and Europe during World War II, and were popular with countries that received them as aid for many years after the war was over. It had a crew of two, driver and assistant. The flat sheet metal military-style cab could be equipped with the circular ring mount for the Browning .50 caliber machine gun.

I.D. Data: — The serial number was located on the identification data plate on the cowl inside the cab, just above the transmission shift lever, and on the right front frame rail directly above the front axle housing.

Model No.	Body Type	Weight	GVW	Prod. Total
AFKWX	Welded Sheet Steel	10,800	16,150	7325

Engine: — GMC model 270, six-cylinder, inline, OHV, four-cycle, cast iron block and head. Displacement: 270 cubic inches. Bore and stroke: 3-25/32 x 4 inches. Brake horsepower: 91.5 at 2750 rpm. Five main bearings. Carburetor: Zenith die cast.

Chassis and Body: — Wheelbase: 164 inches. Overall length: 266.5 inches. Height: 106 inches. Width: 88 inches. Tread center to center: front 62.25 inches. Tires: 7.50 x 20 8 ply military non-directional.

Technical: — Manual constant mesh transmission. Speeds 5F/1R. Two-speed transfer case. Single dry disc clutch. Semi-elliptic leaf spring suspension. General Motors single reduction banjo differentials. Overall ratio: 6.6:1. Hydraulic vacuum-assisted power brakes. Manual steering. Six-volt electrical system. Top speed: 45 mph. Fuel capacity: 40 gallons. Cruising range: 300 miles.

Standard Accessories: — Hand and vehicle tools; spare parts; fire extinguisher; one .50 caliber machine gun with circular ring mount on vehicles so equipped.

Historical: — Designed and ordered by the Quartermaster Corp in 1939. Production models built in 1942 to 1943 by GMC.

PRICE

Model No.	6	5	4	3	2	1
AFKWX	—	—	—	—	—	—

Right side view of I.H.C. Marine Corps M-5-H6 cargo truck. (Shirley Laird, North Bend, Oregon)

Model M-5H-6: — This 2-1/2-ton 6x6 truck was International Harvester's vehicle in World War II. It was used almost exclusively by the Marine Corps and the Navy, although the Army may have used a few.

Again, as in the GMC, Studebaker, and Reo series, this line of trucks had many of the specifications and standardized components the others had. The basic design and construction of these trucks was essentially the same. But here the similarities end. The Marine Corps and Navy wanted a truck to meet their needs, and consequently this was a much more sophisticated vehicle.

The two most notable items were the Hendrickson design rear walking beam suspension, and the Thornton locking rear differentials. The rear suspension was more durable under off-road conditions, and its design allowed more flexibility over uneven terrain. This was an improvement over the six torque rod setup used on most other six-wheel-drive trucks built in World War II, although both did their jobs very well and were a credit to their designers and manufacturers.

The Hendrickson suspension was very successful on civilian trucks before and after the war, and in postwar years has become the most popular model for off-road use in heavy trucks. The Thornton locking differentials were installed in the rear axles, and allowed both axle shafts to lock together, turning all four wheels on each rear axle at one time, thus all eight rear tires together. This provided incredible traction, which helped in the poor soil conditions of beachheads during invasions.

Prior to and during World War II, International Harvester was one of the top truck producers in the country, and this leadership showed in many ways. The power train was made up of the best commercial parts at the time. Eaton differentials were used in the front axle; rear axles had International Harvester's own proven models. A Fuller overdrive transmission with a Rockford three-finger style clutch was used. The transfer case was an International design made for this application.

International's famous Red Diamond engines were used. These had dry sleeves and many forged parts. A gear-driven camshaft was used on this overhead valve model. Delco Remy built all the electrical components — starter, generator, and regulator. Mechanic's universal joints made up the drive shafts. The springs, axles, and frame were heavier than the

other brands of trucks. Larger tires and better brakes were provided. The outer hub and steering knuckles on the front axle could be unbolted and more easily replaced.

The sturdy K model cab was modified with all the necessary military specifications required. The soft cab was quite different from GMC's and Studebaker's in appearance and function, although the end result was the same. It had one-piece glass in the folding windshield, and the top was shaped much more like a roadster top on a car. The bows folded down behind the driver and passenger. The cab actually had doors that operated with handles, but did not have roll up glass. Side curtains were used for the upper halves of the doors when in inclement weather. The gas tank was located under the seat, and most models had an auxiliary tank on the left frame rail behind the driver's running board or behind the cab under the spare tire mount.

The rear bodies were eight or 12 feet long and were different from their counterparts. Most were built in all wood, wood and steel, or all steel. Dump boxes and the other specialty bodies were all steel. Some of the cargo bodies stowed the spare tire on the outside right front corner, vertically in an indentation in the box. The dump bodies had tool boxes made on the ribbing reinforcements on the outside of the box. Pioneer racks were also mounted in different positions compared to GMC and Studebaker. Most of International's bodies were built by Anthony, whereas the GMCs and Studebakers were mostly built by the Budd Co.

Box sizes, construction, latches, seats, racks, bows, and tailgates were all pretty much standardized by the military for all of these trucks, and were quite similar in appearance. Early versions of the M-5H-6 had a different version of the 361 engine, but with the same specifications. These trucks were all open cabs.

Model M-5-6: — This model was the one used by the Army in a 6x4 version, having no driven front axle or propeller shaft. It was built in a hard cab cargo model only. Short and long wheelbases, with and without winches. A 318-cubic inch engine of slightly earlier design provided power to a Borg Warner transmission. The rest of the truck was essentially the same as the M-5H-6.

World War II I.H.C. Marine Corps M-5-H6 2-1/2-ton cargo truck. (Shirley Laird, North Bend, Oregon)

World War II I.H.C. M-5-H6 2-1/2-ton dump truck. (Royce Anderson, Ponderosa Ranch, Incline Village, Nevada)

World War II Marine Corps I.H.C. M-5-H6 6X6 2-1/2-ton cargo truck.

Right side rear view of Marine Corps I.H.C. M-5-H6 cargo truck.

Front winch on Marine Corps I.H.C. M-5-H6.

Model M-5H-6 Dump Truck: — This was the same basic model as the short wheelbase cargo truck, and had a single cylinder hoist and Anthony or Galion dump body. Some models had Heil bodies as well. International made only a rear dumping model without cab shield. Stowage boxes were on the outside of the dump body and were built into the ribbed reinforcements. Stake pockets were provided so the truck could be used as a troop and cargo carrier with side racks and bows.

Model M-5H-6 Tractor: — This was also the short wheelbase model with a stationary fifth wheel assembly, air compressor, air trailer brake controls, and trailer electrical connections. They came with and without winches, spare tire, and gas tank assembly behind the cab. Ramps were on the rear of the frame for loading the semi trailers, and the pintle hitch and bumperettes were excluded on this vehicle.

Model M-5H-6 Oilfield Body: — This short wheelbase chassis was fitted with a front and rear winch, cab rack, rolling tailboard, and a small steel flatbed body. It was used for pipeline construction and repair.

Model M-5H-6 Wrecker: — This again was the short wheelbase model with the front and rear winch. The rear of the truck had fenders with a small bed in between them. Tubular poles with adjustable holes and pins were used in an A-frame capacity with a towing sling. Auxiliary lights were provided. Very few were made.

I.D. Data: — The serial number was located on the identification data plate on the glove box door on the right side of the instrument panel.

Hendrickson rear suspension on I.H.C. M-5-H6.

Model No.	Body Type	Weight	GVW	Prod.Total
M-5H-6	Cargo	—	—	17,010
M-5-6	Cargo	—	—	500
M-5-6x4	Cargo	—	—	3000
M-5H-6	Dump	—	—	16,242
M-5H-6	Tractor	—	—	7300
M-5H-6	Wrecker	—	—	245
M-5H-6	Refueler	—	—	2275

Engine: — M-5-6, International Harvester FBC-318B. Six-cylinder, in-line, overhead valve, four-cycle. Cast iron block and head. Displacement: 318 cubic inches. Bore and Stroke: 3.875x4.5 inches. Compression ratio: 6:1. Brake horsepower: 85 at 2700 rpm. Seven main bearings. Mechanical valve lifters. Carburetor Zenith 63AW12R.
M-5H-6, International Harvester RED-361-B. Six-cylinder in-line, OHV, four-cycle. Cast iron block and head. Displacement: 361 cubic inches. Bore and Stroke: 4-1/8 x 4-1/2. Compression ratio: 6.3:1. Brake horsepower: 111 at 2650 rpm. Seven main bearings. Mechanical valve lifters. Carburetor: Zenith 63AW12R.

Body and Chassis: — Wheelbase: 149 and 169 inches. Overall: length 238-270 inches. Width: 88 inches. Height: 98 inches. Tread center to center front: 64.5 inches. Tires: 8.25 x 20 10-ply nylon military non-directional.

Technical: — Manual constant mesh overdrive transmission. Speeds: 5F/1R. Two-speed transfer case. Single dry disc clutch. Leaf spring suspension front and rear. International Harvester or Eaton banjo spiral bevel differentials. Thornton locking differentials in the M-5H-6 models. Gear ratio: 7.16:1. Hydraulic vacuum assisted power brakes. Manual steering. Six-volt electrical system. Top speed: 46 mph. Fuel capacity: 60 gallons. Cruising range: 350 miles.

Standard Accessories: — Hand, vehicle, pioneer tools; spare parts; fire extinguisher; cab canvas and side curtains; cargo tarp.

Historical: — Designed and built by International Harvester Corporation from 1941 to 1945 in Fort Wayne, Indiana. Quantities sent out on lend-lease programs.

			PRICE			
Model No.	6	5	4	3	2	1
M-5H-6 Cargo	800	1500	3500	6000	9000	12,000
M-5-6 Cargo	—	—	—	—	—	—
M-5-6x4 Cargo	—	—	—	—	—	—
M-5H-6 Dump	—	—	—	—	—	—
M-5H-6 Tractor	—	—	—	—	—	—
M-5H-6 Wrecker	—	—	—	—	—	—
M-5H-6 Refueler	—	—	—	—	—	—

Studebaker US6 2-1/2 ton truck with hard cab. (John Benter)

Model US6: — The Studebaker US6 was another 2-1/2-ton 6x6 version of the cargo trucks built during World War II. Studebaker was enlisted to produce trucks as demand increased, and other manufacturers could not keep up. Much of the truck used standardized components that were on other two-tons of the period, the GMCs in particular. The cargo boxes were either wood or steel with troop seats, bows, and canvas cargo covers. The power train behind the transmission was the same as the Timken split used in the GMCs. This vehicle used a Borg Warner transmission rather than the Clark used in the GMC. The transfer case, drive shafts, and differential assemblies with suspension were the same as the GMC's. The big difference was in the cab and engine.

Studebaker used their cabs from the M model trucks of the period. Some of the modifications were a mesh screen over the rear cab window. The front windshield was hinged at the top, with the hinges on the outside of the cab roof. The interior had military gauges in the center of the instrument panel with the data plates on either side. Hand controls were under the instruments. The steering wheel was a familiar military design, and the cab and doors were larger than the trucks counterparts. The cowl was longer on the front of the cab, and consequently the fire wall had an indentation for the engine to sit in. The bench seat was quite large, and the lower footroom area was very generous. The front sheet metal was different, but similar to the GMC. The heavy metal brush guard and grille with vertical metal bars was used. The standard blackout lighting system was mounted alongside the headlights behind heavy mesh guards.

The hood opened from the front to rear, but was much more sloped than other trucks. The front fenders were distinctly different. They were flat on the top with a square lip on the edge, and they went straight down at the rear with a right angle to the running board. The cab, hood, and front fenders gave the truck a very distinctive appearance.

The engine was a Hercules JXD L-head design. These were very high quality engines with many forged parts and a gear-driven timing and camshaft arrangement. The external appearance was also different as the water pump, distributor, and fuel pump were on the lower left side of

Close-up of unrestored US6.

the block and driven off the timing gears and camshaft. It had a larger displacement, and at 320 cubic inches, had more torque as well. The power train was six-wheel-drive with a two-speed transfer case and shift levers in the cab for engagement of the front axle and high or low range. The transfer case had provisions for one front and two rear-drive shafts. The shaft going to the rear rear axle used a pillow block on the front rear axle. A 6x4 truck was built with the transfer case so both rear axles could be driven, but no front driven axle or drive shaft was used, with only one lever in the cab.

Early units were built with closed cabs, but later with open cabs and canvas tops. The rear of the frame had the bumperettes with a pintle hitch. Most models came equipped with or without a Garwood 10,000-pound front-mounted PTO-driven winch. Hard and soft cabs alike had

Interior view of US6.

the circular ring mount with machine gun for antiaircraft defense. Short and long wheelbase models were built with wood or steel and combination cargo beds. All Studebaker and Reo trucks used the split-type axles. Cargo capacity of the US6 was 5,000 pounds off-road and 10,000 pounds on hard surfaced roads. The Studebakers were built in several different versions, and the Reo was built only as a cargo truck. The variety of models in these trucks was not as large as the GMC's.

Model US6 Dump Truck: — This truck used a different box than the GMC trucks. It was mounted on the short wheelbase model with a conventional metal cab shield rather than the bolt-together wooden model on the GMC. The floor was heavier, and a dump box tailgate was used. The entire box and floor area was used for hauling material, whereas the GMC used only the rear two-thirds of its floor with a divider to keep the material in the rear area of the box, and had a longer wheelbase. A single-cylinder PTO-driven hydraulic hoist was used. The spare tire was behind the cab below the cab shield, and a toolbox was located on the right side of the frame. A second model was built with a side dumping box. The external appearance was nearly identical, but the hoist pushed the box up to the right side.

Model US6 Gasoline Tanker: — This model used two oval shaped 375-gallon tanks with large fill covers on top. Gravity feed and pumping equipment were stowed in the sheet metal cabinets at the rear for dispensing the fuel.

Model US6 Tractor: — This truck was a 6x4 drive cab and chassis with the spare tire behind the cab, and the toolbox was on the right side of the frame behind the running board. There was a stationary fifth wheel assembly with ramps for loading and towing semi trailers. The pintle hitch and bumperettes were excluded. The maximum towed load was about 21,000 pounds. The vehicle was air compressor equipped with a hand brake control on the steering column.

I.D. Data: — The serial number was located on the identification data plate on the left front rail above the front spring.

Model No.	Body Type	Weight	GVW	Prod.Total
US6	Cargo	10,745	16,095	125,711
US6x4	Cargo	9615	19,615	79,102
US6	Tanker	10,585	15,585	2300
US6	Dump	10,760	20,760	100
US6x4	Tractor	8140	17,760	8640

Engine: — Hercules JXD. Six-cylinder, inline, L-head, four-cycle. Cast iron block and head. Displacement: 320 cubic inches. Bore and Stroke: 4 x 4.25 inches. Compression ratio: 6.5:1. Seven main bearings. Mechanical valve lifters. Carburetor: Carter BBR1-5655.

Chassis and Body: — Wheelbase: 148 and 162 inches. Overall length: 220-266 inches. Width: 88 inches. Height: 88-109 inches. Tread center to center front: 62.25 inches. Tires: 7.50x20 8-ply nylon military non-directional.

Technical: — Manual constant mesh transmission with overdrive. Speeds: 5F/1R. Two-speed transfer case. Single dry disc clutch. Leaf spring suspension front and rear. Timken spiral bevel-full floating differentials with split housings. Gear ratio: 6.6:1. Hydraulic vacuum-assisted power brakes. Manual steering. Six-volt electrical system. Top speed: 45 mph. Fuel capacity: 40 gallons. Cruising range: 236 miles.

Standard Accessories: — Hand, vehicle, pioneer tools; canvas top, side curtains, cargo tarp; spare parts; fire extinguisher; rifle racks on open cab models.

Historical: — All models designed and built by Studebaker from 1941 to 1945. Reo also assembled only cargo trucks. Thousands given to lend-lease program countries.

			PRICE			
Model No.	6	5	4	3	2	1
US6 Cargo	500	1500	2500	3500	7000	9000
US6x4 Cargo	—	—	—	—	—	—
US6 Tanker	—	—	—	—	—	—
US6x4 Tractor	—	—	—	—	—	—
US6 Dump	—	—	—	—	—	—

Early 1950s GMC M211 6X6 2-1/2-ton cargo truck with dual rear wheels and winch.

Model M211: — The M211 is an improved six-wheel drive cargo truck that was designed from the GMC CCKW series of trucks used in World War II. It was a much more roadworthy vehicle and had a longer mechanical life than its predecessors. The cab was larger and used heavier sheet metal in all areas of the vehicle. Better seating, interior room and weatherproofing were incorporated. Waterproof sealed ignition, heater kits and hinged doors with roll-up windows helped modernize the trucks.

The engine size was increased, and the block was made of harder cast iron. It was somewhat heavier than the earlier trucks, which made it more practical for commercial use. As with all the M series vehicles designed in the earlier 1950s, the trucks were built to be operated in all climates and weather conditions. An air compressor was added to the engine for trailer towing as well as an air assist brake booster to improve braking performance with the double-wheel cylinders on each drum. Fording kits would allow the trucks to be driven under about five feet of water. The transfer case used a sprag unit to engage the front axle when it was needed. The rear wheels would slip a small amount, and the front axle would be engaged automatically.

Much heavier suspension was used in the rear; it actually had a double set of springs in the rear. The trucks were built with and without front PTO-driven winches, which had an aluminum case. A very nice spare tire carrier was installed which swung out away from the vehicle, and down, which made handling the tire much easier. The unique feature of this truck was the fact that it had an automatic transmission. It was a General Motors Hydramatic modified for heavier use in this truck. A gear reduction unit was added to the rear of the transmission. This gave the vehicle eight speeds forward, four in high range, and four in low range. Then in each range there was a provision for level or hilly driving. This was all performed in the transmission, and this allowed a single-speed transfer case to be used. Different gear ratios and heavier housings were used in the axles. A totally new electrical system was designed and used for better radio suppression, and was made waterproof as well.

It really was an all new truck, built from the experiences in World War II and the needs for the Army's new requirements. A twelve-foot standard military cargo box was used, and the vehicle was operated by one or two men. The cab was built to accept the installation of the .50 caliber ring-mount kit for antiaircraft. A very nice hard top cab kit was available; it could be bolted on. The off-road performance was very good because the

automatic transmission did not allow the truck to lose its momentum, as in shifting in a manual transmission vehicle.

Model M135: — This model was the same basic vehicle as the M211, but had single 11.00 x 20 tires and wheels, rather than the 9.00 x 20 duals used on the M211. A spacer was installed on the rear brake drum to put all tires in line. The tires all being in line gave the vehicle better off-road performance because the wider rear tires had to break a new track. The cargo box was changed and had wheel wells to allow the taller tires to move up and down when going cross country. It was also a little narrower, and had a step in the rear tailgate for ease of entry to the box for troops. Top bows and troop seats were used as in the M211.

Model M215: — The M215 was a dump truck based on the M211 chassis, but with a slightly shorter wheelbase. A 2-1/2 cubic yard body, with a double floor and large cab shield, was used. This sat on a sub frame which was also the hydraulic reservoir. A large single hydraulic cylinder was used, and the entire assembly was built by Garwood. The hydraulic pump was driven from a PTO on the transfer case. Hoist controls were inside the cab.

Model M221: — This semi tractor model used the shorter wheelbase like the dump truck, and was based on the M211 as well. It used a stationary fifth wheel with skid plates on the rear of the frame to stand on. The trailer air and electrical connections were mounted on a flexible stand behind the cab. Air trailer brake controls were on the steering column in the cab. No spare tire or carrier were used on this truck.

Model M220: — The van body truck used the same basic chassis as the M211 model. It was fitted with a twelve-foot steel body that had double walls and insulation. At the rear were double access doors with a ladder for entrance to the body. The electrical system was designed for 24-volt DC or 115-volt AC current. Three windows with slide-up screens and blackout panels were on each side of the body. Heating and ventilation systems were available, usually on the front of the van body above the cab of the truck. The hard top was standard on this model. The interior of the rear body also had a blackout lighting system for night use.

Early 1950s GMC M211 6X6 2-1/2-ton cargo truck with dual rear wheels.

Early 1950s GMC M135 6X6 2-1/2-ton cargo truck with single rear wheels.

GMC M215 6X6 2-1/2-ton dump truck. (Lou Bircheff, Alpaloma, California)

Rear view of GMC M215 dump truck. (Lou Bircheff, Alpaloma, California)

Model M222: — The M222 water tank truck also used the M211 chassis. It was fitted with a 1,000-gallon aluminum tank that was double walled and insulated. It had two compartments, one 400-gallon and one 600-gallon. A transfer case PTO-driven pump, controls and equipment were in the rear cabinets. A rear heating system was under the tank using engine exhaust to keep it from freezing in the winter. The tank was filled with the pump and emptied by gravity, filling done by two large openings in the top of the tank. Each vehicle was equipped with suction and discharge equipment used with the pump.

Model M217: — The M217 was a gasoline tank truck using the M211 chassis. A 1,200 gallon steel tank was used with three compartments, 200-, 400-, 600- gallon. A transfer case PTO-driven pump at the rear in the large cabinet with other items was used for filling and emptying the compartments. Controls, delivery pump, hoses and valves were all mounted in the rear compartment. An insulated wiring harness was used on the rear body to prevent sparks. The truck has no pintle hitch, trailer brake, or electrical connections at the rear of the body. Gasoline could be delivered by pump or gravity. Filling was done by large covers in the top of the body.

I.D. Data: — The serial number was located on the identification data plate on the instrument panel, and on the left front frame rail directly above the front axle housing.

Model No.	Body Type	Weight	GVW	Prod. Total
M211	Cargo	13,170	23,520	—
M135	Cargo	12,740	23,090	—
M215	Dump	14,460	24,460	—
M217	Tank	14,340	22,690	—
M220	Van	15,085	23,085	—
M221	Tractor	11,695	24,045	—
M222	Tank	14,100	22,950	—

Engine: — GMC Model 302, six-cylinder, inline, OHV, four-cycle, cast iron block and head. Displacement: 302 cubic inches. Bore and Stroke: 4 x 4 inches. Compression ratio: 7.2:1. Brake horsepower: 130 at 3400 rpm. Five main bearings. Mechanical valve lifters. Carburetor: Holley.

Chassis and Body: — Wheelbase: 144 and 156 inches. Overall length: 233 to 269 inches. Width: 82.5 to 96 inches. Height: 102 to 130 inches. Tread center to center: 69 inches. Tires: 9.00 x 20 or 11.00 x 20, 8- or 12-ply military non-directional.

Technical: — Automatic transmission, General Motors Hydramatic with torque converter and gear reduction unit attached. Speeds 8F/2R. Single-speed transfer case. Semi-elliptic leaf spring suspension. General Motors hypoid, full floating, single reduction banjo differentials. Overall gear ratio: 6.17:1. Hydraulic air-assisted power brakes. Manual steer-

Early 1950s GMC M220 6X6 2-1/2-ton van. (Chuck Barnett, Upland, California)

Rear view of GMC M220 van. (Chuck Barnett, Upland, California)

ing. Twenty-four-volt electrical system. Top speed: 55 mph. Fuel capacity: 56 gallons. Cruising range: 300 miles.

Standard Accessories: — Canvas for cab and cargo box; troop seats and top bows; hand, vehicle, pioneer tools; spare parts; circular ring mount for .50 caliber machine gun, if so equipped.

Historical: — Designed and built in mass production by GMC truck division of General Motors in Pontiac, Michigan from 1950 to 1955. Competed with and was superseded by the Reo "Eager Beaver" 2-1/2 ton truck. Used by many National Guard units well into the 1960s. Large quantities produced. Saw some combat use in Korean War. Mostly used in the continental United States.

			PRICE			
Model No.	6	5	4	3	2	1
M211	300	800	1500	4000	5000	6000
M135	300	800	1500	4000	5000	6000
M215	300	800	1500	4000	—	—
M217	300	800	1500	4000	—	—
M220	300	800	1500	4000	—	—
M221	300	800	1200	3500	—	—
M222	300	800	1200	3500	—	—

Mid-1950s Reo M356 6X6 2-1/2-ton cargo truck. (Tom Sears, Springfield, Ohio)

Model M35: — The "Reo" was the U.S. military's model of choice for 2-1/2- ton transportation needs, following the veteran CCKW of World War II. The early 1950s brought many changes in the cargo trucks. They were completely new vehicles and were much more roadworthy, and had a longer mechanical life than their predeccessors. The M35 was a ten-wheel truck fitted with the standard 12-foot cargo box. The cab sheet metal was heavier, and it was larger inside. It was more streamlined, and the hood side panels could be folded down for easier servicing. Better weatherproofing was incorporated into the design with hard tops that could easily be installed or removed. Seating was improved, and fender-mounted gasoline-fired or hot-water heater kits were provided.

Waterproof ignition with radio suppression, electrical and fuel systems were designed and installed. Hinged doors with roll-up glass windows were added, and the folding windshields were still used with the removable canvas tops. A blackout light system was used for night driving; red lights were in the instrument panel for easier vision while using the blackout drive system. The engine size was increased, and it was wet sleeved. Synchromesh was made standard in the transmissions. The trucks were heavier in almost all aspects, and were also designed to be used in all climatic conditions with the addition of winterization, or fording kits, or whatever equipment was required. A new compressed air assist system was added to the braking system, making air compressors standard on all trucks. The cooling system was improved, and the fording equipment actually allowed the truck to be driven under water when installed. Usually the depth of water was about five feet.

Larger tire sizes were used, and some models used single wheels on the rear, which followed in the same track as the front and improved the offroad performance. The transfer case design was changed, still using two speeds; the front axle engagement was an automatic feature done by a sprag unit in the front of the case. This eliminated the need for two levers in the cab, consequently only one was used for shifting to high or low range. When the rear wheels began to slip, the front axle was positively engaged by the sprag unit. Stronger leaf spring suspension was used, and the Timken six-link control system was still used. Front

Rear view of Reo M35 cargo truck. (Tom Sears, Springfield, Ohio)

mounted PTO driven winches were used on some models; almost all models had rear pintle hitches for towing. The winches had aluminum cases. Air lines and receptacles were at the rear of the frame for trailer brakes which were air over hydraulic, just like the truck.

Electrical trailer brakes were used very little after World War II. The spare tire system was changed, using a short cable and ratchet mechanism to secure the spare assembly. The axle housings were a square

Late 1960s Kaiser Jeep M36A2 6X6 2-1/2-ton long wheelbase cargo truck with winch. (Jon Bircheff, Fontana, California)

lube design, and the suspension components were clamped to them with bolts, rather than the spring perches being cast to the housings. The differentials were the double reduction type with the pinion shafts going all the way through the carrier. This allowed flanges on both ends, and they could be used in tandem, thus eliminating one set of rear drive shafts, as two sets were used in the World War II trucks. This truck and all the various models were later repowered with multifuel diesel engines in the early 1960s. The new engines required different radiators, clutches, overdrive transmissions and transfer cases. Later models had air shift units rather than the sprag units, and the trucks had different air cleaners. These were the basic differences. There were constant changes of small items on the trucks as the production contracts went on over the years. It was one of the most widely used designs and has enjoyed one of the longest periods of use of any of the U.S. military truck designs to date. Cargo capacity was about 10,000 pounds on the highway and 5000 pounds offroad.

Model M35A1: — Same cargo truck as the M35, but was powered by a Continental multifuel diesel engine, turbocharged model LDS-427.

Model M35A2: — Same cargo truck as the M35A1, but was powered by a Continental LD-465 multifuel diesel, naturally aspirated.

Model M36: — Same cargo truck as the M35, but has a longer wheelbase and a 17-foot cargo box with one side that drops for easier loading from the side.

Model M36A2: — Same cargo truck as the M36, but was powered by a Continental LD-465 multifuel diesel engine. Overall length 344 inches.

Model M34: — This truck was the same basic vehicle as M35, but used single wheels on the rear with a spacer on the rear brake drum. All wheels on the truck had a different offset so they would track the same. Following in the same track provided better traction offroad because dual rear wheels have to fight to break a new track. The cargo box was different. It had wheels for the taller 11.00 x 20 tires, which had a taller travel when moving offroad. It was a little narrower and had a folding step in the tailgate for ease of entry into the box for troops.

Model M47: — This was a dump truck using the same chassis as the M34 cargo truck. A 2-1/2 cubic yard double floor dump box with a large cab shield was mounted on a sub frame with a single cylinder hydraulic

hoist. The hydraulic pump was PTO driven off the transmission. The spare tire and tool box were mounted behind the cab. The hydraulic reservoir was inside the sub frame. Hoist controls were inside the cab.

Model M59: — This dump truck was the same as the M47, but used the same chassis as the M35 cargo with the dual rear wheels. The dump box was a little wider to cover the wider rear tires but was functionally the same in all aspects. Later diesel-powered vehicles such as this used a two cylinder hoist.

Model 342A2: — This was the same truck as the M59 dump truck, but was powered by a Continental LD-465 multifuel diesel engine and had the twin cylinder hoist.

Model M49: — This vehicle was a gasoline tanker using the M35 cargo truck chassis. The 1200-gallon steel tank had three compartments for 200, 400, and 600 gallons. A transfer case-mounted PTO drives the rear delivery pump for filling or emptying the compartments. Controls, delivery pump, hoses, controls and valves were mounted and stored in the rear of the truck in a large cabinet which was part of the body. An insulated wiring harness was used on the rear body to prevent sparks, and no pintle hitch or trailer brake or electrical connections were at the rear of the truck. Gasoline could be delivered by the pump or by gravity. The tank was filled through large covers on the top of the body.

Model M49A1: — This was the same truck as the M49, but was powered by a Continental LDS-427 multifuel diesel engine, turbocharged.

Model M49A2: — This was the same truck as the M49AI, but was powered by a Continental LD-465 multifuel diesel engine.

Model M50: — This was a water truck using the M35 cargo truck chassis with a double-walled insulated aluminum tank with rear cabinets. It had a 1,000-gallon capacity, with one 400 and one 600-gallon compartment. The transfer case PTO driven pump, controls, and equipment were in the rear compartment. A rear heating system was under the tank using heat from the engine exhaust to keep the tank from freezing in cold weather. The tank was filled with the pump and emptied by gravity. Each truck was equipped with suction and discharge equipment.

Model M50A1: — Same truck as the M50, but was powered by a Continental LDS-427 turbocharged multifuel diesel engine.

Mid-1950s Reo 6X6 2-1/2-ton M49 gasoline tanker.

Model M50A2: — This was the same truck as the M50A1, but was powered by a Continental LD-465 multifuel diesel engine.

Model M48: — This tractor was based on the M35 cargo truck chassis. It has a stationary fifth wheel with skid plates on the rear of the frame. The tool box and spare tire were behind the cab. The air and electrical connections for the semi trailer were mounted on the spare tire carrier. The air trailer brake controls were on the steering column.

Model M275: — This truck tractor used the shorter wheelbase, with a stationary fifth wheel and skid plates. With the shorter wheelbase the fuel tank was mounted under the cab where the tool box was normally located, beneath the driver's door. This unit does not carry a spare tire or tool box.

Model M275A1: — Same truck as the M275, but was powered by a Continental LDS-427 multifuel diesel engine.

Model M275A2: — Same truck as the M275AI, but was powered by a Continental LD-465 multifuel diesel engine.

Model M109: — This was the same chassis as the M35 cargo truck. It has a 12-foot all-steel van body with double walls and insulation. In the rear there were double access doors. An access ladder was provided to get on the roof. The electrical system was designed for 24-volt D.C. or 115-volt A.C. current. Five windows and screens were on each of the bodies with blackout panels to cover them. Heating and ventilation systems were available to provide a variety of comfortable working conditions. The hard top cab was standard on this model. The interior of the van body was provided with a blackout lighting system.

Model M109A1: — Same truck as the M109, but was powered by a Continental LDS-427 multifuel diesel engine.

Model M109A2: — Same truck as the M109AI, but was powered by a Continental LD-465 multifuel diesel engine.

Model M108: — This was a crane truck using the M35 cargo truck chassis. A revolving hydraulic crane was mounted on the rear; it could swing 270 degrees between stops. A platform was built around the crane to work or stand on. The single-cylinder lift on the boom was powered by a transfer case PTO driven pump. The winch for the crane was

Left rear view of 1950s Reo M Series gas tanker.

on the rear of the boom. The boom could be extended to a length of 16 feet. The operator's controls and seat were on the side of the main mast of the boom assembly and turned with the crane. Floodlights and manual outriggers were provided, and the rear suspension had a support beam above the rear springs so as to stabilize the truck when the crane was working. Crane capacity was 8000 pounds with the outriggers down, boom elevated and retracted. With the boom extended, the capacity was 4000 pounds.

Model M60: — This was the same truck as the M108, but had a 20,000-pound winch mounted on the frame at the rear of the truck. The platform was changed slightly for some additional tools and equipment because this model was also for salvage and recovery.

I.D. Data: — The serial number was located on the identification data plate on the instrument panel, and on the left front frame rail above the left front spring.

Late 1950s Reo M109 6X6 2-1/2-ton van.

Right rear view of Reo M109 van.

Model No.	Body Type	Weight	GVW	Prod. Total
M34	Cargo	11,775	22,540	—
M35	Cargo	12,465	23,230	—
M35A1	Cargo	13,530	23,530	—
M35A2	Cargo	13,530	23,530	—
M36	Cargo	13,915	23,500	—
M36A2	Cargo	15,750	25,510	—
M47	Dump	13,450	24,210	—
M59	Dump	14,050	24,810	—
M342A2	Dump	15,500	25,500	—
M49	Tank	13,490	21,755	—
M49A1	Tank	16,107	23,365	—
M49A2	Tank	14,740	22,840	—
M50	Tank	15,038	23,688	—
M50A1	Tank	15,255	23,855	—
M50A2	Tank	14,589	22,930	—
M48	Tractor	11,430	24,190	—
M275	Tractor	11,179	23,939	—
M275A1	Tractor	12,534	23,124	—
M275A2	Tractor	12,226	24,226	—
M109	Van	15,231	20,581	—
M109A1	Van	16,296	20,642	—
M109A2	Van	16,296	20,642	—
M60	Crane	23,960	27,810	—
M108	Crane	19,785	23,635	—

Engines: — Reo OA331, gasoline, six-cylinder, inline, OHV, four-cycle, wet sleeved. Cast iron block and head. Displacement: 331 cubic inches. Bore and stroke: 4.125 x 4.125 inches. Compression ratio: 6.75:1. Brake horsepower: 127 at 3400 rpm. Seven main bearings. Mechanical valve lifters. Carburetor: Holley 885FFG.

Continental, multifuel diesel, LDS-427, six-cylinder, inline, OHV, four-cycle, turbocharged, dry sleeved. Cast iron block and head. Displacement: 427 cubic inches: Bore and stroke: 4.31 x 4.87 inches. Compression ratio: 20:1. Brake horsepower: 130 at 2600 rpm. Seven main bearings. Mechanical valve lifters. American Bosch fuel injection.

Continental, multifuel diesel, LD-465, six-cylinder, inline OHV, four-cycle, dry sleeved. Cast iron block and head. Displacement: 478 cubic inches. Bore and stroke: 4.56 x 4.88 inches. Compression ratio: 22:1. Brake horsepower: 210 at 2800 rpm. Seven main bearings. Mechanical valve lifters. American Bosch fuel injection.

Chassis and Body: — Wheelbase: 142, 154, 190 inches. Overall length: 242 to 343 inches with winch. Vehicles without winches were 14 inches shorter. Width: 85 to 98 inches. Height: 97 to 130 inches. Tread center to center front: 67-3/8 or 69-5/8 inches. Tires 9.00 x 20 8-ply or 11.00 x 20 12-ply military non-directional.

Technical: — Manual synchromesh transmission. Overdrive in diesel-powered trucks. Speeds 5F/IR. Two-speed transfer case. Early was sprag type, late was air shift. Single dry disc clutch. Semi elliptic leaf spring suspension front and rear. Timken Rockwell double reduction full floating differentials. Gear ratio: 6.72:1. Hydraulic brakes with air assist. Manual steering. Twenty-four-volt electrical system. Top speed: 60 mph gas, 56 mph diesel. Fuel capacity: 50 gallons. Cruising range: 288 miles gas, 350 miles diesel.

Standard Accessories: — Hand, vehicle, pioneer tools; canvas cab top and cargo box cover; hydraulic jack; fire extinguisher. Other bodies had more specialized equipment, particularly the wrecker, crane, gasoline and water units.

Reo M60 6X6 2-1/2-ton wrecker truck. (Kenosha Military Museum Inc.)

Mid-1950s Reo 6X6 2-1/2-ton compressor truck with winch and hard cab.

Late 1950s Reo 6X6 2-1/2-ton truck with missile launcher.

PRICE

Model No.	6	5	4	3	2	1
M34	400	1500	3500	5000	6000	7500
M35	400	1500	3500	5000	6000	7500
M35A1	600	1800	3500	4500	6000	8500
M35A2	900	2200	4000	5500	7500	9500
M36	800	2000	4000	5500	6500	8500
M36A2	1200	3000	4500	6500	7500	9500
M47	600	1500	3500	5000	6000	7500
M59	600	1500	3500	5000	6000	7500
M49	800	1500	3000	4500	5500	6500
M49A1	1000	1500	3000	3500	6000	7500
M49A2	1500	2000	3500	5000	7000	8500
M50	800	1200	3000	5000	6000	7500
M50A1	1000	1500	3000	5500	6500	8500
M50A2	1200	3000	4500	6500	7500	9500
M48	400	1100	2900	4000	5000	6000
M275	400	1100	2900	4000	5000	6000
M275A1	600	1400	3300	4500	5500	6500
M275A2	900	1700	3600	4800	7000	8500
M109	700	1700	2800	5000	6000	7500
M109A1	1000	2000	3400	4000	6500	8500
M109A2	1300	2300	3900	5000	7500	9500
M60	1200	1800	3500	5500	6800	8000
M108	1200	1800	3500	5500	6800	8000

World War II Diamond T 6X6 four-ton open cab wrecker. (Ralph Doubek, Wild Rose, Wisconsin)

Model Diamond T 969: — The 969 is a six-wheel-drive heavy wrecker used for towing and lifting disabled vehicles and equipment. This was a larger, heavier truck rated at four-ton capacity. The larger engine and improved axles with air brakes made this a versatile truck.

The truck was manufactured with hard and soft cab, and all had a 15,000-pound front winch. The hard cab was a modified civilian model, and the open military cab had the folding windshield and removable canvas top. The power train was conventional layout with a second power take-off on the transfer case to run the wrecker body. The wrecker body was built by the Ernest Holmes Co., model W45, with a military body that had large tool cabinets above the rear tires. The twin power booms could be swung out to the side of the truck, and using the outriggers they had a load capacity of five tons each. A crew of two was usually used to operate the vehicle, as the mechanical controls were on each side of the truck, and the operator had a difficult time seeing the rear when lifting equipment. There were provisions in the body for the antiaircraft ring mount used above the cab. A very large quantity of tools and equipment was carried to facilitate the recovery of a wide variety of vehicles that were serviced by this wrecker.

I.D. Data: — The serial number was located on the identification data plate under the hood on the left side of the cowl, and on the left front frame rail above the front axle housing.

Model No.	Body Type	Weight	GVW	Prod. Total
969	Wrecker	21,350	29,350	6203

Engine: — Hercules RXC, six-cylinder, inline, L-head, four-cycle, cast iron block and head. Displacement: 529 cubic inches. Compression ratio: 5.4:1. Bore and Stroke: 4-5/8 x 5-1/4 inches. Brake horsepower: 106 at 2300 rpm. Seven main bearings. Mechanical valve lifters. Carburetor: Zenith cast iron.

Chassis and Body: — Wheelbase: 151 inches. Overall length: 292 inches. Height: 116 inches. Width: 99.5 inches. Tread center to center front: 73.75 inches. Tires: 9.00 x 20 10-ply military non-directional.

Technical: — Manual constant mesh transmission. Speeds 5F/1R. Two-speed transfer case. Single dry disc clutch. Timken double reduction differentials. Overall ratio: 8.43:1. Semi-elliptic leaf spring suspension. Air brakes with trailer controls. Manual steering. Twelve- and 6-volt electrical. Top speed: 40 mph. Fuel capacity: 60 gallons. Cruising range: 180 miles.

Standard Accessories: — Large quantities of recovery, hand, vehicle, pioneer tools; specialized recovery equipment, air compressor and welding, cutting equipment; spare parts; fire extinguisher, extra spare tire.

Historical: — Design and development began in 1939. Diamond T's model became most successful and was adopted in 1940. Built from 1940 to 1945. Used in all theaters of World War II and by several branches of service.

PRICE

Model No.	6	5	4	3	2	1
969	2000	4000	7000	11,000	14,000	18,000

World War II Diamond T four-ton closed cab wrecker. (George Hilton, North Bangor, New York)

Right rear view of Diamond T closed cab wrecker. (George Hilton, North Bangor, New York)

Model 968A: — The Diamond T 968A was a four-ton six-wheel-drive cargo truck used for general cargo and personnel transportation. It was a standard military unit encompassing all the requirements needed by the armed forces of the period. It was powered by a large L-head gasoline six-cylinder engine. The transmission was a five-speed overdrive unit with a separate two-speed transfer case. The axles in this truck were considerably heavier than the 2-1/2 ton trucks of the period. These were Timken double reduction banjo type using only one drive shaft in the rear. Full air brakes and ten-hole Budd wheels were standard equipment.

Two cabs were used, a modified civilian model and the traditional military unit with folding windshield and canvas top. The open cabs did have small half doors, but no roll up glass. Side curtains were provided for inclement weather.

The cargo trucks came with a front-mounted PTO-driven winch with 15,000 pound capacity. The rear bodies were wood or steel cargo boxes. Troop seats, side racks, top bows, end curtains were standard equipment. A folding rear tailgate with toolbox beneath it was at the rear. Bumperettes, pintle hitch, electrical and air trailer brake connections were at the end of the frame. Air-operated windshield wipers, blackout drive light system, and rearview mirrors were used. The fuel tank was under the driver's door. Step rungs were on the rear mud shield under the box for easier access to the cargo box.

Inside the cab, the driving controls were conventional, and the instrument panel had some additions. A tachometer, viscometer for engine oil, and a manual spark advance for the ignition were added. An air pressure gauge monitored pressurized air for the brake system. A disc parking brake was used, and the electrical system was six-volt with a 12-volt starter. Two batteries were mounted under the passenger's door in a cabinet behind the running board. This model of engine in this series of trucks had two individual cylinder heads. The box was 11 feet long, and the truck could carry about 12,000 pounds of cargo. Two spare tires were mounted in the front of the cargo box. A trailer of about 12,000 pound capacity could be towed, and the open cab had provisions in the body for installing the circular ring mount above the cab for a .50 caliber machine gun used for antiaircraft defense.

Model 970A: — This was the same truck as the 968A but had a longer wheelbase. It was referred to as a "ponton" truck and was used to haul portable bridging equipment for the engineers. The body was 147 inches rather than the 131 inches on the 968A model. The wheelbase was 21 inches longer.

Model 972: — This was the dump truck model and used the chassis of the short wheelbase chassis of the 968A. An all-steel four-cubic yard dump body was used with a single cylinder PTO-driven hydraulic hoist. The rear tailgate of the dump body could be used for spreading or dumping material. The front of the box had a large cab shield, and the spare tire and gas can were mounted on the front of the box in between the back of the cab and front of the dump body. This also came equipped with or without front mounted winch. Only hard cabs were used on this truck. The rear body was 120 inches long with 17-inch high sides.

Model 969A: — This vehicle was the wrecker model. It was equipped with a Holmes W45 wrecker body. It came in hard or soft cab versions. A front-mounted winch was provided; it was driven off the transmission. A second power take-off was on the transfer case for the wrecker winches. The wrecker also had its own transmission with forward and reverse. The two winches and booms could be used together or sepa-

rately. Two hundred feet of cable was on each spool. A gasoline engine-driven air compressor was mounted on the rear body for tire work. A small military body was behind the wrecker assembly with a toolbox on each side and a folding tailgate. The twin power could be swung out the sides of the truck, and a large leg for bracing was provided. The booms had a five-ton capacity or 20 tons with their snatch blocks installed. A crew of two usually operated the truck as the mechanical controls were on each side of the truck, and that person had a difficult time seeing what was going on at the rear of the truck. Ring mount provisions were on this truck as well. A very large quantity of tools and equipment were carried to facilitate the recovery of the wide variety of vehicles that were serviced by this truck.

I.D. Data: — The serial number was located on the identification data plate under the hood on the left side of the cowl and on the left front frame rail above the spring.

Model No.	Body Type	Weight	GVW	Prod.Total
968A	Cargo	18,400	26,400	9794
970A	Cargo	18,800	26,800	852
972	Dump	17,725	25,725	9922
969A	Wrecker	21,700	—	6429
Cab and Chassis for special bodies				2197

Engine: — Hercules RXC, six-cylinder, inline, L-head, four-cycle. Cast iron head and block. Displacement: 529 cubic inches. Bore and Stroke: 4.625 x 5.25 inches. Compression ratio: 5.4:1. Brake horsepower: 119 at 2300 rpm. Seven main bearings. Mechanical valve lifters. Carburetor Zenith Model 29.

Chassis and Body: — Wheelbase: 151 and 172 inches. Overall length: 268-296 inches. Width: 96-101 inches. Height: 111-114 inches. Tread center to center front: 74 inches. Tires: 9.00 x 20 10-ply military non-directional.

Technical: — Manual constant mesh transmission. Speeds: 5F/1R. Two-speed transfer case. Single dry disc clutch. Timken double reduction differentials. Gear ratio 8.43:1. Semi-elliptic leaf spring suspension. Air brakes. Manual steering. Six-volt electrical system, with 12-volt starting system. Top speed: 40 mph. Fuel capacity: 60 gallons. Cruising range: 180 miles.

Standard Accessories: — Hand, vehicle, pioneer tools. Fire extinguisher, grease gun, hydraulic jack, tire chains, spare parts, tow chain, snatch block, engine hand crank. Caband cargo tarps. Wrecker additional equipment: Tow chains, crowbar, 300 feet of rope, second set of pioneer tools, engine driven air compressor with hose. Ground anchors, tow bars, oxygen and acetyline bottles with hoses, torches, welding equipment. Carbon dioxide fire extinguisher, snatch blocks, floodlights.

Historical: — Design and development began in 1939. Diamond T's model was adopted in 1940. Built from 1940 to 1945. Cab and chassis were used for crane equipment, water distributing bodies, map reproduction, van bodies, bituminus supply and distribution bodies.

PRICE

Model	6	5	4	3	2	1
968A	1000	1500	2500	4000	6000	—
970A	1000	1500	2500	4000	6000	—
972	1500	2000	3000	4500	6500	—
969A	2000	4000	6000	8000	11,000	—

World War II Autocar U7144-T four-ton tractor. (Frank Donnelly, LaVerne, California)

Model: — Autocar U-7144T — The Autocar U-7144T was a heavy truck in the four- to five-ton class. It was designed as a tractor for towing semi trailers of different types. Early models were civilian hard cabs fitted with the standard military grille and hardware. Later they were redesigned into open cabs of flat sheet metal with removable canvas tops and folding windshields.

It was a cab-over-engine design with a four-wheel-drive power train beneath it and a conventional channel frame. As a tractor, it was equipped with air brakes, and trailer brake controls, a fifth wheel for towing, and no rear body. A toolbox was carried on the right frame rail behind the cab, and the fuel tank was on the opposite side.

The open cab bodies had brackets for a circular machine gun mount although not all were so equipped. This was above the passenger seat. Two spare tire assemblies were carried behind the cab on a rack. Being a cab-over design and four-wheel-drive, the unit was quite tall. It was not a great problem because the trailers were also tall and the units were used almost entirely in the rear areas away from combat zones. The crew of two were the driver and assistant. Usually one truck out of every four had a machine gun mount, which carried a Browning .50 caliber machine gun. These kits could be installed on any open cab truck.

I.D. Data: — Serial number was on the identification data plate on the instrument panel and on the left front frame rail directly above the front axle housing.

Engine: — Hercules RXC, six-cylinder, L-head, four-cycle, cast iron block. Displacement: 529 cubic inches. Bore and Stroke: 4-5/8 inches x 5-1/4 inches. Brake horsepower: 131 at 2200 rpm. Seven main bearings. Valve lifters: mechanical. Carburetor: Zenith cast iron.

Chassis and Body: — Wheelbase: 134.5 inches. Overall length: 202 inches. Height: 108 inches. Width: 95 inches. Tread center to center rear: 72 inches. Tires: 9.00 x 20 10-ply non-directional.

Technical: — Manual helical gear constant mesh transmission. Speeds: 5F/1R. Two-speed transfer case. Single dry disc clutch. Semi-elliptic leaf spring suspension. Wisconsin double reduction banjo differentials. Overall ratio: 8.43:1. Bendix Westinghouse air brakes with trailer controls. Manual steering. Six-volt electrical system. Top speed: 41 mph. Fuel capacity: 60 gallons. Cruising range: 200 miles.

Standard Accessories: — One .50 caliber machine gun with circular ring mount on vehicles so equipped; hand and vehicle tools; spare parts; fire extinguisher.

Historical: — Originally designed by GMC then Mack, but Autocar's model prevailed and went into production in 1941. White helped with assembly, and Federal made a similar truck with minor sheet metal differences. White's model number was 444T, Federal's was 94x43A.

Model No.	Body Type	Weight	GVW	Prod. Total
U-7144T	Open Cabover Steel	12,200	21,200	—

PRICE						
Model No.	6	5	4	3	2	1
U-7144T	900	1800	3000	6000	—	—

Late 1960s M54A2 6X6 five-ton cargo truck.

Model M54: — The M series "five-ton" was the postwar replacement for the four-, six-, 7-1/2-ton series trucks used in World War II. It was very similar in design and appearance to the 2-1/2-ton series trucks. It, too, was an all-new design that was improved and repowered all through its life. The simple rugged construction was just too good to be cast aside, consequently this truck also had a very long economic life for the military.

The sheet metal, cab and 14-foot cargo box were all new designs, using all steel construction. In World War II many trucks had wood boxes due to the shortage of steel. The driver's comfort was improved with the addition of gasoline or hot water heater kits along with hard top cabs. Hydraulic power steering was added, along with synchromesh transmissions. This M series truck had a great deal of standardization incorporated into the design, appearance, and functions. A blackout drive system, removable canvas tops on the cabs and cargo beds, troop seats, waterproof electrical, and fuel systems were featured as in the other M series vehicles.

The original trucks were powered by a large Continental gasoline engine; later models used a Mack or Continental multifuel diesel engine. The air brake system of the World War II trucks was replaced by an air-over-hydraulic system. This was done with fording in mind because the hydraulic system could be sealed from moisture more easily than the air system. Larger tires were used for better flotation. The two-speed transfer case used a sprag unit for automatic engagement of the front axle when the rear wheels slipped, similar to the 2-1/2 ton series trucks. The Timken six-link torque rod suspension was retained with the double reduction style axles. A 20,000-pound PTO-driven front winch was used on the front of some models. A level wind unit was available to keep the cable on the drum in a correct manner. The wrecker trucks had rear drag winches of 40,000-pound capacity. Pintle hitches were on the rear of the frame along with bumperettes. Air line connections for the trailer brakes were at the rear of the frame. Semi trailers used straight air, and two-wheel trailers usually used air-over-hydraulic systems with an air chamber pushing on a master cylinder to apply the hydraulic pressure to the wheel cylinders. The axles had all the suspension components bolted and clamped to them. The repowering began in the 1960s, making up several more series of trucks. This program extended their life considerably.

The heavy components in the chassis made it a very popular truck in the civilian sector among commercial users. They were capable of carrying cargo loads of up to 25,000 to 30,000 pounds comfortably. The hydraulic brakes did limit the truck somewhat. Loads this heavy require better brakes, preferably the straight air type used on commercial trucks. Almost all the boxes, special beds or equipment on these chassis had more capacity than their earlier predecessors. They were also geared for more road speed, and the overhead valve engines were more efficient than the L-head designs. The diesel-powered trucks had additional changes other than just the engine. Overdrive transmissions, larger cooling and air filtration systems, clutch, and electrical systems were added or upgraded to function with the new engines. This truck was designed at about the same time as the quarter-, three-quarter-, and 2-1/2-ton M series units of the early 1950s were introduced. The M54 was a simple cargo truck with a steel body used for general troop transport and cargo transportation.

Model M54A1: — This is the same truck as the M54, but was powered by a Mack ENDT-673 diesel engine.

Model M54A2: — This is the same as the M54A1, but was powered by a Continental LDS-465 multifuel diesel engine.

Model M41: — This cargo truck used the same basic chassis as the M54 but was equipped with 14.00 x 20 single tires mounted on combat wheels. The front and rear tires, all being in line, provided better traction off-road than the dual tired models. The cargo box was 14 feet long, but had wheel wells built in the sides to accommodate the longer travel of the tires moving up and down in off-road situations. The tailgate had a folding step in it for easier entry into the box. The cargo box was also slightly narrower than the M54's box.

Model M55: — This was the same chassis as the M54, but had a longer wheelbase for the 20-foot cargo box.

Model M55A1: — This was same chassis as the M55, but was powered by a Mack ENDT-673 diesel engine.

Model M55A2: — This was the same truck as the M55A1, but was powered by a Continental LDS-465 multifuel diesel engine.

Early 1950s M51 6X6 five-ton dump truck. (Bob Anderson, McFarland, Wisconsin)

Right rear view of M-51 dump truck. (Bob Anderson, McFarland, Wisconsin)

Model M51: — This dump truck used the same chassis as the M54 cargo truck, but had a shorter wheelbase using a 10-1/2 foot five-yard box. It was made of all-steel construction and had a double floor. A PTO-driven hydraulic pump powered a twin-cylinder hoist; the oil reservoir was in the subframe of the hoist. A large cab shield was mounted on the front of the box, and it could be used as a rocker-type dump box or as a spreader box by changing the tailgate. The spare tire and toolbox were mounted between the cab and dump body.

Model M51A1: — This was the same chassis as the M51 truck, but was powered by a Mack ENDT-673 diesel engine.

Model M51A2: — This was the same chassis as the M51A1 truck , but was powered by a Continental LDS-465 multifuel diesel engine.

Model M52: — This tractor used the same short wheelbase chassis as the M51 dump truck, but had a stationary fifth wheel and approach plates for towing a semi trailer. The spare tire assembly and toolbox were mounted behind the cab. The air trailer brake connections were on the spare tire carrier.

Model M52A1: — This was the same truck as the M52 tractor, but was powered by a Mack ENDT-673 diesel engine.

Model M52A2: — This was the same truck as the M52A1, but was powered by a Continental LDS-465 multifuel diesel engine.

Model M139: — This vehicle was a long wheelbase model originally designed to transport bridge building components. Later it was used for special equipment for the 762mm "Honest John" surface-to-surface rocket. It used 14.00 x 20 dual tires, making it over eight feet wide. The M139C, D, and F models used with the rocket had a lower gear ratio in the axles, 10.26:1, for improved off-road traction.

Model M62: — The M62 wrecker truck used the same chassis as the M54 cargo vehicle. The wrecker was used for towing, salvage and recovery of medium-duty trucks and other equipment. All were equipped with a front-mounted winch and level wind with 20,000 pound capacity. A bumper-mounted vise was at the front. Behind the cab was an area for carrying cutting equipment and for stowage. The rear bed had a frame-mounted Austin Western 20,000-pound hydraulic revolving crane. It had an 18-foot extendable boom, and manual outriggers were provided for stability. The boom was a two-stage unit with power coming from the PTO-driven hydraulic system. It could also swing 270 degrees between stops. Stiff legs and a solid beam above the rear springs limited suspension travel when traveling or using the boom. The truck spare tire assembly was mounted on the left side of the boom, and the operator's controls were on the right side. The main winch for the boom was at the rear of the boom and used a two-part line with a snatch block. The maximum capacity of the boom could only be used with the outriggers down and stiff legs under the boom for support. The boom had to be retracted all the way at its maximum elavation. The boom had limitations, and 20,000 pounds just could not be picked up anytime and swung around at will. This resulted in severe damage to the turntable of the boom and would tip over the truck. The hydraulic reservoir was in the bed of the truck.

Mid-1950s M62 6X6 five-ton wrecker.

Right rear vew of M62 wrecker.

The boom had a single lift cylinder underneath it, which was meant to raise and lower the boom itself, not to lift loads. The boom winch was to be used for raising or lowering the load. On the rear of the bed was a 40,000-pound drag winch equipped with level wind for recovery. Floodlights were on the rear area of the truck for night work. A large quantity of tools and equipment were carried for many types of work.

Model M543: — This wrecker used the same basic chassis as the M62 but as a completely different crane with some improvements. The capacities and performance were the same on both models. This Austin Western crane had the hydraulic reservoir on the side of the boom where the spare tire assembly was mounted on the M62. The winch was under the boom more towards the front, and it had two lift cylinders on the outside of the boom. The spare tire was mounted behind the cab on the M543, next to the cutting equipment. Most other equipment on the truck was the same as on the M62; front and rear winches were provided also. The bed around the crane was slightly different, and floodlights, vise, outriggers, etc. were provided and functioned basically the same as the M62.

Model M543A1: — This was the same truck as the M543 but was powered by a Mack ENDT-673 diesel engine.

Model M543A2: — This was the same truck as the M543A1, but was powered by a Continental LDS-465 multifuel diesel engine.

Model M246: — This crane truck was different from the others. It had a 20,000 pound three-stage boom behind the cab with a stationary fifth wheel behind the crane for towing semi trailers. There was an enclosed cab for the operator. Controls were mounted on the right side of the boom. The spare tire for the truck was mounted on the left side of the boom. The boom winch was at the rear of the mast. A 20,000 pound front PTO-driven winch was used on this model, but there was no rear winch. The truck was used primarily for loading and unloading damaged aircraft and transporting them. All the wreckers and this crane had reinforced frames.

Model M246A1: — This was the same truck as the M246, but was powered by a Mack ENDT-673 diesel engine.

Model M246A2: — This was same truck as the M246A1, but was powered by a Continental LDS-465 multifuel diesel engine.

I.D. Data: — The serial number was located on the identification data plate on the instrument panel, and on the left front frame rail above the left front spring.

Model No.	Body Type	Weight	GVW	Prod. Total
M54	Cargo	19,230	39,230	—
M54A1	Cargo	19,480	39,480	—
M54A2	Cargo	19,800	39,800	—
M41	Cargo	19,190	34,190	—
M55	Cargo	20,000	40,000	—
M55A1	Cargo	20,250	40,250	—
M55A2	Cargo	20,570	40,570	—
M51	Dump	21,980	41,980	—
M51A1	Dump	22,230	42,230	—
M51A2	Dump	22,550	42,550	—
M52	Tractor	18,813	43,818	—
M52A1	Tractor	19,063	44,063	—
M52A2	Tractor	19,383	44,383	—
M139	Cab/Chassis	26,591	46,591	—
M62	Wrecker	32,981	39,681	—
M543	Wrecker	34,440	46,440	—
M543A1	Wrecker	34,670	46,670	—
M543A2	Wrecker	35,010	47,010	—
M246	Wrecker	31,186	43,186	—
M246A1	Wrecker	31,436	43,436	—
M246A2	Wrecker	31,756	43,756	—

Engine: — Continental R6602, gasoline, six-cylinder, inline, OHV, four-cycle. Cast iron head and block. Displacement: 602 cubic inches. Bore and Stroke: 4-7/8 x 5-3/8 inches. Compression ratio: 6.4:1. Brake horsepower: 196 at 2800 rpm. Seven main bearings. Mechanical valve lifters. Carburetor: Holley 885JJSG. Mack ENDT-673 diesel, six-cylinder, inline, OHV, four-cycle. Cast iron block and head. Displacement: 672 cubic inches. Bore and Stroke: 4.875 x 6 inches. Compression ratio: 16.6:1. Brake horsepower: 205 at 2100 rpm. Seven main bearings. Mechanical valve lifters. Mack mechanical fuel injection. Continental LDS-465 multifuel diesel, six-cylinder, inline, OHV, four-cycle. Cast iron block and head. Displacement: 478 cubic inches. Bore and

Late 1950s M289 five-ton truck with Honest John missile and launcher.

Early 1960s M289 6X6 five-ton truck with Honest John missile and launcher.

Stroke: 4.56 x 4.88:1. Compression ratio: 22:1. Brake horsepower: 250 at 2800 rpm. Seven main bearings. Mechanical valve lifters. American Bosch mechanical fuel injection.

Chassis and Body: — Wheelbase: 167, 179, 215 inches. Overall length: 273-386 inches. Width: 96-115 inches. Height: 103-132 inches. Tread center to center front: 73-5/8 and 76-3/8 inches. Tires: 11.00, 12.00, 14.00 x 20 12-ply military non-directional.

Technical: — Manual synchromesh transmission. Speeds: 5F/1R. Two-speed transfer case, early sprag type, late airshift. Single dry disc clutch. Semi elliptic leaf spring suspension front and rear. Timken Rockwell double reduction axles. Gear ratio: 6.443:1. Air assist over hydraulic brakes. Hydraulic power steering. 24-volt electrical system. Top speed: 54 mph. Fuel capacity: 78 gallons. Cruising range: 214 miles gasoline, 400 miles diesel.

Standard Accessories: — Hand, vehicle, pioneer tools; spare parts; fire extinguisher; hydraulic jack; Wreckers had extensive recovery and salvage related tools and equipment.

Historical: — Designed and built by IHC Corporation, Diamond T, Mack, and AM General from the early 1950s to the late 1970s.

Model No.	6	5	4	3	2	1
M54	600	1200	1800	3000	4000	5500
M54A1	900	1500	2300	3700	5500	7500
M54A2	900	1500	2300	3700	5500	7500
M41	600	1200	1800	3000	4000	5500
M51	900	1500	2300	3700	5500	7500
M51A1	1200	1800	3000	5000	7000	9500
M51A2	1200	1800	3000	5000	7000	9500
M52	600	1200	1800	3000	4000	5500
M52A1	900	1500	2000	3800	5500	7500
M52A2	900	1500	2000	3800	5500	7500
M55	900	1200	1800	3000	4000	5500
M55A1	1200	1500	2400	3800	5500	7500
M55A2	1200	1500	2400	3800	5500	7500
M139	900	1200	1800	3000	4000	5500
M62	3000	7000	9000	14,000	19,000	25,000
M543	4000	8000	10,000	15,000	20,000	25,000
M543A1	5000	9000	11,000	17,000	22,000	27,000
M543A2	5000	9000	11,000	17,000	22,000	27,000
M246	3000	7000	9000	14,000	19,000	25,000
M246A1	4000	8000	10,000	15,000	20,000	24,000
M246A2	4000	8000	10,000	15,000	20,000	24,000

Late 1960s M656 8X8 five-ton cargo truck. (Fred Ropkey, Indianapolis, Indiana)

Model M656: — The M656 was an 8x8 or eight-wheel-drive, five-ton cargo truck. It was a cab-over-engine model with a 15-foot box on the rear of the chassis.

This truck was fully amphibious with very little preparation. The cab doors and cargo box sides and rear tailgate were sealed with air pressurized rubber gaskets using 3-5 psi. The truck had a conventional steel ladder type frame, and the cab and box were made of aluminum. The cab was fitted with a canvas top and folding windshield. The spare tire was inside the cab behind the driver's seat. Hard top cab kits were available. The air cleaner was located inside the cab also, behind the passenger's seat.

The engine housing was between the driver and passenger. Engine service could be performed by removing the large cover over the engine inside the cab or through small openings in the cover itself. Standard driving controls were in front of the driver and on his right side. Transmission, winch, and PTO were in this area. Batteries were located under the passenger's seat.

The cargo area had a folding tailgate and sides. This allowed easier loading with forklifts. The all-aluminum seats and racks inside the box seat 16 troops with equipment and can be folded to permit full use of the cargo body. Aluminum top bows and a canvas tarp were used for covering the rear compartment. Mud flaps, bumperettes, pintle hitch, and air trailer brake connections were at the end of the frame.

The power train was composed of a turbocharged diesel engine and automatic transmission with torque converter going into a single-speed transfer case and on to the double reduction axles. These axles used single driveshafts, being the through shaft design. All four axles drove all the time, the front two used for steering. The suspension used was the torque rod type used on most military trucks. The springs were longer and inverted. This allowed the wide tires more room to move up and down and twist over rough terrain. The axles were almost evenly spaced, giving a very comfortable ride. Hydraulic power steering was used; an engine-driven pump provided pressure to a ram on the steering linkage with a sensor. The double reduction axles were a different design than the models used on the 2-1/2 and five-ton M-series trucks. These had the differentials installed from the side, rather than dropped in from the top. The axle housings were also wider for use with single wheels. The two front steering axles used constant velocity joints for movement side

to side inside the knuckles. The air brakes used an outboard drum outside the wheels rather than behind them. The axle shaft was separate from the drum. The brakes were sealed with two air lines going into the backing plates, one for air going in to apply the brakes, the other for exhausting the used air. Two wheel cylinders were used on each hub as well. The tires were tubeless and mounted on special wheels that bolted on a lip on the outside of the drum. The fuel tank was on the left side of the frame, and a storage box was on the right side, each mounted between the front and rear bogie assemblies. The PTO on the transmission for the 20,000-pound front-mounted winch was an air shift unit. Arctic kits with heater and defroster, gun mount, and other kits were provided for use in all climates.

Model M757: — This unit was the same basic vehicle as the M656 cargo truck, but was a tractor model with a stationary fifth wheel at the rear of the frame. The combination toolbox and platform was mounted directly behind the cab along with the air trailer brake connections. The fifth wheel was mounted above the rear axles. This truck used two fuel tanks mounted on the sides of the frame, one left, one right. They sat between the front and rear bogie assemblies. Trailer brake controls were mounted on the steering column. A truck tractor protection control valve was provided in case of trailer air system failure. The tractor models had shock absorbers on all four axles rather than the two used on the cargo model.

Model M791: — This was the same truck as the M656 cargo unit but had a 17-foot expandable van body that was used as a fire direction center for the missile system it serviced. When expanded, the body would become about twice the normal size. In all forms it was a weather-tight enclosure. Leveling jacks were used for stability. A heating, lighting, and air conditioning system was used with a blackout lighting system. Four windows and screens on the sides with blackout panels, and two side and rear doors were used for ventilation. Two aluminum ladders on the rear were used for entry and exit in the rear of the body. Dual electrical systems were available for 24-volt power from the truck and 120-280-volt from an auxiliary generator, three phase.

I.D. Data: — The serial number was located on the identification data plate on the passenger side of the instrument panel.

Late 1960s M757 Ford 8X8 five-ton tractor with hard cab. (Kenosha Military Museum Inc.)

Model	Body Type	Weight	GVW	Prod. Total
M656	Cargo	15,330	25,730	500
M757	Tractor	13,500	45,500	—
M791	Van	20,200	25,000	—

Engine: — Continental LDS-465-2, six-cylinder, inline, diesel, four-cycle, dry sleeved, OHV. Cast iron block and head. Displacement: 478 cubic inches. Bore and Stroke: 4.56 x 4.88 inches. Compression ratio: 22:1. Brake horsepower: 200 at 2800 rpm. Seven main bearings. Mechanical valve lifters. American Bosch fuel injection.

Chassis and Body: — Wheelbase: 148 inches; between bogies: 58 inches. Overall length: 278 inches; with winch: 299 inches. Width: 96 inches. Height: 116 inches. Van body: 141 inches. Tread center to center: 77.25 inches. Tires: 16.00 x 20 tubeless 10-ply military non-directional.

Technical: — Allison automatic transmission with torque converter. Speeds 6F/1R. Dana single speed transfer case. Tapered leaf inverted spring suspension with torque arms. Front shocks on M656 and M791, and rear shocks on M757. Rockwell double reduction axles. Gear ratio: 6.4:1. Air brakes. Hydraulic steering. 24-volt electrical system. Top speed: 50 mph. Fuel capacity: 80 gallons. Cruising range: 375 miles.

Standard Accessories: — Hand, vehicle, pioneer tools; tire repair kits; fire extinguisher, hydraulic jack, snatch block, tow chain, tire chains; life preserver; cab and cargo compartment canvas.

Historical: — Designed and built by Ford in the late 1960s. Other companies also competed with 8x8s, but Ford's model was chosen. It was used with artillery units servicing the Pershing missile system.

PRICE

Model	6	5	4	3	2	1
M656	1000	2000	3000	5000	9000	12000
M757	1000	2000	3000	5000	—	—
M791	1000	2000	3000	5000	—	—

World War II White Model 666 six-ton prime mover.

Model White 666: — The White 666 was a heavy cargo truck in the six-ton class, originally designated as a prime mover for antiaircraft artillery, but it had many other successful uses as well. Several models were built by several manufacturers: cargo, fuel transport, semi tractor, crane carrier, and bridge erection.

The cargo model had an 11-foot standard military body with a 15,000-pound winch mounted between the cab and the rear body, which could be used to the front or the rear of the truck. Some other models had a 25,000-pound front winch with capstans. Early units had an all-steel cab; later units had the standardized military cab with folding windshield and removable canvas top.

The truck was very sophisticated and used many power train items that are seen in modern trucks today. It had a cargo capacity of 20,000 pounds and a towing capacity of 40,000 pounds. The large engine had tremendous torque for pulling these heavy loads. Front and rear pintle hitches were provided for gun placement. Air and electric trailer brakes were used for towing. The cab had provisions for an antiaircraft ring mount, if so equipped. Rear bodies were made of wood or steel and used troop seats and bows. A crew of one or two operated the vehicle.

I.D. Data: — The serial number was located on the identification data plate on the passenger seat base in the cab and on the left front frame rail above the front axle housing.

Model No.	Body Type	Weight	GVW	Prod. Total
666	Cargo	22,900	42,000	3446

Engine: — Hercules HXD, six-cylinder, inline, L-head, four-cycle, cast iron head and cylinders, aluminum crankcase. Displacement: 855 cubic inches. Bore and Stroke: 5-1/2 x 6 inches. Compression ratio: 5.49:1. Brake horsepower: 202 at 2150 rpm. Seven main bearings. Mechanical valve lifters. Carburetor: Zenith Model 29.

Chassis and Body: — Wheelbase: 185 inches. Overall length: 289 inches. Height: 114 inches. Width: 96 inches. Tread center to center front: 73.25 inches. Tires: 10.00 x 22 12-ply highway tread or military non-directional.

Left rear view of White Model 666 prime mover.

Technical: — Manual constant mesh transmission. Speeds 4F/1R. Two-speed transfer case. Single dry disc clutch. Semi-elliptic leaf spring suspension. Timken double reduction differentials. Overall ratio: 7.33:1. Air brakes with trailer controls. Manual steering. Top speed: 35 mph. Fuel capacity: 80 gallons. Cruising range: 300 miles.

Historical: — Design and development began in 1939 by several companies. White began production in 1939 and continued until 1945. Additional production by Corbitt, Brockway, Ward LaFrance, and FWD.

PRICE

Model No.	6	5	4	3	2	1
666	700	1800	4000	6000	8000	10,000

World War II Mack Model NO7 7-1/2-ton cargo/prime mover.

Model NO7: — The Mack NO7 was a large prime mover in the 7-1/2 ton class. It was used to tow the eight-inch howitzer and the 155mm gun. In the front of the truck was a bumper-mounted PTO-driven Garwood 40,000 pound winch. The power train was the conventional automotive layout with a large gasoline engine powering the truck, attached to a combined transmission transfer case assembly. A crew of two was used to operate the truck. The cab was of all-steel construction with the standard folding windshield and removable canvas top and a water heater mounted on the cowl. A blackout drive light system was provided. The rear cargo body was made of all oak wood with top bows and canvas. Two spare tire and wheel assemblies were carried inside the cargo box. In the rear of the box was a three-ton chain hoist assembly mounted on an inverted U-shaped tubular frame.

This assembly was used to raise or lower the trails and the special ordnance-designed pintle and hitch unit for these artillery pieces. A small tool compartment was located under the floor of the cargo box at the rear beneath the tailgate. Hand-controlled trailer brakes were used for the gun by the driver. Provisions were built into the cab for the standard military circular machine gun mount, using the .50 caliber or the .30 caliber guns. This was one of the lowest geared trucks used by the U.S. forces in World War II. Top speed in first gear and low range at full throttle was 1.6 mph.

I.D. Data: — The serial number was located on the identification data plate on the instrument panel, and on the left front frame rail above the left front spring.

Model No.	Body Type	Weight	GVW	Prod. Total
NO7	Cargo	28,675	43,570	2503

Engine: — Mack EY, six-cylinder, inline, OHV, four-cycle. Cast iron block and heads. Displacement: 707 cubic inches. Bore and Stroke: 5 x 6 inches. Compression ratio: 5.35:1. Brake horsepower: 170 at 2100 rpm. Seven main bearings. Mechanical valve lifters. Carburetor: Zenith 63AW16.

Chassis and Body: — Wheelbase: 156 inches. Overall length: 297 inches. Height: 123 inches. Width: 102 inches. Tread center to center front: 76.25 inches. Tires: 12.00 x 24 14-ply military non-directional.

Technical: — Manual constant mesh transmission. Speeds 5F/1R. Two-speed transfer case. Single dry disc clutch. Leaf spring suspension front and rear. Mack double reduction rear axles and triple reduction front axle. Gear ratio: 9.02:1. Air brakes. Manual steering. Six-volt electrical system. Twelve-volt starting system. Top speed: 31 mph. Fuel capacity: 160 gallons. Cruising range: 160 miles.

Standard Accessories: — Hand, vehicle, pioneer tools; tire chains, hydraulic jack, chain hoist; fire extinguisher.

Historical: — Designed and built by Mack Truck Corporation, Allentown, Pennsylvania, from 1942 to 1944.

			PRICE			
Model No.	6	5	4	3	2	1
NO7	1100	2500	3500	5500	—	—

Rear view of World War II Ward LaFrance 6X6 six-ton wrecker. (Chet Krause, Iola, Wisconsin)

Model M1: — The M1 was a heavy wrecker in the six-ton, 6x6 category and was built by Ward LaFrance and Kenworth. It was a powerful truck -- the largest wrecker used by the armed forces on a daily basis during World War II.

The M1 could easily accomplish most tasks that were undertaken. It worked with all types of wheeled vehicles and was even used for towing light and medium tanks. Its maximum towed load was 70,000 pounds. The main part of the vehicle was the large Garwood wrecker body with its heavy tow winch in the rear. The components of the body were powered by a transfer case power take-off. An A- frame main mast supported the boom overhanging the rear. The boom winch capacity was 20,000 pounds or 16,000 pounds, depending on the model. It could lift about eight tons but could tow much more, as previously mentioned. This did require the boom support legs to be in place from the outside rear corners of the bed to the boom itself.

A drag winch, rated at 47,500-pound capacity, was located behind the large mast and boom assembly. This was powered from the transfer case power take-off, which had a small two-speed transmission for better performance. A large roller assembly for the cable was located on the rear of the frame. The main tow bar was carried on the top of the boom. Early models had a manually operated elevation and traverse on the boom; the last model had full power for these functions.

Spare tires, tools and welding equipment were carried on the rear bed, some parts of which were made of wood. Two floodlights were mounted on the top of the mast assembly. Ground anchors, spades and manual outriggers were carried.

The cab was a metal hard top model on the first four models; the fifth model had a standardized open cab with canvas designed for the truck. The metal cab was a Ward LaFrance or Kenworth unit with military front sheet metal added. There was a wooden frame under the sheet metal as

well as wooden doors. The Kenworth truck had a slightly different appearance than the Ward LaFrance. The instruments were civilian until the fifth model.

The power train and chassis were essentially the same from both manufacturers on all five models. Booms were this way as well. A front-mounted 20,000-pound winch was provided on all models. The power train and running gear in these trucks were two of the heaviest built and lowest geared during World War II. Timken Detroit rear axles and a Wisconsin front axle were used on early models; later ones used all Timken Detroit axles. They were double reduction banjo units.

A Timken T-77 transfer case was powered by a Fuller five-speed overdrive transmission. The engine was a Continental 22R and was only used in these trucks. It was an overhead valve model with adequate torque and speed. A fender-mounted siren and light assembly was on the right front, and the standard blackout lighting system accompanied the headlights.

A circular antiaircraft machine gun mount was available and could be installed on both open and closed cab trucks. There were four Ward LaFrance models in the first closed cab body style, and a fifth model in the second open cab style. These were called model 1000, series 1001, 1002, 1003 and 1004. The Kenworths were called models 570, 571 and 572 in the first series with hard cabs, and 573 in the second series. The differences in the first series of trucks were as follows: The first series had a front winch only and two spare tires behind the cab on the mast. The second series had a front winch and a larger rear winch with one spare tire behind the cab and one spare on the side of the mast for the boom. The third series was supposed to be painted tan and came without front and rear air trailer brake connections. The fourth series had a curved boom. A "whiffle tree" front bumper was used on some second and third series units and on all fourth series models.

Right side view of World War II Ward LaFrance 6X6 six-ton wrecker. (James Welty, Ohio Military Museum Inc., Fairborn, Ohio)

Model M1A1: — This was the same chassis as the Ward LaFrance and the Kenworth, but was fitted with an open military style cab. The M1A1 had flat fenders, a folding windshield and removable canvas top. The power train and chassis were unchanged, but the wrecker body had a power boom, traverse, elevation and winch. The Ward LaFrance was called a Model 1000, series 1005, and the Kenworth was a model 573. Spare tires were moved to the sides of the main mast for the boom, and long stiff legs were added to the sides of the main mast for side stability when lifting. The boom on this truck was actually longer as well. Toolbox arrangements were changed, and the boom controls were simplified to three long levers and a small platform on which the operator could stand.

I.D. Data: — The serial number was located on the identification data plate on the instrument panel.

Model No.	Body Type	Weight	GVW	Prod.Total
M1 WF	Wrecker	27,330	35,330	1190
M1 KW	Wrecker	27,330	35,330	308
M1A1 WF	Wrecker	30,000	38,000	3810
M1A1 KW	Wrecker	30,000	38,000	602

Engine: — Continental 22R. Six-cylinder, in-line, overhead valve, four-cycle. Cast iron block and head. Displacement: 501 cubic inches. Bore and Stroke: 4.5 x 5.25 inches. Compression ratio: 5.23:1. Brake horsepower: 145 at 2400 rpm. Seven main bearings. Mechanical valve lifters. Carburetor: Zenith SF-5.

Chassis and Body: — Wheelbase: 181 inches. Overall length: 281 inches. Width: 99.5 inches. Height: 117 inches. Tread center to center front: 73 inches. Tires: 11.00 x 20 12-ply nylon military nondirectional.

Technical: — Manual constant mesh transmission with overdrive. Speeds: 5F/1R. Two-speed transfer case. Single dry disc clutch. Leaf spring suspension front and rear. Timken Detroit double reduction differentials. Gear ratio: 8.27:1. Air brakes. Manual steering. Twelve-volt electrical system. Fuel capacity: 100 gallons. Cruising range: 250 miles.

Standard Accessories: — Hand, vehicle, pioneer tools, spare parts, fire extinguisher, welding and cutting equipment, retrieval, recovery, towing, and salvage equipment. Probably carried one of the largest on-vehicle inventories of tools and equipment in World War II. This made it very versatile for heavy lifting and recovery of all types.

Historical: — Designed and built by Ward LaFrance and Kenworth from 1941 to 1945. Used mainly by the Army in all theaters of conflict in which it was involved.

PRICE

Model No.	6	5	4	3	2	1
M1	1500	2500	4500	8500	11,000	15,000
M1A1	1500	2500	4500	8500	11,000	15,000

Early 1960s Mack M123AI 6X6 ten-ton tractor. (James Welty, Ohio Military Museum Inc., Fairborn, Ohio)

Model M123: — The M123 was a heavy truck tractor in the 10-ton class. Known as the "Dragon Wagon," it pulled the M15A1 or M15A2 semi trailer and was used for heavy recovery operations in tactical and combat situations, mainly for tank transportation. It had a Fruehauf fifth wheel with a larger center pin opening for the large weight of the semi trailer used in conjunction with truck, and two 45,000-pound capacity winches, all mounted behind the cab. The winches were used for pulling disabled vehicles on to the deck of the trailer.

The unit was similar in appearance to the 2-1/2-ton and five-ton trucks in the M series vehicles, and in fact used the same cab, but the rest of the truck was totally different.

The engine, transmission, transfer case, axles, frame, and brakes were all much larger and heavier to move the huge payloads the truck and trailer were capable of hauling. The M123's engine was a Le Roi overhead valve V-8. This was very unusual, as most tactical vehicles had in-line six-cylinder units. The heavy weights being towed required higher horsepower ratings. A peculiar feature of the M123's engine was that the exhaust manifolds were on the top of the engine near the intake manifold. The unusual design gave the truck a sound that was unique.

Mack built the trucks, and the transmission transfer case assemblies were a modified civilian unit from their truck lines. They were bolted together with no drive shaft between them. The rear axles were Mack double reduction models, dropped in from the top, and of 65,000-pound capacity. The front axle was also a Mack model with a double reduction drop-in unit, but it also had planetary hubs, making it a triple reduction unit. Power steering and full air brakes were used.

The truck and trailer with their payload were often in the area of 160,000 pounds. The vehicle carried a large variety of recovery tools and equipment used in the field operations. The power train behind the engine was all built by Mack to military specifications.

Model M125: — This was the same basic truck as the M123 but was the cargo version built in 1957 and 1958. About 550 were manufactured. The M125 had a 40,000-pound front winch and no rear winches. At the rear was an all-steel cargo bed with troop seats, bows and removable canvas top.

The M125 had a special pintle hitch and was used for towing the eight-inch howitzer. A small chain hoist with crane, used for lifting the trails of

the gun off and on the hitch, was located in the rear bed by the tailgate. This arrangement was also used on the World War II Mack NO7 truck.

The M125 had a gasoline engine only. Later models of the M123 trucks had Cummins V-8 diesel engines and different winch configurations behind the cab. Some models had single winches, and most rear winches had aluminum cases.

I.D. Data: — The serial number was located on the identification data plate on the instrument panel inside the cab.

Model No.	Body Type	Weight	GVW	Prod. Total
M123	Tractor	32,250	67,250	—

Engine: — LeRoi T-H844, V-8, 90 Degree OHV, four-cycle. Cast iron block and heads. Displacement: 844 cubic inches. Bore and Stroke: 5-1/4 x 4-7/8 inches. Compression ratio: 6.7:1. Brake horsepower: 286 at 2600 rpm. Five main bearings. Mechanical valve lifters. Carburetor: Zenith Z29D14RZ.

Chassis and Body: — Wheelbase: 181.5 inches. Overall length: 280 inches. Height: 113 inches. Width: 114 inches. Tread center to center: 79 inches. Tires: 14.00 x 24 20-ply military non-directional.

Technical: — Manual synchromesh transmission. Speeds 5F/1R. Two-speed transfer case. Dual disc dry clutch. Semi-elliptic leaf spring suspension. Mack double reduction rear differentials. Mack triple reduction front differential with planetary final drives. Gear ratio: 9.02:1. Air brakes. Hydraulic power steering. Twenty-four-volt electrical system. Top speed: 42 mph. Fuel capacity: 166 gallons. Cruising range: 300 miles.

Standard Accessories: — Hand, vehicle, pioneer tools; extensive recovery towing and retrieval equipment; spotlight, spare tires, fire extinguisher.

Historical: — Several models built by Mack from the mid-1950s to late 1970s. All Mack power train components from the engine back. Replaced World War II M26A1 "Dragon Wagon."

PRICE

Model No.	6	5	4	3	2	1
M123	800	2000	4000	5000	8000	12,000
M125	800	2000	4000	5000	8000	12,000

Left rear view of late 1950s Mack M123A1 ten-ton tractor. (James Welty, Ohio Military Museum Inc. Fairborn, Ohio)

Late 1950s Mack M125 6X6 ten-ton cargo truck. (Tony Roca, Milwaukee, Wisconsin)

Right side view of Mack M125 cargo truck. (Tony Roca, Milwaukee, Wisconsin)

World War II Diamond T Model 980 hard cab 12-ton 6X4. This truck had a Hall Scott engine.

Right rear view of Diamond T M20 Model 980 hard cab truck with Hall Scott engine.

Model M20: — The Diamond T M20 was a 12-ton heavy prime mover used to transport heavy material, mainly tanks, on the 24-wheel trailer model M9. This truck had tandem rear wheel drive only, and was designed earlier in World War II. The front axle was a standard I-beam truck axle. They were manufactured in both the open or hard top cab style. It had a crew of two to operate the unit. A large 40,000-pound winch was mounted behind the cab and was used for pulling damaged tanks onto the trailer but could also be used for winching from the front of the truck. Roller and sheave assemblies in the rear of the frame and in the front bumper were provided for this.

The winch was chain driven from the auxiliary transmission. On the rear of the truck was a large square-shaped ballast box where the spare tires were carried, and weight could be added for better traction. A tailgate was at the rear of the box for easy access. Front and rear pintle hitches were provided for positioning the trailer or general towing use. The truck was geared very low and had tremendous pulling power. It could pull a trailer weighing up to 120,000 pounds. It was manufactured with gas or diesel engines. The hood of the truck was very long, making it easy to spot. The gas engine in this truck was the largest ever put in a World War II military truck.

The vehicle used both the Hercules DXFE diesel engine and the Hall Scott 440 gasoline engine. The Hall Scott model was the same unit in

World War II Diamond T Model 981 6X4 12-ton with Hercules diesel engine, open cab and original rear box. (Dana Zwang, Coalinga, California)

World War II Diamond T Model 981 6X4 12-ton with Hercules diesel engine, open cab and original rear box. (Dana Zwang, Coalinga, California)

the successor to this truck, the M26 and M26A1 Pacific tractors.

The power train was conventional in layout. The large powerful engine was needed for extremely heavy loads. A single dry disc clutch was coupled to the main four-speed transmission, with a separate three-speed auxiliary box behind it. The power take-off for the winch was on top of the rear transmission. The rear differentials were Timken double reduction and were huge. The axle shafts were short because the differentials were so large they filled the housings from spring to spring. They were geared very low because the massive pulling power required this. Full air brakes were used with air connections at the rear for the trailer.

The cab was the same basic design as the four-ton series trucks.

When the Pacifics were issued, these were quickly put into rear echelon areas. They made tremendous ammunition haulers. Their lack of front-wheel drive really hindered their off-road performance, however.

I.D. Data: — The serial number was located on the identification data plate on the left front cowl, ahead of the driver, inside the engine compartment.

Model No.	Body Type	Weight	GVW	Prod. Total
M20	Cargo	26,950	45,000	5871

Engines: — Hercules DXFE diesel, six-cylinder, OHV, inline, four-cycle. Cast iron block and head. Displacement: 895 cubic inches. Bore and Stroke: 5-5/8 x 6 inches. Compression ratio: 14.8:1. Brake horsepower: 185 at 1600 rpm. Seven main bearings. Mechanical valve lifters. Bosch fuel injection.

Hall Scott 440, gasoline, six-cylinder, inline, OHV, OHC. Cast iron block and head. Displacement 1090 cubic inches. Bore and Stroke: 5-3/4 x 7 inches. Compression ratio: 5.7:1. Brake horsepower: 240 at 2000 rpm. Seven main bearings. Mechanical valve lifters.

Chassis and Body: — Wheelbase: 179 inches. Overall length: 280 inches. Height: 100 inches. Width: 100 inches. Tread center to center: 74 inches. Tires: 12.00 x 20 14-ply military non-directional.

Technical: — Manual constant mesh transmissions, main four-speed, auxiliary three-speed. Speeds: 12F/3R. Single dry disc clutch. Leaf spring suspension. Timken double reduction differentials. Overall ratio: 11.66:1. Air brakes. Manual steering. 24-volt electrical system. Top speed: 23 mph. Fuel capacity: 150 gallons. Cruising range: 300 miles.

Standard Accessories: — Hand, vehicle, pioneer tools; spare parts for truck and trailer; towing and winching equipment; engine hand crank and snatch block; fire extinguisher.

Historical: — Designed and built by Diamond T from 1941 to 1945. Originally intended for the British early in World War II, but used by both the United States and England. Very limited off-road performance because there was no front-wheel drive. M26 superseded this vehicle.

PRICE

Model No.	6	5	4	3	2	1
M20	1000	2000	3000	4000	—	—

Model M9: — The M9 trailer was towed by the M20 Diamond T 12-ton truck and was used for transporting heavy material, mainly tanks. An A-frame drawbar and ring hitch was in the front, along with the air brake lines and safety chains. Two axles sat side by side under the turntable on the front, with four tires per axle — a total of eight under the front end. On top of the turntable were roller and sheave assemblies for the truck winch cable to pull disabled units onto the trailer, and the hand brake assemblies for the trailer.

The bed of the trailer was an all-steel welded assembly made of I-beams and plate steel. Under the rear were two tandem axle assemblies sitting side by side. These sat on walking beams and trunions. This enabled axle movement from side to side, as well as front to rear, for use on uneven terrain. Heavy tie down rings were mounted around the outside of the bed with large chock blocks to hold the tank in position when loaded. Folding rear ramps and cable pulleys were mounted in the rear dovetail of the trailer. A total of 24 wheels and tires supported up to 90,000 pounds of cargo. Dayton hubs were used on the axles with spare tires carried on the truck.

I.D. Data: — Serial number is located on the identification data plate on the right front frame rail at the extreme front of the trailer.

Model No.	Body Type	Weight	GVW	Prod. Total
M9	Trailer	22,000	112,000	—

Chassis and Body: — Wheelbase: 187 inches. Overall length: 356 inches. Height: 57 inches. Width: 114 inches. Tires: 8.25 x 15 14-ply highway tread.

Technical: — Solid walking beam suspension with trunions. Air brakes with break-away lock-up features. Hand wheel-operated manual parking brakes. Six-volt electrical system.

Standard Accessories: — Turn buckles, block and tackle, chains, pins, hooks; hydraulic jack, tire wrenches, shackles; sheave blocks.

Historical: — Built from 1941 to 1945 by Fruehauf, Pointer Williamette, Rogers Brothers, and Winter Weiss Company.

PRICE

Model No.	6	5	4	3	2	1
M9	1500	2500	3500	4500	—	—

Left front view of Pacific M26A1 tractor tank retriever. (James Welty, Ohio Military Musuem Inc., Fairborn, Ohio)

Model M26A1: — The M26A1 12-ton 6X6 truck was one of the largest trucks designed, built and used by the Army in World War II. The primary role was to retrieve the heaviest vehicles that were used in combat zones.

The M26 was a semi-tractor used with a large trailer capable of carrying extremely heavy loads. It was a unique, complex and very sophisticated machine. Many of the modern mechanical principles used today were used in this unit. The drivetrain of this specialized vehicle was used only in this model. The Hall Scott engine was a large marine adaptation because of the high horsepower requirements. The truck was capable of moving loads up to 100,000 pounds. The cylinder head on the engine used an overhead camshaft with cross flow combustion chambers, opposed valves and two spark plugs per cylinder.

The single-speed transfer case was attached to the rear of the auxiliary transmission. The parking brake was mounted on the rear differential. The rear differential was mounted on the frame with a walking beam suspension and chain drive to each wheel. Coil springs were used on the rear for stabilization. A 40,000-pound front winch and two 60,000-pound rear winches were on the frame of the truck between the cab and the fifth wheel. A boom and chain hoist were provided for changing tires.

The rear suspension of the M26A1 was basically solid. Oilers were located above each of the rear chain drive units; the constant dripping left a trail everywhere the truck went. The sprockets were mounted on the ends of the upper drive differential, which was bolted solid to the frame under the fifth wheel. The brake drums had the lower sprockets on the inside lip behind the tires. Combat wheels and tires were used on all 10 assemblies.

The front winch was under the front bumper, making it almost unnoticeable. When the rear winches had the cables crossed, each one was hooked onto the opposite corner of the tank. This enabled the winch operator to actually steer the tank onto the trailer. A folding wrecker boom was pinned at the rear of the frame and could be collapsed down onto the frame on the outside of the fifth wheel. When raised, it used the rear winches and made a powerful attachment. The fifth wheel was also a special unit. It could oscillate from left to right and from front to rear.

The pin opening was also much larger to accommodate the huge pin used on the M15A1 trailer.

The M26A1 was the soft top version of the original M26 truck; the M26A1 used a removable canvas cab. The original M26 had an all-armored cab that was dramatically heavier. Entry to the cab was at the rear behind the front tire. Seats were provided alongside the engine and at the rear of the compartment for the crew. The driver sat in the traditional left front position with all his controls. This was one of the few trucks used during World War II that had hydraulic power steering.

A large variety of tools and recovery equipment were carried. The cab was made of armored sheet steel with seats inside for the entire crew. Many of the tools were stowed inside the cab. The roof had a ring mount for a .50 caliber machine gun.

I.D. Data: — The serial number was located on the identification data plate on the back of the engine housing inside the cab.

Model No.	Body Type	Weight	GVW	Prod. Total
M26A1	Tractor	42,960	108,895	1400

Engine: — Hall Scott 440, six-cylinder, inline, OHV, OHC, four-cycle. Cast iron block and cylinder head. Displacement: 1090 cubic inches. Bore and Stroke: 5-3/4 x 7 inches. Compression ratio: 5.7:1. Brake horsepower: 240 at 2000 rpm. Seven main bearings. Mechanical valve lifters. Carburetor: Zenith 151OMS.

Chassis and Body: — Wheelbase: 177 inches. Overall length: 306 inches. Height: 25 inches. Width: 130.5 inches. Tread center to center: 82 inches. Tires: 14.00 x 24 20-ply military non-directional.

Technical: — Manual transmissions, constant mesh, main and auxiliary. Speeds 12F/3R. Single-speed transfer case. Dual disc dry clutch. Timken double reduction differentials. Knuckey chain drive rear bogie. Overall ratio: 7.69:1. Leaf spring suspension front. Walking solid beam

Rear view of World War II Pacific M26A1 6X6 12-ton tractor tank retriever. (James Welty, Ohio Military Museum Inc., Fairborn, Ohio)

Right rear view of Pacific M26A1 tractor tank retriever. (James Welty, Ohio Military Museum Inc., Fairborn, Ohio)

rear suspension with coil springs for stabilization. Air brakes. Hydraulic power steering. Steel combat wheels. Twelve-volt electrical system. Top speed: 28 mph. Fuel capacity: 120 gallons. Cruising range: 120 miles.

Standard Accessories: — Hand, vehicle, pioneer tools; recovery and welding equipment; spare parts, fire extinguishers; first aid kit; crane with chain hoist for tire work; tow cable, chains, hydraulic jacks, vise, rear boom assembly for lifting; floodlights, spotlights, whiffle tree with tow bar; ring mount with .50 caliber machine gun, tripod, ammunition, .45 caliber submachine gun.

Historical: — Originally designed by Knuckey Truck Company of San Francisco, California. Production by Pacific Car and Foundry of Renton, Washington from 1943 to 1945.

Model No.	6	5	4	3	2	1
			PRICE			
M26A1	1500	25,000	5,000	10,000	—	—

Trailers

Front view of World War II MBT quarter-ton jeep cargo trailer.

Model MBT: — This quarter-ton trailer was a small, simply designed unit for transporting all types of cargo. It was primarily towed by the Ford and Willys quarter-ton trucks but was sometimes used behind half-ton Dodges and by the M29 Weasel because it was fully amphibious when loaded.

The body was made of stamped steel panels welded together, with ribbing added for strength. The entire body was then welded to the channel steel frame. Round fenders were bolted to the body, and rope tie-downs were added to hold the tarp in place. Two taillights were provided, along with reflectors for night use. A cord with a plug went to the towing vehicle where it was inserted into a standard military designed socket. The body and frame assembly rode on a pair of leaf springs that flexed on the rear spring shackles.

Grease fittings were on both ends of the springs. Shock absorbers were mounted between the tubular axle and the frame. Brake drums with shoes were fitted for the parking brakes. A hand lever located at the front operated the brake. A military style lunette ring hitch with safety chains and a folding stand were at the very front of the draw bar for towing the trailer.

I.D. Data: — The serial number was located on the identification data plate, on the front panel of the body on the left side near the top edge.

Model No.	Body Type	Weight	GVW	Prod. Total
MBT	Cargo	565	1065	

Chassis and Body — Overall length: 108 inches. Height: 42 inches. Width: 56.5 inches. Body length: 72 inches. Height: 16 inches. Width: 43 inches. Tread center to center: 48 inches. Tires: 6.00 x 16 six-ply military non-directional.

Technical: — Leaf spring suspension. Hand lever-operated mechanical parking brake. Six-volt electrical system.

Rear view of MBT quarter-ton jeep cargo trailer.

Standard Accessories: — Canvas tarp.

Historical: — Built by Willys Overland and Bantam Car Company and numerous other manufacturers from 1941 to 1945.

	PRICE					
Model No.	6	5	4	3	2	1
MBT	100	300	500	800	1100	1300

Front view of M100 quarter-ton cargo trailer.

Model M100: — The M100 is an updated version of the quarter-ton trailer built for use behind the M series quarter-ton trucks that came into use about 1950. This trailer was towed behind the M38 and the M38AI Jeeps. It is an improved model of the World War II quarter-ton amphibious cargo trailer. The same welded steel body with ribbing is welded to the frame. A similar tube-style axle, leaf spring suspension, and shock absorber arrangement is also used.

The familiar A-frame draw bar hitch with lunette, folding support leg, and safety chains was used in the front. The front panel of the body had two additional data plates on the right side and a small storage box on top of the frame channel. A different handle was used on the parking brake mechanism.

The floor had two drain plugs, one in the front and one in the rear, as does the World War II model. Two taillights with waterproof electrical connections were used, and the trailer had larger tires. The familiar round fenders were bolted to the sides. General appearance was almost the same as the World War II models, but there were distinct differences between the two units.

I.D. Data: — The serial number was located on the identification data plate on the front panel of the body, upper left side near the top edge.

Model No.	Body Type	Weight	GVW	Prod. Total
M100	Cargo	550	1050	—

Chassis and Body: — Overall length: 108 inches. Height: 42 inches. Width: 56 inches. Body length: 72 inches. Height: 18 inches. Width: 38 inches. Tread center to center: 49 inches. Tires: 7.00 x 16 six-ply military non-directional.

Technical: —Leaf spring suspension. Hand lever-operated mechanical parking brake. 24-volt electrical system.

Left side view of early 1950s M100 quarter-ton cargo trailer.

Standard Accessories: — Canvas tarp.

Historical: — Built by several manufacturers from the early 1950s to the early 1960s.

PRICE

Model No.	6	5	4	3	2	4
M100	100	300	400	700	1000	1300

M416 quarter-ton trailer. (Jon Bircheff, Fontana, California)

Model M416: — The M416 is the third generation of the quarter-ton trailer used behind the M series vehicles. This trailer was towed behind the M151 or M422 quarter-ton trucks, and as before was used for general transportation of all types of cargo.

This trailer was very different from earlier models. It had fenders made from flat steel rather than the rounded stamped fenders. The data plates were located on the right rear of the body. A different style wheel was used, and the body could be unbolted from the frame. The hand brake lever was changed again, and larger taillights were fitted on the rear. The amphibious steel body with floor drains is still used.

Tube-style axle, leaf spring suspension, shock absorbers, brake drums and shoes similiar to the earlier models were retained. The A-frame draw bar hitch, lunette, saftey chains, and support leg made the front of the trailer complete to military specifications.

From a distance, this trailer's general appearance resembles the earlier models, but parts are not interchangeable. The M416 was painted in very different color schemes compared to World War II and Korean War models. The M416A1 was the same as the M416, but had hydraulic brakes that were activated by a surge-type coupling in the hitch. When the tow vehicle slowed, the pressure of the hitch pushing against itself forced fluid into the wheel cylinders in the brake drums, thus stopping the trailer.

I.D. Data: — The serial number was located on the identification data plate near the top of the right rear panel of the body.

Model No.	Body Type	Weight	GVW	Prod. Total
M416	Cargo	570	1070	—

Chassis and Body: — Overall length: 108 inches. Height: 42 inches. Width: 60 inches. Body Length: 96 inches. Width: 41 inches. Height: 11 inches. Tread center to center: 53 inches. Tires: 7.00 x 16 6-ply military non-directional.

Rear view of M416 quarter-ton trailer. (John Bircheff, Fontana, California)

Technical: — Leaf spring suspension, hand lever-operated mechanical parking brake with cable tensioner in handle. Twenty-four-volt electrical system.

Standard Accessories: — Canvas tarp.

Historical: — Built by several manufacturers from the early 1960s to the present.

	PRICE					
Model No.	6	5	4	3	2	1
M416	100	250	350	500	650	750

Model M101: — The M101 trailer is a three-quarter ton model using a single axle and two wheels. It was normally towed by the M37 three-quarter ton truck. The wheel and tire assemblies were interchangeable. It had an all-steel body with a folding tailgate secured by chains. Wheel wells were built into the body, but otherwise it had a flat floor and smooth sides. Stake pockets were provided for the wooden side racks, with metal posts, and top bows for the cargo canvas. End curtains were standard with the canvas top.

The frame was steel channel, with an A-frame drawbar hitch and lunette. The drawbar was hinged just in front of the front spring shackles with pins at the front of the box. This allowed the box to tip up slightly for ease of loading and unloading. Towing clevises were at the front and rear. A tubular steel straight axle, mounted on leaf springs, carried the frame and body. Each axle hub had a brake drum with a mechanical parking brake. Two levers were at the front of the box to operate each parking brake separately. Rope tie downs were riveted or spot welded all around the body. Data plates were on the lower front corners of the box. A standard lunette, safety chains, and landing-leg were provided. Double acting shock absorbers were mounted on the axle. Standard military electrical connectors and cable moved power to the service, blackout tail and marker lights. Top bows could be stored next to the front of the trailer in racks just behind the front top bow. The M101A1 was the same trailer, but had different hand brake levers.

I.D. Data: — The serial number was located on the identification data plate on the lower outside corners, in front of the box.

Model No.	Body Type	Weight	GVW	Prod.Total
M101	Cargo	1340	3590	—
MI01A1	Cargo	1340	3590	—

Chassis and Body: — Overall length: 147 inches. Width: 73.5 inches. Height: 83 inches. Tread center to center: 72 inches. Tires: 9.00 x 16 8-ply military non-directional.

Technical: — Leaf spring suspension. Hydraulic shock absorbers. Mechanical parking brakes. 24-volt electrical system.

Standard Accessories: — Canvas top, side curtains, bows, racks.

Historical: — Built by several manufacturers from the early 1950s to present in different forms. Chassis and frame were used for a wide variety of functions with special equipment.

Model No.	6	5	4	3	2	1
			PRICE			
M101	200	400	800	1000	1300	1500
M101A1	200	400	800	1000	1300	1500

World War II one-ton cargo trailer with all-steel body. (Jack Tomlin, Tooele, Utah)

Model G518 — This one-ton cargo trailer was one of the most common cargo carriers built during World War II. It was pulled behind almost all large trucks, from one-tons to 7-1/2 tons; even armored vehicles used them. It was a simple box on wheels and was very easy to build. Consequently, it was built by numerous companies.

The chassis on this unit was the same as that used on the water tank trailer. The steel channel frame sat on a pair of leaf springs with a square tube axle. Standard six hole Budd wheels with 7.50 x 20 tires were used. This trailer was built with an all-wood or all-steel body, but wood body models are very rare. The A-frame style hitch was used with a retracting landing wheel and safety chains. The standard military lunette was provided.

Taillights were located on the rear of the frame along with the blackout lighting system. Round sheet metal fenders were bolted to the side of the body. Stake pockets with metal posts and wooden racks and bows held the canvas top in place. A steel or wood folding tailgate with chains made up the rest of the body. Unique reflectors with round glass balls were used on early models; later ones used the plastic type reflector. A hand brake was used, with the controls on the right rear corner of the body.

I.D. Data: — The serial number was located on the identification data plate on the lower left front box panel above frame member.

Model No.	Body Type	Weight	GVW	Prod. Total
G518	Cargo	1300	4300	—

Chassis and Body: — Overall length: 145.5 inches. Height: 73 inches, reducible to 50.5 inches. Width: 71 inches. Box dimensions: 96 x 46 inches. Tread center to center of tires: 59 inches. Tires: 7.50 x 20 8-ply military non-directional.

Technical: — Leaf spring suspension, hand lever-operated mechanical parking brake. Six-volt electrical system.

Standard Accessories: — Canvas cargo cover, side racks with top bows.

Historical: — Built by American Bantam, Ben Hur, Century Boat Works, Checker, Dorsey, Gertenslager, Henney, Hercules Body, Highland Body and Trailer, Hobbs, Hyde, Mifflinburg Body, Naburs, Nash Kelvinator,

Right rear view of one-ton cargo trailer with all-steel body. (Jack Tomlin, Tooele, Utah)

Omaha Standard Body, Pike, Queen City, Redman, Steel Products, Strick, Transportation Equipment, Truck Engineering Corporation, Willys Overland, Winter Weiss, Baker, Covered Wagon, Keystone, and Streich from 1941 to 1945.

Model No.	PRICE					
	6	5	4	3	2	1
G518	200	600	800	1000	1200	1400

Right side view of one-ton cargo trailer with metal body. (Ralph Doubek, Wild Rose, Wisconsin)

World War II one-ton cargo trailer with metal body. (Ralph Doubek, Wild Rose, Wisconsin)

World War II one-ton cargo trailer with all wood body.

Right side view of World War II "water buffalo." (Ralph Doubek, Wild Rose, Wisconsin)

Model G-527: — This 1-1/2-ton trailer is commonly referred to as the "Water Buffalo." Built in World War II, it is used for transporting and dispensing drinking water to troops in the field.

The tank was made from aluminum or steel and sat on a steel channel frame with round fenders bolted to the frame. A square tube axle and leaf springs were used with standard six-hole Budd truck wheels. A hand lever-operated mechanical parking brake was the right rear corner of the frame. Two taillights and four reflectors were on the rear of the trailer. The A-frame hitch with lunette, safety chains, and a retractable wheel stand were on the front. The water tank had drain plugs in the bottom, a large opening in the top with a filtering device, and lid that could be fastened tightly. At the front of the tank a hose and hand pump assembly was attached for filling. Two water boxes were at the front of the frame, one on each side. Inside them were three spigots with handles. This trailer was normally towed by a larger truck, such as the 1-1/2-ton Chevrolet 4x4 or the GMC 2-1/2-ton CCKW 6x6.

I.D. Data: — The serial number was located on the identification data plate on the left front corner of the frame rail.

Another view of the "water buffalo." A complete trailer has a hand-operated pump mounted on the front of the trailer. (Ralph Doubek, Wild Rose, Wisconsin)

Historical: — Manufacurered during World War II by over 15 different companies from 1941 to 1945.

Model No.	Body Type	Weight	GVW	Prod. Total
G-527	Tank	1500	3500	—

Chassis and Body: — Overall length: 136.5 inches. Height: 70 inches. Width: 71 inches. Tank length: 61 inches. Width: 46 inches. Tread center to center: 59 inches. Tires: 7.50 x 20 8-ply military non-directional.

Technical: — Leaf spring suspension, hand lever-operated mechanical parking brake. Six-volt electrical system.

Standard Accessories: —Water hand pump and hose assembly.

			PRICE			
Model No.	6	5	4	3	2	1
G-527	200	500	700	800	900	1100

Left rear view of "water buffalo." (Ralph Doubek, Wild Rose, Wisconsin)

World War II M1 searchlight trailer has a breaking tongue to form a ramp to load the searchlight. It is about 10 inches higher than other models listed below. (Chet Krause, Iola, Wisconsin)

Model M7: — The M7 trailer was an all-steel low profile unit, originally designed for transporting generators. It was a very versatile model and was adapted for many uses.

It was quite different from the other cargo trailers used in World War II. It was used extensively and almost exclusively by the antiaircraft artillery. The body was welded into a one-piece structure and unitized. Two wheel and tire assemblies were mounted on each side on walking beams. The hubs were mounted directly on the walking beams, and no springs were used. This feature provided better travel over uneven ground. Standard Budd wheels were used, the same six-hole models as on the 2-1/2-ton trucks. This trailer had electric brakes.

Each corner of the body had a control on the top for screwing down the four leveling jacks. These allowed the trailer to lift off the ground for stabilization when operating the generators. The front hitch was attached to the standard drawbar-type frame welded to the body. This was a welded unit rather than one built out of channel. The lunette was adjustable for different towing vehicles.

Clearance lights, reflectors, blackout stop and taillights were mounted around the body. Some models were equipped with an adjustable landing wheel under the drawbar. Footman loops and rope tie downs were riveted around the body. The tailgate was heavily constructed for use as a loading ramp when sliding generators in or out of the bed. Some had steel channel, and others had full sheet metal in the tailgates.

The floor was normally made of diamond plate, but some had wooden planks as well. The M18 model used a manually operated winch mounted on the drawbar in front of the cargo box. Two large hand wheels were used on each side of the winch, and a cable went through the box so generators or other cargo could be pulled up into the floor. On some models, M1, M13 and K84, canvas tops with bows were used for covering equipment, while M14 and M22 trailers had fully enclosed metal tops. These usually had two rear doors and full insulation. Five windows with screens and sliding black out panels were provided.

Hand-operated parking brakes were used in conjunction with the standard electrical braking system. The M7 had many uses: antenna mount and radio equipment transport, search light transport, generator transport and general cargo use. The chemical warfare board adopted one to mount a smoke generator; the smoke was used for camouflaging troop movements.

Model M13, M14, M22: — These units housed directors for antiaircraft artillery, along with tools and equipment stowage. The directors were electro-mechanical systems using optical and radar observations for computing gun firing data continuously when engaging enemy aircraft in defensive or offensive fire. Several items made up a director; a computer, power unit, tracker, altitude converter, and optical equipment were needed. These were normally carried in one or more trailers. A generator mounted in another trailer provided power. The M14 and M22 had

Model No.	Body Type	Use	Tongue	Top	Weight	GVW	Manuf.
M1	—	Searchlight	Flexible	Canvas	—	—	Fruehauf
M7	—	Generator	Rigid	Open	—	—	Fruehauf
M7	Cargo	Smoke Generator	—	—	4150	8447	Brill
M13	—	Director M9/M10	Rigid	Canvas	—	—	Brill
M13	Cargo	Director M9/M10	Rigid	Canvas	4400	7850	Fruehauf
M14	Cargo	Director M9/M10	Rigid	Steel	5450	8900	Fruehauf
M14	—	Director M9/M10	Rigid	Steel	—	—	Brill
M17	Cargo	M45 Gun Mount (designated M5)	Rigid	Open	4520	7490	Fruehauf
M18	Cargo	Generator	Flexible	Open	4000	8297	Fruehauf
M21	—	Director	Rigid	Steel	—	—	Fruehauf
M22	Cargo	Director M9/M10	Rigid	Steel	5450	8900	Standard
K84	—	Radio Transport	Rigid	Canvas	—	—	Fruehauf

World War II M1 searchlight trailer. (Chet Krause, Iola, Wisconsin)

World War II M17 trailer with quad .50 caliber antiaircraft gun mount. (Chet Krause, Iola, Wisconsin)

Rear view of M17 trailer with quad .50 caliber antiaircraft gun mount. (Chet Krause, Iola, Wisconsin)

metal tops with insulation, blower ventilation fan, and gasoline heating unit. The M22 also had a wooden floor.

Model M17: — This model was the same basic trailer as the M7 but was modified for carrying the quad .50 caliber machine gun mount, M45. This was the same type mount as the M16 and M16AI half tracks carried.

I.D. Data: — The serial number was located on the identification data plate on the front center of trailer.

Chassis and Body: — Overall length: 189 inches. Width: 96 inches. Height: 98-129 inches. Tires: 7.50 x 20 8-ply military non-directional.

Technical: — Hand-operated mechanical parking brakes. Electric service brakes. Six-volt electrical system. Walking beam suspension, no springs.

Historical: — Built by Fruehauf Trailer Company and J.G. Brill Company during World War II, from 1941 to 1945.

			PRICE			
Model No.	6	5	4	3	2	1
M1	300	600	1000	1500	2500	3000
M7	300	600	1000	1500	2500	3000
M18	300	600	1000	1500	2500	3000
M13	300	600	1000	1500	2500	3000
M14	300	600	1000	1500	2500	3000
M22	300	600	1000	1500	2500	3000
M17	600	900	1300	1800	3000	3500

M151A tank transporter. (James Welty, Ohio Military Museum Inc., Fairborn, Ohio)

Model M15A1: — This semi-trailer was the unit towed by the M26A1 12-ton 6X6 truck tractor for tank retrieval. It was a drop frame style trailer with the cargo deck in the center being lower than the level of the fifth wheel pin at the front.

Eight large combat single wheels and tires at the rear were mounted on solid walking beams with trunion shafts between the tires for better off-road movement when loaded. Compressed air from the tractor operated the trailer brakes. Large hinged ramps at the rear let the tanks be easily pulled onto the main frame rails of the trailer. The ramps allowed the tank tracks to go between the trailer tires. The wheels and tires could be adjusted in or out for different loads or to narrow the unit for transporting it. Its large rear ramps were fastened to the back of the tank when being winched up onto the deck, thus lifting them as it went on the trailer.

Two strut and leg support assemblies at the front held up the trailer when detached from the tractor. The front upper deck of the trailer was used for the larger stowage items used in the recovery operations. Additional stowage compartments were on the side of the main trailer frame rails. Roller assemblies built into the trailer bed were used as cable guides for the winches on the tractor, keeping the cable straight and guiding the tank onto the cargo deck. The front of the trailer had a set of steps up to the top deck. The upper deck was very tall, and these steps provided access to the stowage areas there.

The trailer was rated at 45 tons, but it was not uncommon to see 60 to 100 tons carried. The carrying capacity was tremendous, to say the least.

I.D. Data: — Serial number was located on the identification plate on the outside of the left front frame.

Model No.	Body Type	Weight	GVW	Prod. Total
M15	Semi-trailer	42,370	122,370	—

Chassis and Body: — Overall length: 462 inches. Height: 105 inches. Width: 146 inches. Tread center to center outside tires: 131 inches; inside tires: 45 inches. Tires: 14.00 x 24, 20-ply, military non-directional.

Technical: — Fruehauf solid walking beam suspension with trunion cross shafts for lateral movement. Air brakes. Steel combat wheels. Twelve-volt electrical system. Top speed: 28 mph.

Standard Accessories: — Tool kit, crosscut and hand saws; crowbars, skids, tow chains, rope, anchor and utility chains; tow cables, crane and hoist assembly, planks, chock blocks, single and double pulley snatch blocks; wheel guards and anchor stakes.

Historical: — Built by Fruehauf Trailer Company to be used with the M26 truck tractor from 1943 to 1945.

			PRICE			
Model No.	6	5	4	3	2	1
M15A1	2000	3000	4000	6000	—	—

World War II M10 ammunition trailer with combat wheels. (Ralph Doubek, Wild Rose, Wisconsin)

Model M10: — The M10 ammunition trailer was a unit used mostly by armored units for transporting additional ammunition behind vehicles when needed. It was towed by many types of vehicles, including 2-1/2-ton trucks, half tracks, armored cars, self-propelled artillery, and tanks.

It was basically a welded steel box on wheels, using a solid axle with no suspension, drawbar and hitch. The top of the box had hinged rails for support of the canvas cover. The box itself was just about square in dimension with a series of metal tie-down hooks that were riveted in place on the outside for the canvas tie-down ropes. The interior floor and sides had footman loops that were also riveted into small recessions; these, in turn, were spot welded to the body. This arrangement made the floor and sides smooth for easier loading and unloading.

A large hinged tailgate was at the rear with an opening in it so it could clear the rear pintle hitch in the down position. A small pin and chain assembly held it in place when in the up position. Rear blackout and taillights were provided along with reflectors. An additional rear electrical receptacle was provided for towing the trailers in tandem. The axle was mounted solid to the body, and standard six-hole Budd combat wheels with head locks were used. A metal shield covered the axle so it wouldn't catch on obstacles when traveling cross country.

Each axle hub had a brake drum with a one-piece band inside and parking brake. The two control levers mounted on the drawbar operated cables going back to the drums. A large metal box was mounted at the front of the drawbar and was used for fuse storage, appropriate for the type of ammunition carried. The front of the drawbar had the lunette and hitch with the electrical cord for the lights. A stand was under the hitch for propping up the front when parked, and could be folded up when needed. A manual catch with release mechanism was used. A small caster with wheel was at the bottom of the stand, and later models used a larger wheel, similar to the ones used on the one-ton cargo trailers. The lunette had a small release on it and could be swiveled up or down to adjust for different pintle heights. The frame was a steel channel perimeter type with cross members welded inside it. Some trailers used combat tires that had highway tread; later ones had the standard military tread pattern.

I.D. Data: — The serial number is located on the identification data plate on the left side of the drawbar near the lunette.

Model No.	Body Type	Weight	GVW	Prod.Total
M10	Cargo	2090	5090	—

Chassis and Body: — Overall length: 140 inches. Width: 77 inches. Height: 58 inches. Tires: 9.00 x 20 12-ply military non-directional.

Technical: — Hand-operated mechanical parking brakes. Solid axle. Six-volt electrical system.

Historical: — Built by Fruehauf Trailer Company, Youngstown Steel Door Company, and Schlem Brothers from 1942 to 1945.

PRICE						
Model No.	6	5	4	3	2	1
M10	200	600	1200	1800	2400	—

Interior of M10 ammunition trailer. (Ralph Doubek, Wild Rose, Wisconsin)

Unrestored World War II M10 ammunition trailer.

LIGHT ARMOR

Half-Tracks

World War II M3 half-track. (Ralph Doubek, Wild Rose, Wisconsin)

Model M2: — The M2 half track was a specially designed vehicle to provide improved cross-country performance over the scout cars so troops could give better support to advancing armored columns. It was used as a personnel carrier, prime mover, gun motor carriage, mortar carrier, and antiaircraft weapons station.

Numerous models were built, and standardization was used extensively in the power train and basic chassis. The main differences were in the configuration of the rear body behind the driver's seat. The vehicle was built on a modified truck chassis with driving front and rear axles. The rear axle drove the track with a drive sprocket replacing the wheel, normally used on a conventional truck. The drive sprocket was much smaller than the front wheels, and consequently the front and rear axles had different gear ratios to compensate for this. The rear suspension was a Kegresse design built by Timken. The frame on the early models was a single channel. Later models had a double frame as they had a tendency to brake above the rear axle housing. The power train configuration was a conventional truck design. The axles were both Timken models with a split housing in the front and a banjo type in the rear.

Both were driven from a transfer case-transmission assembly by drive shafts. The rear axle was bolted directly to the frame. Rear suspension was a vertical volute spring model with two per side, and a return roller on the top. The rear idler was a spring type; this kept tension on the track and could be adjusted. Early units had no idler spring at all, and later

World War II half-track suspension, tracks, sprockets and bogies.

Early World War II White M3A1 75mm gun motor carriage.

models had a small single spring. Finally the large spring was adopted and kept until the end of production.

The rubber tired bogie wheels were mounted in clusters of four on tapered roller bearings. The two clusters per side pivoted on arms attached to the suspension frame and springs. Moving independently of each other, they could roll over uneven terrain very easily. The vehicles were built with or without PTO-driven front winches or a roller assembly used for crossing ditches, preventing the front end from digging in. The L-head engine used in the White, Autocar, and Diamond T models was designed just for these vehicles and was used after in civilian trucks after the war. The body was made of flat face-hardened quarter-inch armor plate held together by armored screws that were counter sunk.

The front, back and sides used armor plate, but the floor was made of sheet metal, much of it being a smaller pattern of diamond plate. A large variety of stowage cabinets were in the rear bodies and floors had a different configuration depending on the model. Large metal cabinets were provided for radios, which were usually behind the driver and assistant driver seats. Rubber-coated fuel tanks were inside the body above the tracks, and were mounted forward or rearward, depending on the model.

Rifle racks were provided for carrying small arms. Many models had mine racks on the outside and rear stowage racks used for personal gear. Gas can carriers were mounted on the side of the cowl. The windshield was fitted with fold-down armor, and three collapsible legs held it up when not in use. The top half of the door armor was hinged and could be folded down and secured. The body had a series of footman loops and top bows to secure the canvas top when used. Pioneer tools were carried on the outside below the front doors on each side. Combat wheels were used on the front axle, and the tracks were rubber with steel cross bars and had cable reinforcements. The track guides in the center could be replaced by unbolting them. The M2 half track was equipped to carry 10 men and had rear-mounted fuel tanks.

A skate or gun rail ran around the interior, from which machine guns could be fired. This body was about 10 inches shorter than later models. On the rear of the body were small ledges above the taillights, upon which equipment was carried. Some of the M2s had short mine racks on the sides, and all had access doors on the outside for the radio and

World War II half-track stowage and mine racks.

stowage boxes. Early units had truck-style headlights with wire mesh over them and were fender mounted. Later models had the standard socket type with a brush guard. This pedestal style could be removed when necessary and plugs put in place of them. Cargo capacity was approximatly two to three tons. The M2 had no rear door and carried two .30 caliber and one .50 caliber machine guns and a variety of other small arms.

Model M2A1: — This is the same basic vehicle as the M2, but had the circular ring mount above the assistant driver's seat and three fixed pintle sockets, one on each side and one in the rear of the body. The skate rail was not used in this vehicle.

Model M3: — The M3 used the same basic chassis as the M2 but had a different rear body, which extended to the rear of the frame and had a

World War II White M3A1 half-track.

World War II M3A1 half-track. (George Hilton, North Bangor, New York.)

rear door. A single tall pedestal mount for the machine gun was bolted to the frame above the rear drive axle. No skate rail, fixed pintle sockets or circular ring mount was used on this model. The fuel tanks were forward mounted behind the driver's seats. Seating capacity was for 13 men. This model was used extensively in modified form for a large variety of gun motor carriages and other experimental uses.

Model M3A1: — This was the same vehicle as the M3, but the pedestal mount was eliminated and the vehicle was fitted with a circular ring mount and three fixed pintle sockets. The M3 models as well as the M2 models were built with and without winches, mine racks, and rear stowage racks.

Model M4: — This half track used the same basic body as the M2, but was modified to carry 81mm mortar, ammunition, crew and section equipment. The mortar was to be fired mostly from the ground but could be fired from the vehicle in extreme situations, as the traverse was very limited and a heavy base was not mounted in the body. The interior stowage was changed slightly, and ammunition boxes were added. The skate rail gun mount was used in this model.

Model M4A1: — The M4A1 was the same vehicle as the M4, but the mortar was permanently mounted in the rear of the body with a heavy base plate attached to the frame and fired forward. This allowed greater traverse. Interior ammunition stowage was improved and rearranged. Stowage boxes were added to the rear of the body on the outside.

Model M5: — The M5 vehicle was similar in rear body configuration to the M3 models, but this truck was built by International Harvester Corporation and shared only a few parts with the vehicles built by White, Autocar, and Diamond T. Most were sent overseas for the Lend Lease programs with England, France, and Russia. Some remained in the United States for training purposes. The armor was thicker, and rear body sides were one piece rather than bolted together like the other models. All interior and exterior sheet metal was different. The entire power train, fuel, and electrical systems were different. Almost the entire vehicle was different. The engine was an OHV model; front and rear differentials had banjo housings and were built by IHC. The only things

that were interchangeable were the frame, bogies, track, idler and drive sprockets, front wheels, winches and rollers, and the transmission transfer case assembly. The ring mounts, pedestal mounts, and fixed pintle sockets would interchange as well. Many of the changes were improvements over the earlier models.

Model M5A1: — This was the same vehicle as the M5 but the pedestal mount was eliminated, and the unit used the circular ring mount and three fixed pintle sockets. The weapons stations and interior seating arrangement were equivalent to the M3A1 model. One .50 caliber and two .30 caliber machine guns were used on this model.

Model M9: — This was the same basic vehicle as the M5 series, but the interior stowage was arranged to the same specifications as the M2, but access to the stowage and radio cabinets was from the interior of the vehicle, not from the outside. All of the IHC half tracks had rear doors for easier entry and exit. A pedestal mount was used for the machine guns.

Model M9A1: — The M9A1 was the configuration as the M9, but the pedestal mount was eliminated, and the standardized ring mount and three fixed pintle sockets were added. The M9 and M9A1 were able to carry 10 men and equipment.

Model M15: — The M15 was a multiple gun motor carriage based on the M3 half track chassis. It was designed for antiaircraft defense and to engage ground targets in support of armored columns.

The body from the driver's compartment rearward was changed, and a flat floor with a manually operated 360-degree revolving gun platform was installed. The gun mount consisted of a 37mm automatic cannon and two water-cooled .50 caliber machine guns. These were mounted just above the main gun. The mount had a maximum elevation of plus 85 degrees and depression of minus five degrees. The rate of fire of the main gun was 120 rounds per minute, and the machine guns were 500 rounds per minute.

The fuel tank was moved to just behind the cab, with ammunition storage boxes on each side of it. The 37mm gun was fed with clips of 10 rounds, and the .50 caliber guns used the larger 200 round reel style chests. A loader was on each side of the platform for each gun, and the

Left front view of White M4 mortar carrier showing winch. (David Wright, Wright Museum, Shrewsbury, Massachusetts)

Left side view of early World War II White M4 mortar carrier. (David Wright, Wright Museum, Shrewsbury, Massachusetts)

World War II I.H.C. M5 half-track with winch. (David Wright, Wright Museum, Shrewsbury, Massachusetts)

Right side view of I.H.C. M5 half-track. (David Wright, Wright Museum, Shrewsbury, Massachusetts)

Rear view of I.H.C. M5 half-track. (David Wright, Wright Museum, Shrewsbury, Massachusetts)

assistant gunner and gunner sat on seats behind the loaders and the machine guns. Here they operated the hand and foot controls of the gun mount. The rate setter sat in the center of the platform at the rear and operated the gun sight and computation systems.

Model M15A1: — This is the same basic vehicle as the M15, but some improvements were made. An armored shield assembly was installed around the gun platform to protect the crew, and the ammunition storage was rearranged on the floor of the platform. Ammunition boxes for loaded 37mm clips were on the inside walls of the armor for ease of access by the loaders. A hand rail was added to the platform to assist in getting on and off. The .50 caliber machine guns were air cooled. Communications and gun sighting systems were improved.

Model M16: — The M16 was a modified M3 chassis that carried a power operated turret with four .50 caliber machine guns that were used for antiaircraft defense and ground troop support. Power for the Maxson turret was provided by a gasoline engine-driven generator mounted on the back side of the turret. Voltage was 850 watts, 12 volts.

The basic chassis was the same as the other White model half tracks, with the differences mainly in the rear body behind the driver's compartment. No rear door was provided, and the top six inches of armor was

Left side view of I.H.C. M9A1 half-track. (Reg Hodgson, Jim Fitzgerald, Edmonton, Alberta, Canada)

Right side view of I.H.C. M9A1 half-track. (Reg Hodgson, Jim Fitzgerald, Edmonton, Alberta, Canada)

Left side view of early World War II White M15A1 antiaircraft half-track gun motor carriage.

Right side view of White M15A1 antiaircraft half-track gun motor carriage.

Close-up of M15A1 antiaircraft gun motor carriage with 37mm gun.

hinged and could fold down to allow the guns to clear when traversing. Two large cabinets were fastened to the rear of the body for stowage. The fuel tanks were forward mounted with ammunition can and radio storage in between them. The gunner sat inside the turret in a semi-reclining position with firing controls in front of him. The generator charged two large six-volt batteries, and power was drawn from them for the turret. The turret was capable of 360-degree traverse, and plus 90 degree to minus 10 degree elevation. The truck's electrical system could also power the turret, but only for very short periods. To service the machine guns, loaders could stand on a large step on the back side of the turret just behind the generator. The turret sat on a large single ring spacer to raise it up sufficiently to traverse. This turret could be manually operated as well.

Model M16A1: — This model was similar to the M16 and used the same basic gun turret as the M16, but had improvements in the communications and weapons systems. These models were built on reconditioned chassis of different models. The M3 and M15 models were often used.

This model was different in the following ways. The folding side and rear armor was eliminated. A rear access door was used. Ammunition stowage was changed to be more convenient. Radios and mounts were repositioned for a larger set that could communicate between infantry, armor, artillery, and air to ground troops. This vehicle used two spacer rings under the turret; one was slightly taller than the other so the turret could clear the non-folding side and rear armor. "Batwing" armor was fitted to the turret for added protection of the gunner and loaders. The gunner's communication system and the turret electrical system were changed, and a slip ring box was added to insure constant electrical connections between the truck and the turret. A crew of five operated the vehicle: commander, gunner, two loaders, and the driver. Two large cabinets were on the rear corners of the body for personal stowage.

I.D. Data: — The serial number is located on the identification data page on the instrument panel, and on the left front frame rail above the front spring.

Model No.	Body Type	Weight	GVW	Prod. Total
M2	Armored	14,160	17,800	11,415
M2A1	Armored	14,600	19,600	1643
M3	Armored	15,000	20,000	12,499
M3A1	Armored	14,800	20,500	2862
M4	Armored	14,000	17,850	572
M4A1	Armored	15,320	20,140	600
M5	Armored	15,400	18,900	4625
M5A1	Armored	16,175	19,675	2959
M9	Armored	15,975	19,475	2026
M9A1	Armored	16,950	19,050	1407
M16	Armored	18,640	21,640	2877
M16A1	Armored	18,250	21,250	—

With winch, add 500 pounds.

Engine: — White 160AX, six-cylinder, inline, four-cycle, L-head, cast iron block and head. Displacement: 386 cubic inches. Bore and Stroke: 4 x 5-1/8 inches. Compression ratio: 6.3:1. Brake horsepower 128 at 2800 rpm. Seven main bearings. Mechanical valve lifters. Carburetor: Stromberg AAV2. International Harvester Corporation RED 450B, six-cylinder, inline, four-cycle, OHV, sleeved cast iron block and head. Displacement: 450 cubic inches. Bore and Stroke: 4-3/8 x 5 inches. Compression ratio: 6.3:1. Brake horsepower: 130 at 2600 rpm. Seven main bearings. Mechanical valve lifters.

Chassis and Body: — Wheelbase: 135.5 inches. Overall length: 235-249 inches. Width: 88 inches. Height: 89-120 inches. Tread center to center front: 64-1/2-66-1/2 inches. Tires: 8.25 x 20 (White), 9.00 x 20 (IHC) military non- directional 12-ply.

Technical: — Manual constant mesh transmission. Speeds 4F/IR. Two-speed transfer case. Single dry disc clutch. Leaf spring suspension front, vertical volute coil spring suspension rear. Timken spiral bevel split front, banjo rear differentials (White). International Harvester Corporation bevel banjo front and rear differentials (IHC). Overall ratio: 6.8:1 (White), 7.17:1 (IHC). Hydraulic vaccum assisted power brakes. Manual steering. Front combat wheels. Twelve-volt electrical system. Top speed: 45 mph (White), 42 mph (IHC). Fuel capacity: 60 gallons. Cruising range: 175 miles (White), 125 miles (IHC).

Top view of M15A1 half-track gun motor carriage.

Rear view of White M16 half-track with quad .50 caliber machine guns. (David Wright, Wright Museum, Shrewsbury, Massachusetts)

Standard Accessories: — Hand, vehicle, pioneer tools; fire extinguisher; tire chains; track chains; tow cable; canvas top; radios with antenna; weapons depended on the model -- most carried .30 caliber or .50 caliber machine guns with tripods, pintles, cradles or skates; .45 caliber submachine gun, .30 caliber carbines, grenades, mines, 2.36-inch rocket launcher; appropriate ammunition for weapons according to the model and numerous spare parts for the weapons; mortar carriers used the 81mm mortar with sighting equipment, spare parts, and section equipment; quad machine gun vehicles used four .50 caliber air-cooled heavy barrel machine guns with large quantities of ammunition, spare parts and section equipment.

Historical: — Designed by White Motor Company, using a modified M2 and M3 scout car in 1938 to 1939. Production by White Motor Company of Cleveland, Ohio, Diamond T Motor Company of Chicago, Illinois, and Autocar Company of Ardmore, Pennsylvania from 1940 to 1944. International Harvester Corporation from 1943 to 1944. Many other models built on these chassis, and much experimentation with these vehicles for other uses.

			PRICE			
Model No.	6	5	4	3	2	1
M2	1000	3000	7000	11,000	17,000	25,000
M2A1	1000	3000	7000	11,000	17,000	25,000
M3	1000	3000	7000	11,000	17,000	25,000
M3A1	1000	3000	7000	11,000	17,000	25,000
M4	1000	3000	7000	11,000	17,000	25,000
M4A1	1000	3000	7000	11,000	17,000	25,000
M5	2000	4000	9000	13,000	19,000	25,000
M5A1	2000	4000	9000	13,000	19,000	25,000
M9	2000	4000	9000	13,000	19,000	25,000
M9A1	2000	4000	9000	13,000	19,000	25,000
M16	2000	4000	10,000	14,000	20,000	28,000
M16A1	2000	4000	10,000	14,000	20,000	28,000

World War II White M16 half-track with quad .50 caliber machine guns and mount. (David Wright, Wright Museum, Shrewsbury, Massachusetts)

Post-World War II White M16A1 quad mount half-track. (George Rabuse, St. Paul, Minnesota)

Post-World War II M16A1 quad mount half-track. (George Rabuse, St. Paul, Minnesota)

Post-World War II M16A1 quad mount half-track. (George Rabuse, St. Paul, Minnesota)

Post-World War II M16A1 quad mount half-track. (George Rabuse, St. Paul, Minnesota)

Armored Cars

World War II Ford M-20 armored car. (Ralph Doubek, Wild Rose, Wisconsin)

Model M20: — The M20 armored utility car was a lightly armored personnel and cargo carrier with a circular ring mount above the open center crew compartment. It was used primarily for field command, reconnaissance and scouting duties, with defensive antiaircraft capabilities.

The M20 had a welded one-piece armored hull with a modified six-wheel drive power train beneath it. The armor varies from one-quarter to three-quarters of an inch thick. A crew of six operated the vehicle. Four of the personnel sat in the center compartment on small seats under the ring mount. The driver and assistant sat in front under the left and right hatches. The driver and assistant used periscopes when the hatches were closed. A hood was used when inclement weather was encountered. The hood covered each hatch opening and had a glass window with a defroster and windshield wiper. A siren was mounted on the front next to the headlight on the right side. The headlights were removable, and a dummy plug was used to plug the socket, keeping out water and dirt when in combat.

Pioneer tools were carried on the outside of the body on each side of the ring mount. Mine racks were located on each side of the body between the front and first rear tire; they were also used as a step to get up into the vehicle.

The front fenders were made of three separate pieces. The rear fenders were long one-piece units with ribbing stamped in them for reinforcement. Toolboxes with lids and a radio antenna mounted between them were located above the rear fenders. The rear fenders or sand shields were usually removed in combat.

The gas tank was mounted between the crew compartment, and the engine compartment was mounted above the transmission. A double wide radiator was at the very rear behind the engine. Two belt-driven fans pushed air out the rear through the radiator. Sheet metal pans covered the bottom of the engine compartment, acting as dust shields. Fresh air was drawn through the raised deck lids above the engine and fuel tank.

A different pintle hitch was used on these vehicles. A lever was located on the top so a rope could be run forward to the driver; he could pull the rope and remotely disconnect the trailer if needed.

The power train was unique to the M20 and M8. The engine in the rear was a standard truck model, but all the external accessories and fittings were designed for this installation only. The transmission was designed this way also. It used a remote shifter in the driver's compartment, and the linkage went back to the shift tower on the side of the transmission, rather than on the top, which is the normal position for a truck. The transmission was synchromesh in all four gears. The transfer case was again designed for the reverse power train; it had two rear outlets for the double driveshafts to the rear axles, plus the input for the driveshaft from the trasmission. One outlet was on the front side for the drive to the front axle.

The axle assemblies were wider than others on World War II vehicles. The housings were armored, and there were armored covers over the brake lines. Two wheel cylinders were used on each hub; these, too, were special models used for this application only. Combat wheels with the "run flat" capability were used, so no spare tire was carried.

The interior was cramped with many brackets and fittings for the items stowed inside. Radios, weapons, ammunition and personal items were stored here, along with all the other accessory equipment. The driver controls were the same as in a normal truck, but as the engine and transmission were behind the driver, all the foot controls were remote and run by hydraulics. The reservoirs and mechanisms were near the pedals with lines, which were enclosed in the armor of the body, running to the rear. The accelerator, clutch and brakes used these systems. Radios were carried in the sponsons behind the passengers seats. The personnel who rode inside faced each other, their backs to the outside of the vehicle. The circular ring mount above the crew compartment had a trolley and skate assembly for a .50 caliber machine gun. Carbines, rocket launcher, grenades and mines were carried as well.

Model M8: — This was the same basic vehicle as the M20, but it had a turret with a 37mm gun and a coaxially mounted .30 caliber machine gun. In the M8, the turret sat in the center of the body, where the crew was located. A turret basket was suspended below and could move with the turret in a 360-degree circle. It had a manual traversing mechanism with two speeds. The commander and gunner sat on each side of the gun. A .50 caliber machine gun was mounted on the rear of the turret, although occasionally a ring mount was fastened just above the top of the turret. Ammunition was stored in clips around the interior of the turret, and in one sponson.

I.D. Data: — The serial number was located on the identification data plate in the driver's compartment, behind the driver's head on the roof, in between the hatches.

Engine: — Hercules JXD, six-cylinder, in-line, L-head, four-cycle. Cast iron block and head. Displacement: 320 cubic inches. Bore and Stroke: 4 x 4.25 inches. Compression ratio: 6.5:1. Brake horsepower: 110 at 2800 rpm. Seven main bearings. Mechanical valve lifters. Carburetor: Zenith Model 29.

Chassis and Body: — Wheelbase: 104 inches. Overall length: 197 inches. Width: 100 inches. Height: 90 inches. Tread center to center: 76 inches. Tires: 9.00 x 20 12-ply military non-directional.

Technical: — Selective sliding gear manual transmission, synchromesh. Speeds: 4F/1R. Two-speed transfer case. Single dry disc clutch. Leaf spring suspension front and rear. Timken spiral bevel full floating axles with split housings. Gear ratio: 6.66:1. Hydraulic vacuum-assisted power brakes. Hydraulic adjustable shock absorbers on all wheels. Manual steering. Combat wheels. Twelve-volt electrical system. Top speed: 56 mph. Fuel capacity: 54 gallons. Cruising range: 250 miles.

Standard Accessories: — Hand, vehicle, pioneer tools; canvas top for vehicle; machine gun; seat cushions; radios, mines, grenades, smoke pots, fire extinguisher; spare parts; map table; .50 caliber machine gun with tripod, pintle and cradle assembly, five .30 caliber carbines, one 2.36-inch rocket launcher. The M8 had one additional .30 caliber machine gun and carried four .30 caliber carbines.

Historical: — Designed and built in St. Paul, Minnesota by the Ford Motor Company from 1943 to 1945.

Model No.	Body Type	Weight	GVW	Prod.Total
M20	Armored	12,250	15,650	3791
M8	Armored	14,500	17,200	8523

			PRICE			
Model	6	5	4	3	2	1
M20	1500	4000	11,000	15,000	25,000	33,000
M8	3000	9000	13,000	18,000	28,000	38,000

Rear view of Ford M-20 armored car. (Ralph Doubek, Wild Rose, Wisconsin)

Left front view of Ford M8 armored car. (David Wright, Wright Museum, Shrewsbury, Massachusetts)

World War II Ford M8 armored car. (David Wright, Wright Museum, Shrewsbury, Massachusetts)

Early World War II White M3 scout car. (David Wright, Wright Museum, Shrewsbury, Massachusetts)

Model M3A1: — The scout car was a fast, lightly armored vehicle designed for scouting and reconnaissance duties in combat.

The M3A1 gave its crew high mobility with armor plate and a variety of weapons. It was built on a specifically modified truck chassis with a conventional channel-type frame designed to accept a four-wheel drive power train.

The entire body was constructed of quarter-inch face-hardened armor plate, with the exception of the windshield armor, which was a half-inch thick. The driver and commander sat in front; the rear compartment had seats for six additional crew members for a total of eight men. The radiator was covered with armored shutters, which were controlled from the driver's compartment.

The windshield and side door armor could be raised or lowered depending upon combat conditions. The vehicle was radio equipped and carried two machine guns and one submachine gun.

Stowage cabinets were in the floor and above the wheel wells in the rear. A skate rail, on which the machine gun trolleys operated, ran around the entire interior. A roller on the front of the vehicle prevented the truck from getting stuck in steep ditches.

The power train layout was standard "truck" for the period. A Hercules L-head JXD engine with dry disc clutch, four-speed non-synchromesh transmission and two-speed transfer case powered the unit. The transfer case had no disengagement feature, thus giving the truck full-time four-wheel drive. The axles were Timken split housing models mounted on conventional leaf spring suspension. This made the scout car a simple armored truck.

Combat wheels were used on all models. Vacuum-assisted brakes improved stopping ability. The battery box was located on the right runningboard.

The vehicle was actually designed before World War II (one of the earliest pieces of armor designed) and put into use just prior to the war. The half-track vehicles were designed from the scout car, but really were completely different units with virtually no parts interchangeability. They have many visual similarities, but they are not the same in any way. This is somewhat surprising as both were built by White.

Left rear view of White M3 scout car. (David Wright, Wright Museum, Shrewsbury, Massachusetts)

I.D. Data: — The serial number was on the identification data plate on the instrument panel inside, and stamped on the left front frame rail directly above the front axle housing or centered between the front and rear front spring hangers in the same area.

Model No.	Body Type	Weight	GVW	Prod. Total
M3A1	Armored	8900	11,750	20,918

Engine: — Hercules, six-cylinder, in-line, four-cycle, L-head, model JXD. Cast iron block. Displacement: 320 cubic inches. Bore and stroke: 4x4-1/4 inches. Compression ratio: 6.5:1. Brake horsepower: 110 at 2800 rpm. Seven main bearings. Valve lifters: mechanical. Carburetor: Zenith model 29, cast iron.

World War II White M3A1 scout car. (David Wright, Wright Museum, Shrewsbury, Massachusetts)

World War II White M3A1 scout car with skate rail. (David Wright, Wright Musuem, Shrewsbury, Massachusetts)

Chassis and Body: — Wheelbase: 131 inches. Overall length: 222 inches. Height: 79 inches. Width: 80 inches. Tread front: 65-1/4 inches. Tread rear: 65-1/4 inches. Tires: 8.25x20 12-ply nylon combat non-directional.

Technical: — Manual constant mesh transmission. Speeds: 4F/1R. Two-speed transfer case. Single dry disc clutch. Semi-elliptic leaf spring suspension front and rear. Timken spiral bevel full floating axles with split housings. Gear ratio: 5.14:1. Hydraulic vacuum-assisted power brakes. Lever action front and rear shocks. Manual steering. Twelve-volt electrical system. Steel combat wheels. Top speed: 55 mph. Fuel capacity: 30 gallons.

Standard Accessories: — Canvas top, side curtains; pioneer tools, seat cushions; one .50 caliber and one .30 caliber machine gun, tripods, cradle and carriage assemblies; one .45 caliber submachine gun; radio with antenna; hand and vehicle tools; fire extinguisher.

Historical: — Design began in 1937; production began in 1940 in Cleveland, Ohio by White Motor Company.

PRICE

Model No.	6	5	4	3	2	1
M3A 1	1000	2000	6000	13,000	18,000	24,000

Armored Personnel Carriers

Early 1960s Cadillac M114 all-aluminum armored personnel carrier.

Model M114: — The M114 was a small armored personnel carrier used for reconnaissance. It had an all-aluminum welded body and was fully amphibious when its front surfboard was used with propulsion generated from its shroud-covered tracks. Its light weight and low ground pressure allowed it to be transported by air and operated in numerous types of soft terrain in nearly all climates and temperatures.

The engine and transmission were from Chevrolet. Their well-proven 283 cubic inch V-8 and Hydramatic transmission were adapted to the vehicle with different accessories, manifolds, pans, mounts, etc. Carburetion, ignition, exhaust and intake systems were modified. The crankshaft was also longer for use with a larger pulley. Almost everything was changed other than the basic block and heads. This was common with civilian engines adapted for military use.

A small drive shaft went from the transmission to the geared steer differential in the front of the hull. This was a mechanically controlled hydraulic unit; power was then conveyed to the final drives by drive shafts.

Torsion bar suspension was used with four pairs of road wheels on each side. No return rollers were used, and the adjustable idler was at the rear for controlling track tension. Road wheels were aluminum with rubber attached to them. The track was the only type like this ever used on an armored vehicle. It was built in sections with cable reinforced rubber belts. Aluminum cross bars, with small rubber pads, were riveted to it. They were easily replaced as the sections were about four feet long.

The engine had a coaxial fan for the cooling system. When spinning, the engine had a sound similar to a supercharger, especially when combined with the deep throaty sound of the exhaust system. In reality, it was just naturally aspirated with a carburetor.

The M114 was a very compact vehicle and operated with a crew of three: driver, commander and observer. There was room for one more passenger, if neccessary. Entrance and exit were through three hatches in the roof of the vehicle (one for each crew member) and through a large round door in the rear of the body. The driver sat in the left front beside the engine in the right front. The commander sat directly behind the driver in the center, beneath his vision cupola and machine gun mount outside and just in front of his hatch. The observer sat in the right rear with a vision periscope in his hatch and a machine gun mount on the roof just in front of his opening.

The vehicle was equipped with a large variety of gear used in reconnaissance work. An air purification system was provided for use in nuclear, biological, and chemical warfare situations. A .50 caliber machine gun was used by the commander, and an M-60 7.62mm machine gun was used by the observer. Full radio communications were installed in each vehicle. Infrared night vision equipment was carried. Rifles, grenade launchers, rocket launchers and appropriate ammunition, as well personal items, complemented the on-vehicle supplies.

I.D. Data: — The serial number is located on tbe identification data plate inside the vehicle, on the left side of the body near the driver's seat.

Model No.	Body Type	Weight	GVW	Prod. Total
M114	Armored	12,900	14,750	—

Rear hatch on early 1960s Cadillac M114 all-aluminum armored personnel carrier.

Engine: — Chevrolet Military V-8, OHV, cast iron block and beads. Displacement: 283 cubic inches. Bore and Stroke: 3-3/8 x 3 inchess. Compression ratio 8:1. Brake horsepower: 160 at 4600 rpm. Hydraulic valve lifters. Five main bearings. Carburetor: Holley military.

Chassis and Body: — Ground contact length xx inches. Overall length: 176 inches. Height: 92 inches. Width: 92 inches. Tread center to center of tracks: 73 inches. Tracks: Replaceable sectionalized band with metal cross bars and cable reinforcements. Width: 16.5 inches.

Technical: — General Motors 305MC Hydramatic transmission. Speeds: 4F/1R. Allison GS-100-3 geared steer differential. Hand lever-controlled mechanical-hydraulic steering. Mechanical pedal-operated brakes. Overall ratio: 4.17:1. Torsion bar suspension with dual rubber tired road wheels. Twenty-four-volt electrical system. Top speed: 36 mph. Fuel capacity: 110 gallons. Cruising range: 300 miles.

Standard Accessories: — A .50 caliber machine gun, M-60 7.62mm machine gun, M14 rifle, M79 grenade launcher, M72 rocket launcher; radios, ammunition, tow cable, fixed and portable fire extinguishers, periscopes, infrared vision equipment; hand, vehicle, pioneer tools, spare parts and personal stowage items.

Historical: — Built by Cadillac from the late 1950s to the early 1960s. Saw some use in the early Vietnam conflict.

			PRICE			
Model No.	6	5	4	3	2	1
M114	4000	12,000	18,000	24,000	30,000	35,000

Late 1950s FMC M59 armored personnel carrier.

Model M59: — The M59 was a full-tracked armored personnel carrier. The entire body was of welded steel construction, thus making the vehicle fully amphibious on inland waterways. A trim vane positioned on the front improved movement in the water.

The unit was powered by two six-cylinder engines located on the sides above the tracks. The engines used were GMC 302s with Hydramatic transmission. These were similar units to the power train used in the M series GMC trucks of the mid-1950s. They were used as a money-saving feature. The M59 was designed and built to replace the M75, which used the very costly M41 tank tranmssion and engine. The M75 was also not amphibious, whereas the M59 was fully amphibious without preparation. With two engines, one on each side of the vehicle, and two drive lines going forward to the front differential, synchronization was critical. Automatic transmissions provided power forward to right-angle drive boxes in the front corners of the hull, then by propeller shafts to the controlled differential. Power train components were serviced from the inside by removing large sealed panels.

The fuel cell was a large rubber unit located under the floor near the rear of the vehicle, with filler tube on the top of the hull. The road wheels, tracks, rear idler and drive sprockets were from the M41 tank family.

The M59, with its two small engines, was very underpowered and never saw combat. It was replaced by the M113 in the early 1960s.

A crew of two operated the vehicle; the driver was in the left front and the commander was in the right front. Bench seats inside had capacity for 10 troops with equipment. Entry was from the rear through a door in the rear ramp, or by lowering the ramp. Track shrouds were located on the sides of the body to cut down on dust and to aid propulsion in water.

The vehicle had an infrared night vision system. A .50 caliber machine gun was carried on a pintle mount in front of the commander's hatch, and a large quantity of ammunition was carried.

Model M59A1: — This was the same basic unit as the M59, but rather than having a commander's hatch, with a pintle mounted .50 caliber machine gun in front of it, a revolving small turret with the machine gun mounted in it was used. The back half of the turret lifted up as the commander's hatch. Rotation was by means of a manual crank. Ammunition was belt-fed from a stowage bin under the commander's seat. The seat, bin and turret assembly all moved together.

FMC M59A1 armored personnel carrier.

I.D. Data: — The serial number was located on the identification data plate inside the vehicle on the left side near the driver's seat.

Model No.	Body Type	Weight	GVW	Prod. Total
M59	Armored	39,504	42,600	—

Engine: — General Motors Model 302, six-cylinder, in-line, OHV, four-cycle, cast iron block and head. Displacement: 302 cubic inches. Bore and Stroke: 4 x 4 inches. Compression: ratio 7.2:1. Brake horsepower: 127 at 3350 rpm. Four main bearings. Mechanical valve lifters. Carburetors: Holley downdraft.

Chassis and Body: — Ground contact length: 121 inches. Overall length: 221 inches. Height: 94 inches. Width: 128.5 inches. Tread center to center of tracks: 103 inches. Tracks steel shoe, rubber bushed steel pin with removable rubber pads: 21 inches wide.

Front view of FMC M59A1 armored personnel carrier.

Interior of late 1950s FMC M59A1 armored personnel carrier.

Technical: — General Motors Hydramatic 301MG transmissions. Speeds: 4F/1R. Mechanical controlled differential. Overall ratio: 4.25:1. Hand lever-controlled steering and braking. Torsion bar suspension with dual rubber tired road wheels. Twenty-four-volt electrical system. Top speed: 32 mph. Fuel capacity: 136 gallons. Cruising range: 120 miles.

Standard Accessories: — One .50 caliber machine gun and one M3A1 submachine gun with ammunition; hand and vehicle tools; spare parts;

fire extinguisher; pioneer tools; infrared vision equipment.

Historical: — Built by FMC Corp. in San Jose, California from 1952 to 1957.

PRICE						
Model No.	6	5	4	3	2	1
M59	1500	2500	5000	9000	13,000	—

Left rear view of early 1950s I.H.C. M75 armored personnel carrier.

Model M75: — The M75 was an armored personnel carrier with a full track chassis. It was capable of transporting 12 men, including the crew, into combat zones with light armor protection.

The M75 was powered by a large horizontally opposed, air-cooled engine in the front. This vehicle could ford water with some preparation, but was not fully amphibious. The M75 used the engine power plant assembly of the M41 tank family. The entire unit could be slid out to the front for service or replacement. Although a sophisticated vehicle, it had a very tall silhouette, and combined with its lack of fully amphibious capability and the prohibitive cost to build, it was soon replaced by the less expensive amphibious M59 vehicles.

The driver sat in the left front and the commander sat directly behind the engine compartment in the center of the vehicle. Each had a hatch above them; the commander's hatch had a pintle mount for a machine gun. A row of personnel seats ran along each side and could seat 10 troops. There were two doors in the rear from which the troops exited, but no ramp. Large hatches in the roof also permitted entrance or exit. The body or hull was a one-piece all-welded structure.

The power plant and drive train were very sophisticated and were used in several other vehicles from the same time period. This vehicle was very expensive to manufacture and was dropped after a short while. The less expensive M59 was adopted by the U.S. Army. These units were radio and interphone equipped, and had an auxiliary generator in the right front corner of the hull.

I.D. Data: — The serial number was located on the identification data on the right wall of the driver's compartment.

Engine: — Continental AO-895-4 six-cylinder, horizontally opposed, air-cooled, OHV, OHC, four-cycle. Aluminum alloy block and heads. Displacement: 895 cubic inches. Bore and Stroke: 5.75 x 5.75 inches. Compression ratio: 6.5:1. Brake horsepower: 295 at 2700 rpm. Mechanical valve lifters. Seven main bearings. Carburetors: Bendix Stromberg NA-Y5G-3. Magneto ignition.

Chassis and Body: — Length of track on ground: 120 inches. Overall length: 204 inches. Height: 120 inches. Width: 112 inches. Steel shoe,

Right rear view of early 1950s I.H.C. M75 armored personnel carrier.

rubber bushed steel pin tracks with replaceable rubber pads. Width: 21 inches.

Technical: — General Motors Allison CD-500-4 cross drive transmission and differential with torque converter. Speeds: 2F/IR. Overall ratio: 22.7:1. Torsion bar suspension with dual rubber tired road wheels. Hand lever-operated hydraulic steering in differential. Pedal-operated service brakes. Twenty-four-volt electrical system. Top speed: 45 mph. Fuel capacity: 150 gallons. Cruising range: 115 miles.

Standard Accessories: — Hand, vehicle, pioneer, track tools; spare parts; radios, vision periscopes; one .50 caliber machine gun, one .45

Mid-1950s I.H.C. M75 armored personnel carrier.

View through the rear doors of early 1950s I.H.C. M75 armored personnel carrier.

caliber submachine gun, one 3.5-inch rocket launcher; auxiliary generator; fixed and portable fire extinguishers.

Historical: — Developed and built by International Harvester Corporation in the early 1950s as a smaller, improved version of the M44. It was succeeded by the less expensive M59, which was fully amphibious without preparation.

Model No.	PRICE					
	6	5	4	3	2	1
M75	4000	7000	9000	12,000	—	—

World War II M39 armored utility vehicle blanketed with snow.

Model M39: — The M39 was a full-tracked utility vehicle with a fully armored hull. Its original design and use was that of a prime mover for the three-inch gun, the M6. The M39 was later used for reconnaissance, cargo and troop transport in combat zones where armor protection was required.

The vehicle was a derivative of the M18 "Hellcat" 76mm gun motor carriage. The chassis was basically the same as the M18, however, there was no turret and there were extensive modifications for better stowage in the M39. The driver and assistant sat under hatches in the front of the vehicle. There were dual driving controls in front of them. The transmission and differential sat between them. The driveshaft to the engine went back under the center compartment where seven additional crew members were seated where the communications equipment, munitions, small arms, personal stowage and much more were carried.

The radial engine was at the rear with the fuel cells and oil reservoir. The differential in the front and the engine at the rear were serviced by lowering their armored covers and sliding them out on rails provided on the back sides of the covers. The armor on the vehicle was one-quarter inch to one-half inch thick, depending on the area. A .50 caliber machine gun was carried on a ring mount at the front of the crew compartment. Independently sprung torsion bar suspension was used with early steel or late rubber track. The vehicle was capable of extremely high speeds to 60 mph.

The armored hull of the M39 was a one-piece welded unit using torsion bar suspension. The suspension was an improvement over the vertical and horizontal volute spring types used on earlier tanks and armored vehicles. The original track was steel shoe with rubber bushed steel pins. Later tracks were rubber covered shoes with the same steel pins. Dual rubber tired road wheels, with a rear idler assembly, and front drive sprockets were used. A track tensioning device was between the front drive sprocket and the first set of road wheels. This kept the track at the proper tension at the high speeds the vehicle could obtain.

Sitting in the rear, the nine-cylinder radial engine had a torque converter and flywheel assembly. The drive shaft going forward to the automatic transmission had overdrive in the top gear selection; this is where the unit got its tremendous speeds. The driver's and assistant's steering levers were mounted upside-down on the roof of their compartment. Steer-

ing was accomplished by simply pulling on them. This was the same lever set up on the M5 series of light tanks.

The M39 was a new concept in armored fighting vehicles — very fast and light. Reconnaissance was one of its objectives. The vehicle was equipped with a very good set of radios.

I.D. Data: — The serial number was located on the identification data plate inside the driver's compartment on the hull near the left side of the driver's seat.

Model No.	Body Type	Weight	GVW	Prod. Total
M39	Armored	—	35,500	640

Engine: — Continental R975C4, nine-cylinder, radial, air-cooled, four-cycle. Steel block with aluminum cylinders and heads. OHV. Displacement: 973 cubic inches. Bore and Stroke: 5 x 5-1/2 inches. Compression ratio: 5.7:1. Three main bearings. Mechanical valve lifters.

Chassis and Body: — Ground contact length: 131.5 inches. Overall length: 214 inches. Height: 77.5 inches. Width: 113 inches. Tread center to center of tracks: 94.5 inches. Tracks: steel or rubber shoe with rubber bushed steel pins, 14.5 inches wide.

Technical: — Torqmatic automatic transmission with torque converter. Speeds: 3F/1R. Single-speed transfer case. Torsion bar suspension with dual rubber tired road wheels. Mechanically controlled differential with hand lever-controlled steering and braking. Overall ratio: 3.13:1. Magneto ignition. Twenty-four-volt electrical system. Top speed: 60 mph. Fuel capacity: 165 gallons. Cruising range: 155 miles.

Standard Accessories: — Canvas top cover, .50 caliber machine gun, two .30 caliber carbines, tow cable, hand, vehicle, pioneer tools, spare parts, track sections, fire extinguishers, radios, periscopes for vision and fire control, smoke pots, grenades, munitions, gun section equipment.

Historical: — Built by the Buick Division of General Motors from October 1944 to March 1945. Used extensively in the Korean conflict.

PRICE

Model No.	6	5	4	3	2	1
M39	9000	12000	18,000	24,000	—	—

World War II M39 armored utility vehicle.

Rear view of World War II M39 armored utility vehicle.

Another view of snow-covered World War II M39 armored utility vehicle.

World War II Ford T16 universal carrier.

Model T16: — The T16 universal carrier was the improved version of the Bren gun carrier used by the British before and during World War II. It was basically longer with a bogie wheel added on each side and a refined suspension system for stability. An improved engine, better steering system and a simplified welded hull were also incorporated.

The T16 was a full-track cargo and personnel carrier capable of high speeds on improved roads. It had light armor: 7/32-inch to 9/32-inch thick in various areas. The carrier was used for a great variety of tasks, some of which were transporting cargo and troops, towing anti-tank guns, transporting mortar carriers, laying communications cable and numerous other duties.

The T16's rear-mounted engine was a Ford L-head V-8 with small modifications for this installation. A manual truck transmission with a remote linkage to the front was attached to the rear of the engine. A short drive shaft went to the rear differential. From the back, the differential looked like a truck unit but was quite different for use in a tracked vehicle.

The suspension was a prewar Horstmann design originally used on the British Bren gun carrier. This unit used only three bogie wheels. The tracks were unusual for an Allied forces vehicle. They were of a very short pitch, with all-metal shoes and dry steel link pins. Most other tracks used by the United States and its Allies were rubber bushed with a much longer life.

The T16 had a crew of four people. The driver sat in the right front, steering the vehicle. The assistant manned the weapons station in the left front position. The other two rode in back, one on each side above the tracks, as the engine, radiator and transmission were in the center of the unit. Wooden troop seats were located in the rear alongside the engine. The radiator was in front of the engine between the driver and assistant. Two machine guns, two rifles, one smoke mortar and an anti-tank projector were carried as standard issue weapons. This vehicle could float and propel itself by its tracks.

Model T16E2: — This was the same basic vehicle as the T16, but was a few inches longer with the suspension bogies repositioned farther back and apart. The rear bogie was reversed for a different action of the suspension. The rear differential was also moved back as well.

I.D. Data: — The serial number was on the identification data plate inside the driver's compartment.

Model No.	Body Type	Weight	GVW	Prod. Total
T16	Personnel	7756	9440	13,893

Engine: — Ford, 90 degree V-8, four-cycle, L-head, cast iron block. Displacement: 239 cubic inches. Bore and stroke: 3-1/16 x 3-1/4 inches. Compression ratio: 6.4:1. Brake horsepower: 100 at 3800 rpm. Three main bearings. Carburetor

Chassis and Body: — Track on ground: 78 inches. Overall length: 153 inches. Height: 61 inches. Width: 83 inches. Tread center of track to center of track: 62.5 inches. Tracks: 9.5 inches wide, steel shoe, dry steel pin.

Technical: — Manual selective sliding gear transmission. Speeds: 4F/1R. Single dry disc clutch. Horstmann double coil spring suspension, two per side with four bogie wheels per side. Front idler wheel, rear drive sprocket. Mechanically controlled differential. Lever steering with lever- and pedal-controlled brakes. Twelve-volt electrical system. Top speed: 33 mph. Fuel capacity: 24 gallons. Cruising range: 120 miles.

Standard Accesories: — Canvas covers for front and rear; two machine guns, one infantry anti-tank projector (PIAT), two service rifles; radio and antenna, if applicable; hand and vehicle tools; vehicle spare parts; fire extinguisher.

Historical: — Designed in the 1930s, it originally had only three bogie wheels per side. Several manufacturers made many improvements and changes. The T16 was the final basic design that was produced in mass quantities, mainly for the British. Various models were built in Great Britain, Canada, and the United States until the end of World War II.

PRICE

Model No.	6	5	4	3	2	1
T16	2000	6000	9000	12,000	14,000	—

Rear view showing tools on the Ford T16 universal carrier.

HEAVY ARMOR

Light Tanks

World War II M3A1 light tank. (Fred Ropkey, Indianapolis, Indiana)

Model M3A1: — The M3A1 light tank was the U.S. Army's standard model after the beginning of World War II. Its origins dated back to the M1 and M2 tanks of the mid to late 1930s. The designs were created and improved as the Army's philosophies changed, particularly as they saw the war begin in Europe and witnessed early advances with occupation in the Pacific theater.

The M1 and M2 tanks had the same basic power train layout as the M3 series vehicles. The radial air-cooled engine was in the rear of the tank with the driveshaft going forward under the turret to the front-mounted transmission differential assembly. The early tanks were equipped with machine guns only, and some had two turrets as well as one.

The M2A4, the last model of its series, introduced the 37mm gun, which was used with different mounts on all of the M3-M5 series tanks. A very distinctive characteristic of the M1-M2 tanks was that the rear idler wheel was smaller and off the ground. The M3s had the large trailing idler wheel, so this gave the vehicle more ground contact length, improving ground pressure and stability. The M1, M2, and the early M3s had riveted hulls; welded hulls began with the M3A1s and were used from that point on.

The armor in the M3s was 5/8 inch to 1-3/4 inches thick in front, 1 inch thick on the sides and rear, 3/8 inch thick on the top, and 3/8 to 1/2 inch thick on the bottom. The turret was 1-1/4 to 1-1/2 inches thick. The suspension on the tanks was a vertical volute design with two bogie clusters per side (each cluster having two springs and two road wheels) and a trailing idler wheel that kept the track tension correct.

Tracks came in four styles. First was the smooth rubber block; then steel bar cleat and steel chevron; and finally rubber chevron. Bolt-on steel track grousers were stored on the outside of the turret for added protection when not needed.

The tank was operated by a crew of four. Driver and assistant were in the lower front, and the gunner with commander loader were in the turret. Vision was by means of periscopes.

Armaments consisted of the 37mm main gun with a coaxial .30 caliber machine gun. A bow machine gun was operated by the assistant driver. An exterior-mounted machine gun for antiaircraft use was located on the commander's cupola. A variety of grenades and a .45 caliber submachine gun were provided for crew use.

Left front view of M3A1 Stuart light tank. (Fred Ropkey, Indianapolis, Indiana)

The turret was powered by an electric hydraulic unit for a 360-degree traverse. Manual traverse could be used as well. The 37mm gun was stabilized by a gyroscope. Radios and an interphone system were used by all members of the crew.

The engine was an aircraft design seven-cylinder air-cooled radial with a manual clutch mounted on the forward side of the engine; the driveshaft went forward under the turret basket to the five-speed manual synchromesh transmission. The transmission was bolted directly to the differential, which was a mechanically controlled unit, using wet bands actuated by two hand levers for steering and braking.

The exterior of M3 was quite boxy; most surfaces were flat and vertical. The turret sides were vertical as well, but the turret itself was a round type with a flat plate on which the mantlet was mounted. The M3A3, M5 and M5AI had improved armor with more slope for better deflection of projectiles. The M3 also had external air cleaners. The vertical front hatches made it very difficult for the driver and assistant to enter and exit. Large headlights were fender mounted in the front of the vehicle. Jettisonable auxiliary fuel tanks were used on the M3 vehicles; the tanks could be dropped quickly when entering a combat zone. As usual, the armaments, communication equipment, mechanical and electrical systems and other aspects of the vehicle were improved when the M3AI replaced the M3.

Model M3A3: — The M3A3 used the same chassis as the M3A1; tracks, suspension, hull bottom, differential, transmission and engine were retained. The all-welded hull from the tracks upward, as well as the turret, were completely revised. The hull front was extended forward, and the driver and assistant's hatches were installed in the top plate for easier entry and exit and much better protection. The sides and rear of the body were also sloped for much improved ballistics. The sponsons were lengthened, which added more room for ammunition and fuel. A bustle or storage box was usually on the rear above the engine access doors. The turret was redesigned with a bulge for radios in the rear and larger hatches for the commander and gunner. This tank used all periscopes for vision. Sand shields were used on this model. An auxiliary generator provided power for heavy electrical loads.

Model M5: — The M5 was a model that came about due to the shortages of radial engines that occurred when the M3s were being built. Radial engine production was needed for aircraft use. Consequently, Cadillac Division of General Motors suggested using two car V-8s, side by side, with their new Hydramatic automatic transmissions. They promptly built a prototype and drove it without any problems from their factory to Aberdeen, Maryland for tests.

The upper hull of the tank was modified by raising the deck in the rear to accommodate the radiators, which were mounted above the engines. The front armor was one piece and had a very nice slope, much better than the M3 tanks. This was the same front as the M3A3 tank. The side armor was vertical rather than sloped on the M3A3. The turret of the M3A1 was also used, but the driveshafts were lower in the hull; this allowed the turret traverse mechanism to be located under the turret basket rather than in it. The armament and suspension were the same as the M3AI's. This tank was much easier to drive. The engines and transmissions were modified somewhat for use in the tank. An auxiliary generator was used in this tank as well.

Model M5A1: — The M5A1 was the same basic vehicle as the M5 but had the improved turret of the M3A3 with radios in the rear bulge and larger hatches in the top of the turret. An improved gun mount for the 37mm gun and a new antiaircraft machine gun mount was installed on the outside of the turret. The armor on the M5 was slightly thicker than on the M3; this increased the weight by several thousand pounds. The front hull was 1-1/8 to 2-1/2 inches thick, the sides and rear were 1 to 1-1/8 inches, the top was 1/2 inch and the bottom was 3/8 to 1/2 inch. The turret was 1-3/4 inches thick in front, 1-1/4 inches on the sides and 1/2 inch on top. There was an escape hatch in the hull floor. The M5 and M5A1 both had different vision and fire control systems as well as different main gun mounts. As usual, the tanks were constantly improved as the models changed.

Model M8: — The M8 Howitzer motor carriage used the M5 tank chassis with a 75mm pack Howitzer in a revolving open-topped turret. The driver and assistant's hatches were moved to the front hull plate because of the larger turret overhang. The chassis was designed to tow an ar-

World War II M3A3 light tank.

Right rear view of M3A3 light tank.

mored ammunition trailer because interior space was more limited with the larger ammunition. A ring mount for the .50 caliber machine gun was in the right rear corner of the turret. These vehicles were replaced by the M7 Priest with the 105mm Howitzer.

I.D. Data: — The serial number was located on the identification data plate in the driver's compartment by his left leg.

Model	Body Type	Weight	GVW	Prod. Total
M3	Armored	—	27,400	5811
M3A1	Armored	—	28,500	4621
M3A3	Armored	—	31,752	3427
M5	Armored	—	33,000	2074
M5A1	Armored	—	33,907	6810
M8	Armored	—	34,600	1778

Engines: — (M3, M3A1) Continental W670-9A, seven-cylinder radial, air-cooled, OHV, four-cycle. Cast iron block with steel sleeved aluminum cylinders. Displacement: 670 cubic inches. Bore and Stroke: 5-1/8 x 4-5/8 inches. Compression ratio: 6.1:1. Brake horsepower: 250 at 2400 rpm. Three main bearings. Mechanical valve lifters. Guiberson T-1020-4 nine-cylinder radial, air-cooled diesel, OHV, four-cycle. Cast iron block with steel sleeved aluminum cylinders. Displacement: 1021 cubic inches. Bore and Stroke: 5-1/8 x 5-1/2 inches. Compression ratio: 14.5:1. Brake horsepower: 245 at 2200 rpm. Three main bearings. Mechanical valve lifters. Bosch fuel injection. (M5, M5A1, M8) Cadillac V-8, eight-cylinder, 90-degree, L-head, four-cycle. Cast iron block and heads. (TWO) Series 42. Displacement: 346 cubic inches each. Brake horsepower: 110 at 4000 rpm each. Bore and Stroke: 3-1/2 x 4-1/2 inches. Compression ratio: 6.7:1. Five main bearings. Mechanical valve lifters.

Chassis and Body: — Track on ground: 117 to 121 inches. Overall length: 174 to 178 inches. Width: 88 to 95 inches. Height: 90 to 99 inches. Tread center to center of tracks: 73 inches. Tracks: double pin rubber bushed, smooth rubber block, steel chevron or bar cleat or rubber chevron. Width: 12 inches.

Technical: — M3's manual synchromesh transmission. Single dry disc clutch. Speeds: 5F/1R. M5's Hydramatic automatic transmissions. Two-speed transfer case. Speeds: 8F/2R. Torque converters. Vertical volute spring suspension. Eight spoked or solid bogie wheels both sides. Mechanically controlled differential, with two levers for steering and braking.

Planetary final drives with herringbone gears. Twelve-volt electrical systems. Top speed: 36 mph. Fuel capacity: 56 gallons (M3); 89 gallons (M5). Cruising range: 70 miles (M3); 100 miles (M5).

Standard Accessories: — Hand, vehicle, pioneer, track tools; tow cable, fire extinguishers; vehicle and weapons spare parts; section equipment for main gun; machine guns, small arms, grenades, tripods for .30 caliber machine guns; telescope sight, periscopes with spare heads; first aid kits, radios, interphone systems; canvas tarp; ammunition for all weapons; personal stowage.

Historical: — The M3 was built by American Car and Foundry of Berwick, Pennsylvania from 1941 to 1943. The M5 and M8 were built by American Car and Foundry; Cadillac in Detroit, Michigan and Southgate, California; and Massey Harris of Racine, Wisconsin, from 1942 to 1944.

PRICE

Model	6	5	4	3	2	1
M3	—	—	—	—	—	—
M3A1	15,000	20,000	25,000	30,000	35,000	—
M3A3	—	—	—	—	—	—
M5	15,000	20,000	25,000	30,000	35,000	—
M5A1	15,000	20,000	25,000	30,000	35,000	—
M8	—	—	—	—	—	—

Front view of M3A3 light tank.

World War II M5A1 light tank. (Joe McLean, McLean Museum, Vincennes, Indiana)

World War II Cadillac M5 light tank. (James Welty, Ohio Military Museum Inc., Fairborn, Ohio)

Right side view of M24 "Chaffee" light tank with twin Cadillac V-8s. (David Wright, Wright Museum, Shrewsbury, Massachusetts)

Model M24: — The M24 "Chaffee" was a light tank used in combat zones for offensive or defensive operations, with full armor protection for the crew of four. It was designed as a replacement for the M3 and M5 series light tanks.

The Chaffee had many improvements: torsion bar suspension, wider center guide tracks, larger gun and turret, thicker armor with better angles for deflection, easier maintenance of power train components, easier access through hatches for the crew, more stowage, better communications, and improved vision and fire control systems. In short, a great deal of redevelopment went into this model.

The biggest improvement was the 75mm main gun mounted in an all-new cast turret with a .30 caliber coaxial machine gun and a .50 caliber machine gun on the outside of the turret for antiaircraft use. An additional .30 caliber machine gun was used in a bow mount on the right front by the assistant driver. The hull was a one-piece welded unit with the differential in the front, the fighting compartment and the turret in the center, and the power plants in the rear.

The dependable Cadillac engine and Hydramatic transmission was retained on this tank. Two engines were used, mounted side by side with a transfer case to combine their power for the all-new differential and final drives in the front. Larger radiators were fitted and moved so service would be easier. The modified torsion bar suspension of the M18 Hellcat built by the Buick Division of General Motors was used. A new transfer case was also used; it tied the two engines together and had a manual reversing feature with two forward speeds. It was synchronized as well. The transfer case was mounted on the rear of the engine and transmission assemblies. This made it possible to use one drive shaft to the differential. The M5 series tank used two drive shafts, and the synchronizer unit was mounted on the differential.

The all cast steel turret used the ring from the M5 tank, but the turret itself was much larger. The 75mm gun required much more room inside. This gun fired the same ammunition as the 75mm gun in the M4 series Shermans. Radios were in the rear bustle of the turret. No turret basket was used, but the seats were set up to move when the turret revolved. The main gun ammunition was carried in liquid-filled stowage boxes under the floor. The turret was traversed by power or manually, the drive shaft beneath it. This vehicle was wider and longer than the previous light tanks, but its wider tracks gave it better off-road performance.

The armor was thicker on the M24 than on the M5 tanks, and the hull itself was a welded unit, made of mostly flat plates. The silhouette was lower and sleeker than its predecessors. This was due to better deflection angles of the unit. The front of the tank had a distinctive octagonal plate bolted to it for access and service to the differential.

The assistant driver had a ball-mounted .30 caliber machine gun mounted in front of him, and he had a set of driving controls as well as the driver.

The track, suspension, road wheels, etc. were all entirely different from the M5 tanks. Most noticeably, the track was a center guide design that used dual tired road wheels. The sprockets engaged the track shoe rather than engaging the end connectors as it did on the M5. Large shock absorbers were used on the two front and rear sets of road wheels. The center set had none.

I.D. Data: — The serial number was located on the identification data plate inside the driver's compartment on the hull.

Model No.	Body Type	Weight	GVW	Prod. Total
M24	Armored	—	40,500	4070

Engine: — Two Cadillac 90-degree V-8s, Model 44T24. L-head, four-cycle. Cast iron block and heads. Displacement: 349 cubic inches each. Bore and Stroke: 3.5 x 4.5 inches. Compression ratio: 7:1. Brake horsepower: 110 at 3400 rpm each. Five main bearings. Mechanical lifters. Carburetors:

Chassis and Body: — Length of track on ground: 123 inches. Overall length: 216 inches. Height: 97 inches. Width: 112 inches. Tread center to center of track: 96 inches. Steel and rubber block track, with rubber bushed steel pin. Width: 16 inches.

Technical: — General Motors Hydramatic transmissions. Speeds: 4F/1R. Two-speed transfer case. Torsion bar suspension with dual rubber-tired road wheels. Mechanical controlled differential. Overall ra-

Cadillac/Massey-Harris M24 "Chaffee" light tank. (David Wright, Wright Museum, Shrewsbury, Massachusetts)

Left front view of M24 "Chaffee" light tank. (Fort DeRussy, Hawaii)

Top view of M24 "Chaffee" light tank.

tio: 70:1. Hand lever- operated steering and brakes. Twenty-four-volt electrical system. Top speed: 30 mph. Fuel capacity: 110 gallons. Cruising range: 100 miles.

Standard Accessories: — Hand, vehicle, pioneer, track tools; spare parts; fixed and portable fire extinguishers; tow cable, auxiliary generator; vision periscopes, gun sight; one .50 caliber machine gun; two .30 caliber machine guns, one .45 caliber submachine gun, one .30 caliber carbine, grenades; radios.

Historical: — Built by Cadillac Division of General Motors and Massey-Harris Corporation from 1944 to 1945, in Detroit, Michigan and Milwaukee, Wisconsin.

PRICE

Model No.	6	5	4	3	2	1
M24	15,000	25,000	35,000	45,000	—	—

Another top view of M24 "Chaffee" light tank.

Medium Tanks

World War II M43 self-propelled eight-inch howitzer built on an M4 Sherman chassis.

Model M4: — The M4 "Sherman" tank was a medium tank used during and after World War II. It was the culmination and successor to earlier versions dating back to 1938.

The design began with the M2, which had the same basic power train as the later model M4s, but the superstructure from the tracks up was completely different. The familiar vertical volute suspension, nine-cylinder radial engine and five-speed transmission with front-mounted differential were used from the beginning.

The M2 had several machine guns and a 37mm cannon in a small turret that was welded together from flat plates. The next model of the M2 had a 75mm pack Howitzer mounted in the right sponson above the track. This later M2 evolved into the M3 series "Lee" tank. A variety of manufacturing techniques was used in the construction of the M3's hulls. The first ones were riveted, the second ones were cast, and the third ones were of all welded plates. Armament in the M3 consisted of a 75mm gun in the right sponson, a 37mm gun in a small cast turret in the top center of the hull, and a .30 caliber machine gun in a second smaller turret mounted on top of the first one. This gave the M3 a very high profile.

The M3 was the first U.S. tank to use a power turret and gyro stabilized gun. A crew of six men operated the M3: driver, radio operator, 75mm gunner, 37mm gunner and loader, and commander. The M2 tank was obsolete before the war began because the gun was too small. The M3 was declared obsolete before the end of World War II because of the limited traverse of the gun.

The M3 was used by England, Russia and the United States in some combat situations. Its shortcomings led to the M4 design. The M3 was used for training and was converted to other uses. The M3 was introduced in June 1941; work was already in progress on the M4, which was introduced in October 1941.

During World War II, more M4 series tanks were used than any other medium tank, which made it the most familiar to the public. It probably is yet today. The M4 vehicles were built in the thousands, in many models and configurations. Many were used for experimental problems. So many changes were made from the beginning to the end of its production that, despite it looking nearly the same, it was, in fact, a completely different vehicle by the end of its production. The M4 tracks, sprockets, bogie wheels and vertical volute suspension were borrowed from the

World War II early Sherman M4 split differential housing.

M2. Frame work, bogie wheels and track support rollers were modified several times through production. Early bogie wheels were spoked; later ones were solid. The upper hull was of welded material with a cast turret. Second models had a cast hull and turret. The last models had all-welded hulls. Early front differentials were three-piece housings bolted together.

Second models were a round-nosed one-piece unit. The last models were a sharp-nosed one-piece unit. The round- and sharp-nosed units were used on all models as the war progressed or as the vehicles needed repairs or rebuilding. The M4's armament consisted of a 75mm gun in the power-operated turret with a coaxial-mounted .30 caliber machine gun, and a ball-mounted .30 caliber machine gun. An exterior mount was provided for an antiaircraft machine gun, usually a .50 caliber, located near the commander's cupola. All models were radio equipped with the radios in the rear of the turret.

A crew of five people operated the M4: commander, driver, assistant driver who operated the bow machine gun, gunner and loader. The M4

Rear view of M43 self-propelled eight-inch howitzer built on an M4 Sherman chassis.

World War II late Model M4 Sherman sharp-nosed differential housing.

and M4A1 models were powered by the nine-cylinder radial engine, but production problems due to aircraft demands quickly led to alternative power plants and many improvements. A dry disc clutch was mounted on the rear of all the engines, with a driveshaft going under the turret basket to the synchromesh five-speed transmission, which was attached to the front differential. The differential pinion gear was in the transmission, and the ring gear was in the differential itself. The steering and braking was done by two levers operating the oil-bathed contracting bands inside the differential housing. An escape hatch was located in the bottom of the hull behind the assistant driver's seat.

Auxiliary power was required when all systems were operating. A generator set -- powered by a two-cycle gasoline engine, which had its own separate fuel tank -- was located in the left side of the hull. It could be started electrically or manually. Fuel tanks were in the rear of the hull for added protection. Early radial-engined models had externally mounted air cleaners, but most were in the engine compartment.

Several types of track were used on the early vertical volute suspension models: rubber chevron or smooth block, or steel chevron or bar cleat. Extended end connectors were added on the outside of the track for better flotation. Some rebuilt tanks had the extended end connectors on the inside, also; the suspension was spaced out, away from the hull, for the extra width of the track. Tow cables, pioneer tools, track tools and spare track blocks were frequently carried on the exterior of the hull. Applique armor was on the outside of the hull over the ammunition storage areas for extra protection. Approximately ninety rounds of main gun ammunition was carried, as well as several thousand rounds of machine gun ammunition. Small arms and different types of grenades were also carried.

The M4 series vehicle's armor had actual thicknesses of 2 inches in the front upper hull, 1-1/2 to 2 inches in the lower hull, 1-1/2 to 2 inches on the sides, 1-1/2 inches in the rear, 1 inch on the top, and 1/2 to 1 inch thick on the bottom. The turret had 3 inches of armor in the front, 2 inches on the sides, and 1 inch on top.

Two different types of gun were used on the M4 models. The first was a 75mm that used dry storage for the ammunition; later, a wet type of storage was used to help prevent interior fires when hit by an enemy shell. A liquid-filled case surrounded the ammunition; the liquid was usually water and anti-freeze solution, which kept well for winter and summer use. When the liquid-filled jacket was punctured, it supposedly extinguished the fire. Many times extra ammunition was stowed outside the protected bins, and when hit, the extra ammunition would explode.

Later in the war a better gun was needed as enemy armor was not being penetrated, and a 76mm model was designed with a new turret. It was first installed in the original turret but did not fit well; consequently, a new turret, mantlet and mount were designed with the same turret ring diameter, which allowed it to be installed on existing M4 hulls. Once accepted, it was used on all M4 models and was retrofitted when tanks were rebuilt. The new gun and turret was a significant improvement.

A redesigned 105mm Howitzer was also used with a new mount in the early turret; these were built in quantity. The model equipped with the

Unrestored World War II M4A1 Sherman tank with flame thrower and extended tracks. (Fred Ropkey, Indianapolis, Indiana)

Rear view of M4A1 Sherman tank with flame thrower and extended tracks. (Fred Ropkey, Indianapolis, Indiana)

Left rear view of M4A1E8 Sherman tank with H.V.S.S., wide tracks and radial engine.

World War II M4A1E8 Sherman tank with radial engine, H.V.S.S. and wide tracks.

higher velocity 76mm gun, wider tracks and suspension, powered by the Ford V-8 engine, was preferred during World War II. It was the final model of M4, and was the one adopted for postwar use. It also served in Korea.

Three types of hulls were used. The first type was a combination of welded and cast materials; the second type was an all-cast hull; and the third type was all welded. The suspension originally had a 16-inch wide track with six bogie wheels per side. The later development of the horizontal volute spring suspension was quite different. The track was 23 inches wide with three bogie clusters per side, but these had four wheels per cluster rather than the earlier two per cluster on the vertical spring suspension. With 12 wheels per side and horizontal springs, the tanks had better flotation ability and a much better ride.

The M4 tank went through countless changes based on engineering and experience in combat from 1941 to 1945. These changes included all aspects of the vehicle -- hull, suspension, turret, armaments and power plants.

There were five engines that were used in the M4 series. All were adaptations of either aircraft or automotive designs. The first tanks used the Continental radial air-cooled nine-cylinder engine.

The second group used a twin six-cylinder diesel unit using two General Motors commercial truck engines. These were two-cycle 6-71s used in buses as well. They were tied together at the rear with a common bell housing, and drove a single driveshaft to the differential.

The third engine was the Chrysler multibank. This was an adaptation of five modified car engines to a common crankcase. The rear ends of each of the five crankshafts had a small gear. These gears ran a large sun gear behind the flywheel and clutch assembly. This was a complicated unit to maintain, thus, a relatively quick disconnecting system was designed so the whole engine, radiator and clutch assembly could be removed at one time for easier maintenance. It did, in fact, meet the requirements needed for a tank power plant, and a large number were produced. Most of the models equipped with this engine, as well as the twin diesel en-

gine, were given to the lend-lease countries.

The fourth engine used was an adaptation of a Ford V-12 aircraft model, however, the engine was shortened to a V-8 as the V-12 was too long for the hull of the M4. This was probably the most reliable and widely used engine in the medium tanks; it was used after World War II as well. It was a 60-degree unit with an all-aluminum block and cylinder heads. The cylinders were sleeved. Dual overhead camshafts were used with four valves per cylinder and cross flow opposed valve combustion chambers. It had forged steel connecting rods and crankshaft, forged aluminum pistons with full floating pins, twin magnetos with two plugs per cylinder, stellite valves in the cylinder heads, dual carburetors, and head studs rather than head bolts.

Much of this sophisticated technology was not seen in racing circles and production cars in the United States until the mid-1960s. The fifth engine was a conversion of a Wright radial (by Caterpillar Company) to a diesel model. It was air-cooled and the largest of the five in cubic inches. Very few were built, but in trials it did turn out to be the best performing of the five engines installed in the M4. Due to the availability of gasoline, this engine was dropped for the sake of standardization, and the Ford V-8 became the most widely used model. The radial diesel was used in the longer M4A4 hull because of its size. Today, diesel power is used in most tanks because of fuel economy, flammability and durability.

The differential in the M4 tank was located in the lower front of the vehicle. It was a mechanically controlled type that used two contracting bands bathed in oil. It was pretty much the same from the beginning to the end of production, although the housing itself was modified three times. The first model was a three-piece unit that was bolted together. The second was a one-piece cast unit with a round nose. The third was a one-piece all cast unit with a sharp nose for better deflection of shells. The round nose and the sharp nose units were added to earlier models as these models were repaired or replaced.

Steering and braking were accomplished by using two levers, operated by hand, to actuate the bands. The unit was very large and had a tre-

World War II M4A3E8 Sherman tank with 76mm gun and Ford GAA V-8 engine.

Left rear view of M4A3E8 Sherman tank with 76mm gun and Ford GAA V-8 engine.

mendous oil capacity. The five-speed Spicer synchromesh transmission is bolted directly to it. An external shift lever is on the left side for the driver to operate. A foot pedal with mechanical linkage runs back to the clutch on the rear of the engine. Except for the levers, the controls are similar to those used to operate other automotive type vehicles.

The crew of five men consisted of the driver, assistant driver who manned the bow machine gun, gunner, loader, and commander. The driver and assistant sat in the left or right front of the tank; the loader sat on the left side of the main gun, the gunner sat on the right side of the gun, and the commander sat just behind and a little above the gunner so he could see vision blocks or periscopes from his hatch. The driver and assistant had their own hatches while the commander and gunner used the commander's hatch. The loader had his own hatch on later model vehicles.

In summary, the M4 series used four different hull styles; two different turrets; three guns; three different mantlets; five different types of bogies, four with the earlier narrow track, one with the wide tracks; four different types of track, one narrow, three wide; three types of differential housings; five different engines; two different types of ammunition storage; and countless other changes too numerous to mention.

Although they looked remarkably like the first models, the last models of the M4 were completely different. The basic design was simple, rugged, very reliable and easy to manufacture. The M4 served with the United States and foreign countries for many years after World War II. Thousands were manufactured, many were converted to other uses, and the chassis is still used today in the logging industry.

Model M4: — Welded and cast hull, cast turret, 75mm or 105mm gun, dry ammunition storage, narrow track, vertical suspension, radial gas engine, three- or one-piece differential housing.

Model M4A1: — Cast hull, cast turret, 75mm gun dry storage, 76mm wet storage, narrow or wide track, vertical or horizontal suspension, radial gas engine, three- or one-piece differential housing.

Model M4A2: — Welded hull, cast turret, 75mm gun dry storage, narrow track, vertical suspension, twin 6-71 Detroit diesel engines, three- or one-piece differential housing.

Model M4A3: — Welded hull, cast turret, 75mm dry or wet stowage, 76mm wet stowage gun or 105mm dry stowage gun; narrow or wide track, vertical or horizontal suspension, Ford V-8 gasoline engine, one-piece differential housing.

Model M4A4: — Welded hull, cast turret, 75mm gun dry storage, narrow track, vertical suspension, Chrysler multibank engine, longer hull, three-piece differential housing.

Model M4A6: — Welded hull, cast turret, 75mm gun dry storage, narrow track, vertical suspension, caterpillar radial diesel engine, longer hull (same as M4A4), three- or one-piece differential housing.

Model M7: — The M7 "Priest" was a self-propelled artillery piece based on the M4 and M4A3 tank chassis. The radial engine, transmission, differential, tracks, suspension, etc. were identical to the M4 tank. However, the superstructure from the tracks upward was changed. Some early models had riveted hulls; later ones were all welded. The Priest was used when needed to support advancing tanks with artillery. A standard 105mm Howitzer with a modified carriage was installed in the front center of the hull, just to the right of the driver. A circular ring mount for a machine gun was located at the right front corner of the vehicle. It looked like a pulpit, consequently the name "Priest." The vehicle was open topped with the gunner on the left side of the gun and assistant gunner on the right side. Ammunition was stored on the sides of the fighting compartment at the rear of the piece. Three- or one-piece differential housings were used. Certain areas of the hull on this vehicle were made of soft steel.

Model M7B1: — This was the same basic vehicle as the M7, but it had the M4A3 chassis with the Ford V-8 engine, all-welded hull, one-piece differential housing, narrow track and vertical suspension. Some improvements were made to the gun for better traverse and elevation.

Model M32: — The M32 series was a group of M3 and M4 chassis that were converted to or built as tank retrievers. The series was used for a variety of recovery purposes, but mainly for recovering disabled tanks. The turret was removed, and a 60,000-pound winch was installed in the floor of the vehicle. A different fixed, lightly armored turret was added; it had a machine gun mount on the top for the commander to

World War II M4A3 Sherman jumbo assault tank built for assault of the Siegfried Line.

use. A smaller winch raised and lowered the large A-frame boom, which was used for heavy lifting. A much larger pintle hitch and tow bar were located at the rear for towing heavy loads cross-country. There was lots of space for external stowage on this vehicle; this space was used mostly for spare parts and recovery equipment.

There were several models in this series, and as they were built, they were modified and improved and consequently given new model numbers. The power train and suspension were also upgraded as time went on. The V-8 gas engine and wider tracks with horizontal suspension were used.

Model M74: — This was a tank retriever built from reconditioned M4A3 chassis with wide tracks and V-8 engine. The M74 was built in the early 1950s and served the same purpose as the M32 series, but again was improved. A 90,000-pound winch replaced the one in the M32, with a auxiliary winch mounted on the front of the turret for a lighter load of work. The A-frame booms were operated by the hydraulic system, making them easier to use. Stowage on the outside of the hull was changed. A hydraulic front spade was added in front for light dozing work and heavy winching. The boom winch was inside the turret. All the winches on the M32 and M74 were hydraulically operated. The main cable came through the front hull above the transmission. This was quite a different vehicle compared to the M32 models. Its need was created as a result of the needs of the M26 and M47 heavy tanks.

I.D. Data: — The serial number was located on the identification data plate in the driver's compartment by his left arm, and stamped in the hull directly under the same data plate.

Model	Body Type	Weight	GVW	Prod. Total
M4	Armored	62,800	66,900	8389
M4A1	Armored	62,700	66,800	9707
M4A2	Armored	66,000	70,200	10,968
M4A3	Armored	62,500	66,700	12,342
M4A4	Armored	65,400	69,700	7499
M4A6	Armored	65,800	70,000	75
M7	Armored	43,200	50,600	3490
M7B1	Armored	45,400	52,000	826
M32	Armored	—	61,700	1599
M74	Armored	—	93,750	—

Engines: — Continental R975 C-1 or C-4, radial, air-cooled, nine-cylinder, four-cycle, OHV, forged steel block, steel-sleeved aluminum cylinders. Displacement: 975 cubic inches. Bore and Stroke: 5 x 5.5 inches. Compression ratio: 5.7:1. Brake horsepower: 400 or 450 at 2400 rpm. Three main bearings. Mechanical valve lifters. Carburetor: Stromberg NA-R9G.

General Motors 6046 diesel, 12-cylinder (two 6-71s), in-line, OHV, two-cycle, cast iron blocks and heads. Displacement: 850 cubic inches (425 per engine). Bore and Stroke: 4.25 x 5 inches. Compression ratio: 16:1. Brake horsepower: 375 at 2100 rpm. Seven main bearings. Mechanical valve lifters.

General Motors fuel-injection. Ford GAA V-8, OHV, OHC, four-cycle. Steel-sleeved aluminum block, aluminum heads. Displacement: 1100 cubic inches. Bore and Stroke: 5.4 x 6 inches. Compression ratio: 7.5:1. Brake horsepower: 450 at 2600 rpm. Five main bearings. Mechanical valve lifters. Carburetors: Stromberg NA-Y5G.

Chrysler A57 multibank, 30-cylinder, four-cycle, cast iron crank case, blocks, heads. Displacement: 1253 cubic inches. Bore and Stroke: 4.37 x 4.25 inches. Compression ratio: 6.2:1. Brake horsepower: 370 at 2400 rpm. Four main bearings per block. Mechanical valve lifters. Carburetors: Carter TD-1.

Caterpillar (Ordnance) RD1820 radial, air-cooled, diesel, nine-cylinder, OHV, forged steel block, aluminum steel-sleeved cylinders. Displacement: 1823 cubic inches. Bore and Stroke: 6.1 x 6.9 inches. Compression ratio: 15.5:1. Brake horsepower: 450 at 2000 rpm. Three main bearings. Mechanical valve lifters. Caterpillar fuel injection.

Chassis and Body: — Length of track on ground: 147 inches or 160 inches. Overall length: 230 to 239 inches. Width: 103 to 118 inches. Height: 108 to 117 inches. Tread center to center of tracks: 83 or 89 inches. Tracks, narrow: 16.5 inches wide in rubber chevron or smooth block, steel chevron or bar cleat. Tracks, wide: 23 inches wide in steel chevron, steel or rubber chevron.

Technical: — Manual synchromesh transmission with overdrive, Spicer. Speeds: 5F/1R. Dry disc clutch. Vertical or horizontal volute spring suspension. Mechanically controlled differential. Twin lever-type steering

World War II M4A3 Sherman tank with Ford V-8 engine and 75mm gun.

Left rear view of M4A3 Sherman tank with Ford GAA V-8 engine.

World War II M4A4 Sherman tank with Chrysler multi-bank engine. (George Rabuse, St. Paul, Minnesota)

Chrysler multi-bank engine for M4A4 Sherman tank.

and braking. Overall gear ratio: 10.03:1. Twenty-four-volt electrical system. Top speed: 24 to 26 mph. Fuel capacity: 160 to 175 gallons. Cruising range: 100 to 120 miles.

Standard Accessories: — Hand, vehicle, track, pioneer tools; Tow cables, fire extinguishers; vehicle weapons, spare parts; section equipment for main gun; machine guns, small arms, grenades, tripods for .30 and

.50 caliber periscopes with spare heads; first aid kit, radios with spare parts; telescopic sight for main gun; canvas tarps, driver's hatch cover for inclement weather; ammunition for .45, .30, .50, 75mm guns; personal stowage.

Historical: — Built by Baldwin Locomotive Works, American Locomotive Company, Detroit Tank Arsenal (Chrysler), Pressed Steel Car Company, Pullman Standard Car Company, Lima Locomotive Works, Inc., Pacific Car and Foundry Company, Fisher Tank Division of General Motors Corp., Federal Machine and Welding Company, Ford Motor Company from 1941 to 1945. Many more models were built in different configurations and types using the same chassis and power train. Thousands were distributed to lend-lease countries. Over 57,000 of this type and its derivatives were produced. It was used by the U.S. Army and National Guard, and foreign countries for years after World War II. The constant improvements made during its production actually made the last models totally different from the first.

PRICE

Model	6	5	4	3	2	1
M4	10,000	17,000	25,000	35,000	45,000	—
M4A1	10,000	17,000	25,000	35,000	45,000	—
M4A2	—	—	—	—	—	—
M4A3	10,000	17,000	25,000	35,000	45,000	—
M4A4	—	—	—	—	—	—
M4A6	—	—	—	—	—	—
M7	10,000	17,000	25,000	—	—	—
M7B1	10,000	17,000	25,000	—	—	—
M32	20,000	25,000	30,000	—	—	—
M74	20,000	25,000	30,000	—	—	—

World War II M7 Priest 105mm self-propelled gun carriage on M4 Sherman chassis.

Right side view of M7 Priest 105mm self-propelled gun carriage on M4 Sherman chassis.

World War II M7B1 Priest M4 on Sherman chassis with 105mm gun. (Fred Ropkey, Indianapolis, Indiana)

Front view of M7B1 Priest. (Fred Ropkey, Indianapolis, Indiana)

World War II M32B1 retriever on M4 Sherman chassis. (David Wright, Wright Museum, Shrewsbury, Massachusetts)

World War II M32A1B3E8 retriever on Sherman M4 chassis. (Fred Ropkey, Indianapolis, Indiana)

Rear view of World War II M74 tank retriever on M4 Sherman tank chassis.

Left rear view of M74 tank retriever on M4 Sherman chassis.

Early World War II Lee M3A1 tank.

M4A4 Sherman tank with Chrysler multi-bank engine. (George Rabuse, St. Paul, Minnesota)

Early 1950s Cadillac M41 Walker Bulldog light tank.

Model M41: — The M41 "Walker Bulldog" was a light tank designed to provide mobile fire power in combat and fully enclosed protection for the crew. Its light weight allowed it to be air transportable.

The design was similar to other tanks used by the U.S. armed forces. This tank's design began in 1949 to replace the M24 Chaffee unit of World War II. It was named after Gen. W.W. Walker, who was killed in a Jeep accident in the Korean War. The Walker Bulldog was the first tank that was actually designed around a power plant, which was a Continental flat opposed six-cylinder engine. An Allison cross drive transmission was attached to it. This was the steering unit and transmission combined — quite a compact unit. All of this was located at the rear of the vehicle. The Walker Bulldog was quite different from other World War II tanks as almost all of the others had the differential at the front of the tank. Planetary final drives were used as well. The cross drive allowed the vehicle to pivot in place.

The driver's compartment was in the front, the fighting compartment with turret was in the center, and the power train components were in the rear. Eleven more vehicles were built using the same basic power train and suspension systems.

The turret was quite long with a large bustle at the rear where the radios were enclosed. A large stowage box was added on the outside, giving the turret an even longer appearance.

A crew of four men operated the vehicle. The commander, gunner and loader were in the turret with the driver below them in the left front of the hull. The main armament was a 76mm high velocity gun that was quite a bit longer than the 75mm used in the Chaffee. The original tank had a fully automatic loader, but the design was dropped for the sake of room in the turret. The 76mm gun was the first to use a bore evacuator and muzzle deflector. Later models were equipped with Xenon light systems for night shooting. Sixty-five rounds of ammunition were carried. A .30 caliber coaxial machine gun was located in the mantlet alongside the main gun. Two pintle mounts on the outside of the turret could be used for a .50 caliber machine gun fired by the commander for antiaircraft use or ground support. The turret had power or manual traverse.

An auxiliary generator furnished power for the radios and other electrical equipment. Armor thickness on the all-welded hull ranged from 25mm in the front to 15-20mm on the sides and rear. Fenders carried stowage boxes on top of them. Ammunition was carried in the turret and on the floor of the vehicle. Radio equipment was in the rear of the turret. The unit was equipped with infrared night vision systems. This power train was used in several different armored vehicles.

Some Walker Bulldogs saw action in Vietnam and other Middle East conflicts. They were used by many countries around the world. Diesel repower units were designed for them by aftermarket companies and were quite successful.

I.D. Data: — The serial number was located on the identification data plate in the driver's compartment on the hull wall to the left of the driver's seat.

Model No.	Body Type	Weight	GVW	Prod. Total
M41	Armored	—	51,800	

Engine: — Continental or Lycoming AOS-895-3. Six-cylinder, horizontally opposed, air-cooled, supercharged, OHV, OHC. Four-cycle. Aluminum alloy block and heads. Displacement: 895 cubic inches. Bore and Stroke: 5.75 x 5.75 inches. Compression ratio: 5.5:1. Brake horsepower: 500 at 2800 rpm. Four main bearings. Mechanical valve lifters. Carburetors: Bendix Stromberg NA-Y5G-3.

Technical: — General Motors Allison CD-500-3 cross drive transmission and differential with torque converter. Speeds: 2F/1R. Overall ratio: 22.7:1. Torsion bar suspension with dual rubber tired road wheels. Rear mounted final drives and drive sprockets. Hand lever-operated hydraulic steering in the differential. Pedal operated as service brakes. Twenty-four-volt electrical system. Top speed: 45 mph. Fuel capacity: 140 gallons. Cruising range: 100 miles.

Chassis and Body: — Length of track on ground: 128 inches. Overall length with gun: 323 inches; without gun: 229 inches. Height: 108 inches. Width: 126 inches. Tread center to center of track: 102.5 inches. Steel shoe, rubber bushed steel pin tracks with replaceable rubber pads. Width: 21 inches.

Standard Accessories: — Hand, vehicle, pioneer, track tools; spare parts; fixed and portable fire extinguishers; radios, periscopes, range finder; one .50 caliber machine gun, one .30 caliber machine gun, one .30 caliber carbine, one .45 caliber submachine gun; grenades; tow cable, auxiliary generator; infrared vision equipment.

Historical: — Built at the Cleveland tank arsenal in the early 1950s by Cadillac Division of General Motors.

PRICE

Model No.	6	5	4	3	2	1
M41	20,000	30,000	40,000	50,000	60,000	70,000

Left rear view of M41 Walker Bulldog light tank.

Early 1950s Cadillac M41 Walker Bulldog light tank.

Right side view of Cadillac M41 Walker Bulldog light tank.

Heavy Tanks

Right rear view of Pershing M26 tank. (David Wright, Wright Museum, Shrewsbury, Massachusetts)

Model M26: — The M26 "Pershing" tank was a heavy tank whose design began in 1942. Its development period went through several models, and the M26 was the final model that went into production.

In the beginning of World War II, it was soon learned that a tank heavier than the Sherman was needed, as well as a larger gun. The main armament on the M26 was a 90mm with a muzzle velocity of 3350 feet per second; it could penetrate about seven inches of armor at 1000 yards. It could compete very well with the German guns of the period.

The whole vehicle was a complete new design compared to the Shermans. The M26 was wider, longer and had a lower profile than the M4. Although it was heavier, it still had good cross-country performance and flotation. The front hull armor was 3-4 inches deep, sides were 2-3 inches, the rear was 2 inches, and the top and bottom were 1/2-1 inches. The turret was 3-4 inches thick on the front and sides, and the top was 1 inch thick.

There were two machine guns: One was coaxially mounted with the 90mm main gun in the bow for the assistant driver; the second .30 caliber gun was in the bow for the assistant driver. An exterior mount for a .50 caliber machine gun was provided for antiaircraft use on the outside of the turret. Five .45 caliber submachine guns were provided for the crew, along with a .30 caliber carbine for a grenade launcher. Radios were mounted in the rear of the turret. The hull was a welded unit made up of armored castings and flat plate. Torsion bar suspension was used with a series of five top return rollers. Dual rubber tired road wheels, six per side, were used with a wide center guide track. Four shock absorbers, and volute spring bumpers for limiting road wheel

travel, were installed on each side of the hull. The hull used a more modern power train layout; the power plant was in the rear with the differential and transmission for added protection. The large V-8 engine was a modified GAF from the Sherman with a new automatic transmission.

The crew of five sat in the usual positions. The driver and assistant in the lower front of the hull, each with his own set of controls. The commander, gunner and the loader sat in the turret. There were two escape hatches in the bottom of the hull for the driver and assistant.

In the engine compartment, an auxiliary generator was located on the right side just below the turret ring. Fuel tanks were mounted alongside the engine. Two radiators were used; each fan was driven from a right drive off the front of the engine, with a propeller shaft to each fan hub. The mechanically controlled differential was attached to the transmission and connected to the final drives with double U-joints.

Three types of track were used. The first was all steel, the second was steel chevron, and the third was rubber chevron. All the road wheels, return rollers and idler wheels were rubber tired. The main gun stowage for ammunition was under the turret; it was the "wet" type of stowage used in the later M4 -- thin water tanks which surrounded the ammunition bins.

In later production, other vehicles were built on the same chassis. An eight-inch 240mm gun carriage, cargo carrier, and a tank recovery vehicle were the principal models. None of these were built in large quantities. The M26 was one of very few vehicles built after the hostilities ended in World War II.

World War II Pershing M26 medium tank. (David Wright, Wright Museum, Shrewsbury, Massachusetts)

Left rear view of Pershing M26 tank. (David Wright, Wright Museum, Shrewsbury, Massachusetts)

Model M26A1: – This was the same basic vehicle as the M26, but a new, improved 90mm gun was installed with a new mount. This came about because of widespread dislike for the two-piece ammunition used in the M26. The M26A1 main gun used a shorter one-piece case and projectile, but the case was larger in diameter, which made for much easier handling. The barrel had a bore evacuator added as well to reduce fumes in the turret after firing the main gun.

Model M45: — This also was the same basic vehicle as the M26, but it had a 105mm howitzer in a modified 90mm mount. This came about from the success of and the need for the tank columns in combat to have artillery support when advancing and running into enemy personnel supporting their tanks with light armored vehicles, or to soften up enemy positions before attacking them.

Model M46: — The M46 used the same hull, turret and main gun as the M26 models. A larger Continental V-12 air-cooled engine with a General Motors cross drive transmission differential was fitted to the tank with some minor modifications. This made for a significant increase in performance. External mufflers were used on this tank, and a small compensating idler wheel was addeed between the drive sprocket and rear road wheel. Some of these were built new, and some were built from M26 tanks. These were built from 1949 to 1951.

Model M46A1: — This was the same vehicle as the M46, but it had small differences in the electrical system and some minor mechanical improvements.

Model M47: — This vehicle used the hull of the M46 with armor improvements and the Continental power plant of the M46 vehicles. A new turret was built with better sloping slides; range finder capabilities were designed into its top. The turret had quite a different appearance from the types used on the M26 and M46. Ballistics were better on the entire body of the M47. These tanks were newly manufactured units, not converted models. Large quantities were built from 1951 to 1953. The M47 served as an interim model until the all-new M48 models came out in the late 1950s. The 90mm gun was again improved on the M47, and these guns were built by the Detroit Tank arsenal and the American Locomotive Company.

Left side view of mid-1950s M47 medium tank.

I.D. Data: — The serial number was located on the identification data plate inside the driver's compartment on the left side of the hull.

Model No.	Body Type	Weight	GVW	Prod. Total
M26	Armored	84,850	92,355	2212
M26A1	Armored	87,000	94,600	—
M45	Armored	86,000	93,000	—
M46	Armored	86,500	94,000	760
M46A1	Armored	86,700	94,200	—
M47	Armored	89,800	97,200	8576

Engines: — M26, Ford GAF, V-8, 60-degree, eight-cylinder, OHV, OHC, four-cycle, steel sleeved aluminum block, aluminum heads. Displacement: 1100 cubic inches. Bore and Stroke: 5.4 x 6 inches. Compression ratio: 7.5:1. Brake horsepower: 450 at 2600 rpm. Five main bearings.

Right side view of mid-1950s M47 medium tank.

Mechanical valve lifters. Carburetors: Stromberg NA5YG. M46, M47 Continental AV-1790, V-12, 90-degree, 12-cylinder, air-cooled, OHV, OHC, four-cycle, steel block with steel sleeved aluminum cylinders. Displacement: 1790 cubic inches. Bore and Stroke: 5.75 x 5.75 inches. Compression ratio: 6.5:1. Brake horsepower: 704 at 2800 rpm. Seven main bearings. Mechanical valve lifters. Carburetors: Stromberg NA5YG.

Chassis and Body: — Length of track on ground: 148-160 inches. Overall length: 251-278 inches. Width: 137-139 inches. Height: 109-117 inches. Tread center to center of tracks: 110 inches. Track width: 24 inches, all steel, steel chevron, rubber chevron.

Technical: — M26: Torqmatic automatic transmission with torque converter. Speeds: 3F/1R. M46, M47: General Motors cross drive with torque converter. Speeds: 2F/1R. Torsion bar suspension with six dual rubber tired road wheels per side with three or five return rollers. M26: Mechanical controlled differential; M46, M47: cross drive transmission differential. M26: Twin lever steering and braking; M46, M47: hand lever controlled hydraulic disc steering, pedal operated as service brakes. Overall gear ratio: 13.47, M26; 22.04, M46, M47. Twenty-four-volt electrical system. Fuel capacity: 191 or 233 gallons. Cruising range: 70-100 miles.

Standard Accessories: — Hand, vehicle, pioneer, track tools; tow cable, fire extinguishers; vehicle and weapons spare parts; section equipment for main gun; .30 and .50 caliber machine guns, ammunition for weapons; telescopic sight, periscopes with spare heads; grenades, radios, first aid kits and personal stowage.

Historical: — Built by Fisher Tank Division of General Motors at Grand Blanc Arsenal, and by Chrysler at the Detroit Tank Arsenal, from 1944 to 1945 (M26), 1949 to 1951 (M46), 1951 to 1953 (M47). M26s and M46s saw action in World War II and Korea.

Model No.	PRICE					
	6	5	4	3	2	1
M26	20,000	30,000	40,000	—	—	—
M26A1	—	—	—	—	—	—
M45	—	—	—	—	—	—
M46	—	—	—	—	—	—
M46A1	—	—	—	—	—	—
M47	25,000	35,000	45,000	—	—	—

Another mid-1950s M47 medium tank.

Left front view of M47 medium tank.

Self-Propelled Guns & Howitzers

World War II M19A1 Duster twin 40mm self-propelled gun carrriage.

Model M19A1: — The M19A1 "Duster" was self-propelled, lightly armored antiaircraft gun motor carriage. The Bofors twin 40mm automatic guns were mounted in a power-operated turret at the rear of the vehicle.

This vehicle was designed to replace the M15A1 half track antiaircraft system. The chassis was a modified M24 tank unit with engines and radiators moved forward to the center of the hull, with driver and assistant in the front to operate the vehicle.

Armor on the hull and turret varied from 1/3- to l/2-inch thickness, depending on the area. This vehicle had two V-8 engines with a transfer case to combine power to a single drive shaft into the differential, in between the driver and assistant. Final drives and sprockets were at the front of the hull.

The turret of the vehicle had belt armor around it for crew protection. Shield armor was used above the gunner and assistant when the guns were elevated.

The guns used armor-piercing rounds and high explosives. The armor-piercing rounds had a range of 9475 yards horizontal at 2870 feet per second. This would pierce 1.6 inches of armor at 1000 yards. High explosive shells had a vertical range of 7625 yards at 2870 feet per second. The rate of fire was 240 rounds per minute, and the turret could traverse at 40 degrees per second. The damage this system could inflict on ground targets was almost beyond description.

The two engines were the Cadillac models used in the M24 tank. All the power train components would interchange with the tank. The hulls was almost the same, but the engines were moved to the center, just behind the driver's compartment. The fuel tanks were repositioned as well. The auxiliary generator was mounted on the right fender, about in the middle of the vehicle.

A large stowage area was under the turret in the rear and accessed by two large doors on the back of the hull. Weatherproof cabinets around the turret on the outside were used for ammunition storage. The auxiliary generator sits on the right fender, alongside the engine compartment. Spare barrels were carried on top of the radiator grates, above the motors. A crew of six operated the vehicle when fighting. The driver's compartment was armored, enclosing him and the assistant with hatches. The other crew members sat in the open topped turret. The radio equipment was carried inside the front compartment.

I.D. Data: — The serial number was located on the identification data plate inside the driver's compartment on the hull.

Model No.	Body Type	Weight	GVW	Prod. Total
M19A1	Armored	38,500	41,165	285

Engines: — Two Cadillac 90-degree V-8s, Model 44T24. L-head, four-cycle. Cast iron block and heads. Displacement: 349 cubic inches each. Bore and stroke: 3.5 x 4.5 inches. Compression ratio: 7:1. Brake horsepower: 110 at 3400 rpm. each. Five main bearings. Mechanical valve lifters.

Chassis: — Length of track on ground: 123 inches. Overall length: 218 inches. Height: 117 inches. Width: 115 inches. Tread center to center of track: 96 inches. Steel and rubber block track, with rubber bushed steel pins. Width: 16 inches.

Technical: — General Motors Hydramatic transmissions. Speeds 4F/1R. Two- speed transfer case. Torsion bar suspension with dual rubber tired road wheels. Mechanical controlled differential. Overall ratio 70:1. Hand lever operated steering and brakes. Twenty-four volt electrical system. Top speed: 30 mph. Fuel capacity: 110 gallons. Cruising range: 85 miles.

Standard Accessories: — Hand, vehicle, pioneer, track tools; spare parts; portable and fixed fire extinguishers; tow cable, auxiliary generator; gun section equipment, gun sights, spare 40mm barrels; canvas cover for turret; vision periscopes; four .30 caliber carbines, one .45 caliber submachine gun, munitions, and grenades.

Historical: — Built by Cadillac Division of General Motors and Massey-Harris Corp. in 1944 in Detroit, Michigan and Milwaukee, Wisconsin.

PRICE

Model No.	6	5	4	3	2	1
M19A1	5000	9000	15,000	18,000	22,000	25,000

Mid-1950s M42A1 Duster twin 40mm self-propelled gun carriage.

Model M42: — The M42 "Duster" was a mobile, lightly armored antiair-craft and ground support weapons station mounted on a modified tank chassis.

The driver's compartment was in front, the fighting compartment was in the center with the turret, and the power train components were in the rear. The turret was power operated by an auxiliary generator.

The fully automatic twin 40mm guns were a Swedish design by Bofors, firing at the rate of 240 rounds per minute, with the turret traversing at a rate of 40 degrees per second.

The chassis of this vehicle was from the same family as the M41 tank. Power pack, including engine and transmission, were interchangeable, as well as the suspension components, road wheels, support rollers, sprockets and the track itself. Armored shields were provided to protect the gunners, with belt armor around the turret to protect the rest of the crew as they worked. Ammunition boxes were mounted around the turret for stowage. These were weather-tight units.

A crew of six was used to operate the system: commander, two gunners, two loaders and driver who acted as radio man. This weapons system was the same basic model as used on the World War II M19AI model but with improvements. The commander and driver's positions were in the front of the vehicle; each had a top hatch for entry. A large front hatch also permitted exit or entry. The other four members of the crew rode in the open top turret.

Stowage compartments were located on top of the fenders. The power train at the rear was the same basic unit that was used in the M41 "Walker Bulldog" tank. The M42 was radio equipped and could track targets up to 600 mph. It was outfitted with infrared night vision equipment and was designed to operate in all types of climates.

I.D. Data: — The serial number was located on the identification data plate in the driver's compartment on the hull to the left of the driver's seat.

Model No.	Body Type	Weight	GVW	Prod. Total
M42	Armored	—	49,500	—

Engine: — Continental AOS-895-3. Six-cylinder, horizontally opposed, air-cooled, OHV, OHC. Four-cycle. Aluminum alloy block and heads. Displacement: 895 cubic inches. Bore and Stroke: 5.75 x 5.75 inches. Compression ratio: 5.5:1. Brake horsepower: 500 at 2800 rpm. Seven main bearings. Mechanical valve lifters. Carburetors: Bendix Stromberg NA-Y5G-I3.

Chassis and Body: — Length of track on ground: 128 inches. Overall length: 229 inches. Height: 112 inches. Width: 127 inches. Tread center to center of tracks: 102 inches. Steel shoe, rubber bushed steel pin tracks with replaceable rubber pads.

Technical: — General Motors Allison CD-500-3 cross drive transmission and differential with torque converter. Speeds: 2F/IR. Overall ratio: 22.7:1. Torsion bar suspension with dual rubber tired road wheels. Hand lever-operated hydraulic steering in the differential. Pedal-operated as service brakes. Twenty-four-volt electrical system. Top speed: 45 mph. Fuel capacity: 140 gallons. Cruising range: 100 miles.

Standard Accessories: — Hand, vehicle, pioneer, track tools; spare parts; tow cable, radios, vision periscopes, fixed and portable fire extinguishers; gun section equipment, gun sights, spare barrels; one .30 caliber machine gun, grenades; ammunition for weapons; auxiliary generator.

Historical: — Built by Cadillac Division of General Motors at the Cleveland tank arsenal in the early 1950s. Used in Korea and Vietnam.

PRICE

Model No.	6	5	4	3	2	1
M42	4000	10,000	15,000	25,000	35,000	—

Early 1950s M42A1 "Duster" twin 40mm gun motor carriage.

Right side view of M18 "Hellcat" tank destroyer.

Model M18: — The M18 "Hellcat" is a full-tracked, high-speed tank destroyer. The vehicle has a lightly armored all-welded steel hull with well sloped armor plate 1/4 to 1/2 inch thick, depending on the area. The thin armor and light weight permitted speeds up to 45 mph.

The turret contained the main armament which was a high velocity 76mm gun. The muzzle velocity was 2,600 feet per second, and could penetrate four inches of armor at 1,000 yards. A .50 caliber machine gun was used on a ring mount in the open top turret for antiaircraft defense.

A crew of five operated the vehicle, with driver and assistant sitting in the front of the hull, one on each side of the transmission-differential unit, with dual driving controls. The commander gunner and loader were in the power-operated turret. An auxiliary generator was used for the hydraulic, electrical and communication equipment.

A radio set with an interphone system were in the rear of turret. The engine in the rear and transmission-differential in the front were serviced by removing their armored covers and sliding them out on rails, mounted on the back side of the covers. This was a forerunner of the quick disconnect system used in today's modern vehicles. The M39 armored utility vehicle is a derivative of the M18, but has no turret, and consequently has a higher top speed.

I.D. Data: — The serial number is located on the identification data inside the driver's compartment on the hull near the left side of the driver's seat.

Engine: — Continental R975C4, nine-cylinder, radial, air cooled, four-cycle. Steel block, aluminum cylinders, steel heads. OHV. Displacement: 973 cubic inches. Bore and stroke: 5 x 51/2 inches. Compression ratio: 5.7:1. Brake horsepower: 400 at 2400 rpm. Magneto ignition. Three main bearings. Mechanical valve lifters.

Chassis and Body: — Length of track on the ground: 131.5 inches. Overall length: 214 inches. Height: 101 inches. Width: 113 inches. Tread center to center of track: 94.5 inches. Tracks: steel or rubber shoe with rubber bushed steel pins. Width: 14.5 inches.

Technical: — Torqmatic automatic transmission with torque converter. Speeds 3F/IR. Single-speed transfer case. Torsion bar suspension with dual rubber-tired road wheels. Mechanically controlled differential. Hand-lever operated steering and brakes. Overall ratio: 15.56:1. Twenty-four-volt electrical system. Top speed: 45 mph. Fuel capacity: 170 gallons. Cruising range: 105 miles.

Standard Accessories: — Hand, vehicle, pioneer, track tools; tow cable; spare parts and track blocks; fire extinguisher; radios; periscopes for vision and fire control; gun section equipment; grenades; smoke pots; one .50 caliber machine gun; one .30 caliber carbine; 76mm, .50 caliber and .30 caliber ammunition; telescopic gun sight.

Historical: — Designed and built by Buick Division of General Motors from July 1943 to October 1944.

Model No.	Body Type	Weight	GVW	Prod. Total
M18	Armored	—	37,600	2507

PRICE

Model No.	6	5	4	3	2	1
M18	—	—	—	—	—	—

World War II M18 "Hellcat" tank destroyer.

Early 1950s M56 Scorpion self-propelled 90mm gun.

Model M56: — The M56 "Scorpion" was a self-propelled 90mm gun that could be used for indirect fire as artillery or as direct fire for use against tanks and other stationary targets. It was an extremely compact and light vehicle that was designed for air drop capabilities.

The high velocity gun was very effective in defensive and offensive roles. It was quite unique in many ways. It was designed to be used over all types of terrain — sand, mud, snow, marsh — and all climates as well. The chassis was a water-tight unit made of an aluminum framework with aluminum panels riveted to it. There were accesses in neccessary places to allow for service work when needed.

The tracks were made of steel crossbars with guides welded to them. These were riveted to reinforced rubber belts and bolted together in sections. These sections of track were easily replaced when needed. They were very wide, and by using aluminum, the ground pressure was very low. The drive sprockets were steel but had a heavy rubber coating on them. The idler wheel was also rubber tired. Torsion bar suspension with two shock absorbers per side were used. Each torsion bar had a pneumatic tire and wheel running on it. The tires had no tread and were a 7.50 x 12 12-ply that carried 75 pounds of air pressure. The pneumatic tire system used on the Scorpion was also used on the M76 Otter, but only on these two vehicles.

A blackout lighting system was provided for night driving, and the vehicle also had an infrared lighting system for night driving. The entire electrical system was sealed, as all M series vehicles were. The radio was mounted on the left fender behind the driver and alongside the stowage box. The battery box was on the same fender, but in front of the stowage box, just ahead of the driver.

The 90mm gun sat on its mount in the center of the chassis, directly above the gas tank. The gun was manually traversed and elevated. The breech was at the rear on a small folding platform. The ammunition was stored below the gun mount at the rear, which was accessed from this platform by the loader. The 29 rounds were stowed in individual containers, and sealed. The pioneer tools were stowed at the rear of the vehicle on the back side of the loader's platform. The crew actually sat,

rode and worked in the open as there was no provision for any type of enclosure, just a cover for the gun.

The engine was a flat opposed unit that was air-cooled by a gear-driven fan. Indirect fuel injection was used. The automatic cross drive transmission differential assembly was at the very front of the vehicle with an air intake grille above it that could be raised for service. The engine was attached directly to it, and was located near the driver. Air was drawn down over the transmission and back over the engine and exhausted upwards through the engine grille in front of the driver. The driver sat in the left front alongside the gun, the commander sat behind him, and the gunner sat on the right side with the loader behind him. The driver's controls were in front of him, and he used a small steering wheel to brake each track for turning the vehicle. A foot pedal operated the brakes for stopping. A structural bulkhead separated the engine transmission compartment from the gun mount fuel tank area.

I.D. Data: — The serial number was located on the identification data plate on the bulkhead, just to the right of the driver and just ahead of the gun mount.

Model No.	Body Type	Weight	GVW	Prod. Total
M56	Unitized	12,750	15,500	325

Engine: — Continental AOI-402-5. Six-cylinder, flat opposed, air-cooled overhead valve, overhead camshaft. Four-cycle. Aluminum cylinders and heads, cast iron block. Displacement: 402 cubic inches. Bore and Stroke: 4.625 x 4.00 inches. Compression ratio: 6.9:1. Brake horsepower: 200 at 3000 rpm. Seven main bearings. Mechanical valve lifters. American Bosch indirect mechanical fuel injection.

Chassis and Body: — Length of track on ground: 115 inches. Overall length: 180 inches, chassis; 230 inches, chassis and gun. Width: 101.5 inches. Height: 81 inches. Tread center to center of track: 78 inches. Tracks: Sectionalized reinforced rubber belts with steel grousers and guides. Width: 20 inches. Ground pressure: 4.5 pounds per square inch. Bogie tires: 7.50 x 12 12-ply nylon smooth tread.

Another early 1950s M56 Scorpion self-propelled 90mm gun.

Technical: — Allison CD-150-4 cross drive transmission differential assembly with torque converter. Speeds: 2F/1R. Torsion bar suspension. Mechanical steering with steering wheel. Foot pedal-operated mechanical wet disc brakes. Gear ratio: 66.96:1. Twenty-four-volt electrical system. Top speed: 28 miles per hour. Fuel capacity: 55 gallons. Cruising range: 140 miles.

Standard Accessories: — Hand, vehicle, pioneer, track tools; spare parts, fire extinguisher; gun sighting, fire control, section equipment; radio, canvas cover for gun; personal stowage for crew; four M2 .30 caliber carbines; 20 rounds of 90mm gun ammunition.

Historical: — A small quantity were produced by Cadillac Division of General Motors in the mid to late 1950s. They were used mostly by airborne Army units and the Marine Corps. Discontinued use because of light weight and too much gun recoil and blast; vehicle was unstable when firing.

Model No.	6	5	4	3	2	1
M56	3000	8000	13,000	18,000	—	—

AMPHIBIOUS VEHICLES

World War II Ford GPA "Seep" quarter-ton amphibious truck.

Model GPA: — The GPA was a small amphibious truck in the quarter-ton class. It had a boat-style body made of a one-piece all-steel welded unit built on a four-wheel drive Ford GPW chassis. It was often used for river crossings on advanced scouting missions. Extensive ribbing was stamped in the body for added strength. This gave the vehicle a very distinct appearance.

The GPA was longer in wheelbase and overall length than a standard Ford GPW. The front of the vehicle had a surf shield to prevent water from splashing over the bow. Directly behind was a 3500-pound capacity capstan winch that was driven off the front of the engine by a pulley system. A small door could be opened for radiator air intake on the front deck ahead of the hood opening. Warm radiator air was exhausted through vents on the lower sides of the cowl below the folding windshield.

Access to the drive train components for replacement of parts or major service was accomplished by removing the front deck lid, rear deck lid or the floor coverings in the passenger compartments.

Drain plugs were located at the bottom of the hull for fluid services. There were large openings for the drive shafts, which were enclosed in

hollow tubes with flexible rubber seals at each end. A rear pintle hitch was provided as well as a front tow ring at the bottom of the bow.

The GPA's 12-volt electrical system used two six-volt batteries which were mounted under the rear deck behind the seat. Pioneer tools were carried under the rear seat. Extensive use of bonding straps eliminated radio interference.

The interior had a conventional layout with two front seats and a full-width rear seat for two to three additional passengers. There was an indented step on the side of the body for entering the vehicle. The gas can, spare tire and anchor were carried on the rear deck. The propeller and bilge pump were driven by a power take-off unique to the GPA. The rudder for steering was cable-controlled from the steering column. A large pull-type knob on the instrument panel engaged the winch. Two additional levers for the propeller and bilge pump were located behind the transmission shift lever. The power take-off was mounted on the rear of the transfer case.

The vehicle was approximately 1200 pounds heavier than the standard Ford GPW. Many power train components were the same as the Ford GPW. Cargo capacity was 800 pounds, including passengers.

Rear view of World War II Ford GPA "Seep" quarter-ton amphibious truck.

I.D. Data — The serial number was located on the identification data plate on the instrument panel and on top of the frame on the left side of the engine.

Model No.	Body Type	Weight	GVW	Prod. Total
GPA	Amphibious	3660	4460	12,778

Engine: — Ford GPA, four-cylinder, L-head, four-cycle, cast iron block. Displacement: 134 cubic inches. Bore and Stroke: 3-1/8 x 4-3/8 inches. Brake horsepower: 54 at 4000 rpm. Three main bearings. Mechanical valve lifters. Carburetor: Carter W05395.

Chassis and Body: — Wheelbase: 84 inches. Overall length: 182 inches. Height: 69 inches. Width: 64 inches. Tread center to center: 49 inches. Tires 6.00x16 six-ply non-directional.

Technical: — Manual synchromesh transmission. Speeds: 3F/1R. Two-speed transfer case. Single dry disc clutch. Semi-elliptic leaf spring suspension. Dana Spicer differentials. Gear ratio: 4.88:1. Hydraulic brakes. Manual steering. Twelve-volt electrical system. Top speed: 55 mph land, 5.5 mph water. Fuel capacity: 15 gallons. Cruising range: 250 miles land, 35 miles water.

Standard Accessories: — Canvas top and bows; life preservers, anchor; hand and vehicle tools; spare parts; fire extinguisher.

Historical: — Originally designed by Marmon-Herrington and Sparkman-Stephens. Prototype built on Ford GPW chassis. Produced by Ford Motor Company in 1942-1943.

			PRICE			
Model No.	6	5	4	3	2	1
GPA	6000	12,000	19,000	24,000	30,000	35,000

World War II Studebaker M29 "Weasel" cargo carrier. (Fred Ropkey, Indianapolis, Indiana)

Model M29: — The M29 "Weasel" was a small, light cargo carrier that was a full-track model with all-terrain and fully amphibious capabilities.

The all-one-piece welded steel hull allowed it to float without preparation. It was originally designed for use in snow, but it quickly became popular for use in all climates. The 20-inch wide tracks gave it extremely low ground pressure, actually less than a man standing. This made crossing mud, sand and marsh very easy. The vehicle was very small and compact, making it very maneuverable and easy to transport. It was used widely by many branches of the armed forces and was known as a "go anywhere" vehicle.

The power train layout was simple. The driver sat in the left front. The radiator and engine were on the right alongside him. The fuel tank was on the right side in front of the engine. The engine was an L-head gasoline six-cylinder with a clutch and three-speed transmission attached. The driveshaft led to the rear to the two-speed controlled differential. The drive sprockets were in the rear to propel the tracks. Planetary final drives were not used in this vehicle as they were in so many other models of tracked vehicles. The electrical system was fully suppressed for the use of radio equipment. Up to three radios could be installed; they could be used separately or simultaneously. This could reduce the number of passengers to the operator and the driver, depending on the number carried.

The watertight hull had a series of drain plugs for use after amphibious operations. Early models had a plug in the front of the body for the hand crank used to start the engine, and there were 15-inch wide tracks. Snow camouflage paint schemes were put on the early models; later models were painted in the flat olive drab colors.

Safety belts were provided for all of the personnel in the vehicle. Spotlights were used in early production, but a headlight was substituted later on. A gasoline-fired auxiliary kit could be installed in the lower hull, alongside the drive shaft.

The tracks and suspension were used only on this vehicle series. They were made of stamped and welded metal shoes with small rubber pads

Suspension and tracks of Studebaker M29 "Weasel."

on the outside surface. They were connected by an endless rubber band or belt that had four steel cables molded inside of it. A small cable was near the outside of the track alongside the large belts for additional stability. Tension was provided by the idler wheel at the front of the vehicle, using an adjustable leaf spring. Correct track tension was critical for track longevity. The small rubber tired bogie wheel ran on the main rubber belts. There were four clusters on each side with four wheels on each cluster. Each cluster was mounted on the end of a transverse inverted leaf spring that ran from the right to left side. The bogie clusters could move up and down and had side flex as well. Steering and braking were done by two levers with mechanical linkage to the rear differential. A

World War II Studebaker "Weasel" cargo carrier. (George Rabuse, St. Paul, Minnesota)

Passenger compartment of Studebaker M29 "Weasel."

folding canvas top with bows gave cover to the crew. Cargo capacity was 1200 pounds.

Model M29C: — This was the same basic vehicle as the M29, but it had front and rear flotation tanks bolted to the hull with rudders in the rear for steering in amphibious operations. A surf guard was located on the front of the front flotation cell. The cells were watertight with their own separate drain plugs. The bow-mounted capstan winch was used for recovery of vehicles when needed, using a long rope provided with this model. The winch was driven off the front of the crankshaft by a shaft, pulley and belt arrangement with a clutch. A boat hook was carried on the left side of the body, near the driver. Hinged track shrouds or aprons were fastened to the side of the body above the tracks. These were needed to propel the vehicle forward in the water by means of the track movement. Speed in the water was about four mph. Strong currents and surf were avoided as the freeboard was only about 8-10 inches. The slow movement and low freeboard made moving water dangerous. The vehicle performed excellently in cross-country movement. The rear cell had two rudders which could be folded up for land operations. A pintle hitch was used for towing. Rudder steering was performed by the driver who operated a small tiller in front of him at the base of the windshield.

I.D. Data: — The serial number was located on the identification data plate behind the driver's seat.

Model No.	Body Type	Weight	GVW	Prod. Total
M29	Amphibious	4077	5277	4476
M29C	Amphibious	4771	5971	10,647

Engine: — Studebaker Champion 6-170, six-cylinder, in-line, L-head, four-cycle. Cast iron head and block. Displacement: 170 cubic inches. Bore and Stroke: 3 x 4 inches. Compression ratio: 7:1. Brake horsepower: 65 at 3600 rpm. Four main bearings. Mechanical valve lifters. Carburetor: Carter BBR1-577S.

Chassis and Body: — Ground contact length of track: 78 inches. Overall length: 126 inches. Width: 61 inches. Height: 71 inches. Tread center to center of track: 45 inches. Tracks: Steel shoe connected with endless rubber belts with cable reinforcements, 15 inches wide on early models, 20 inches on late models. Ground pressure: 1.6 pounds per square inch.

Technical: — Manual synchromesh transmission. Speeds: 3F/1R. Clark two-speed mechanically controlled differential. Single dry disc clutch. Transverse leaf spring suspension. Gear ratio: 4.87:1. Lever-actuated steering and braking in differential. Twelve-volt electrical system. Top speed: 36 mph. Fuel capacity: 35 gallons. Cruising range: 175 miles.

Standard Accessories: — Hand, vehicle, pioneer tools; canvas top, side curtains, seat cushions; spare parts; track tools; tow rope, capstan rope, bilge pump; fire extinguisher.

Historical: — Design and development began in May 1942, the first prototype appeared in August 1942, and mass production continued from 1942 to 1945 by Studebaker Corporation of South Bend, Indiana.

PRICE

Model No.	6	5	4	3	2	1
M29	600	2000	4000	6000	9000	—
M29C	600	2000	4000	6000	9000	—

World War II Studebaker M29C "Weasel" amphibious vehicle. (Royce Anderson, Ponderosa Ranch, Incline Village, Nevada)

Rear view of Studebaker M29C "Weasel." (Royce Anderson, Ponderosa Ranch, Incline Village, Nevada)

Front deck of Studebaker M29C "Weasel." (Royce Anderson, Ponderosa Ranch, Incline Village, Nevada)

Rear flotation tank on Studebaker M29C "Weasel." (Royce Anderson, Ponderosa Ranch, Incline Village, Nevada)

Rear view of Studebaker M29C "Weasel." (Royce Anderson, Ponderosa Ranch, Incline Village, Nevada)

Controls of Studebaker M29C "Weasel." (Royce Anderson, Ponderosa Ranch, Incline Village, Nevada)

Pontiac M76 Otter amphibious cargo carrier.

Model M76: — The M76 "Otter" was a fully amphibious cargo carrier that could be operated in almost all climatic conditions. Its fully enclosed, insulated aluminum body with its wide tracks allowed it to function in tropic, arctic and a variety of temperate climates.

The power train of the vehicle consisted of a four-cylinder, air-cooled, opposed engine and cross drive transmission that sat vertically in the front of the vehicle. A large stack, used for engine cooling and exhaust functions, sat between the driver and assistant in the driver's compartment.

The rear compartment could seat eight men. There were doors at the rear and top of the body for entry or exit. A 5000-pound winch was in the rear compartment near the bottom of the rear doors. A retractable propeller mechanism was located on the rear of the vehicle, below the rear doors near the pintle hitch.

Being amphibious, bilge pumps were provided. The fuel cells, spare tire and other tools were on the outside of the body toward the rear on each side. Independently sprung torsion bar suspension was used with dual pneumatic rubber tired road wheels providing for the use of the wide tracks. Provisions were made for the unit to carry radio equipment and small arms. Payload capacity was 3300 pounds.

I.D. Data: — The serial number was located on the identification plate in the driver's compartment on the wall of the air stack.

Model No.	Body Type	Weight	GVW	Prod. Total
M76	Amphibious	8813	12,162	500

Engine: — Continental AOI-268-3A, four-cylinder, opposed, air-cooled, OHV, cast iron block with aluminum cylinders and heads. Displacement: 269 cubic inches. Bore and Stroke: 4-5/8 x 4 inches. Compression ratio: 6.9:1. Brake horsepower: 127 at 3200 rpm. Seven main bearings. Mechanical valve lifters. Fuel injection.

Chassis and Body: — Ground contact length: 96.5 inches. Overall length: 188 inches. Height: 108 inches. Width: 98 inches. Tread center to center of tracks: 68 inches. Tracks: Reinforced rubber belts with

Rear PTO-driven propeller on M76 Otter.

riveted metal crossbars, bolted together in removable sections, 30 inches wide.

Technical: — General Motors CD-150-3 combination automatic cross drive transmission with torque converter and controlled differential. Speeds: 2F/1R. Overall ratio: high range, 18.4:1; low range, 42.2:1.

Right rear view of M76 Otter.

Front drive sprocket on M76 Otter.

Torsion bar suspension. Pedal-operated brakes in differential. Manually operated mechanical steering in differential. Magneto ignition. Twenty-four-volt electrical system. Top speed: 28 mph land; 4.5 mph water. Fuel capacity: 70 gallons. Cruising range: 160 miles land; 5.8 hours water.

Standard Accessories: — Hand, vehicle, pioneer tools; spare parts, tires, track sections; spotlight, small arms, radios.

Historical: — A small quantity were built by the Pontiac Division of General Motors in the early 1950s. It was the sophisticated replacement for the "Weasel."

	PRICE					
Model No.	6	5	4	3	2	1
M76	2000	4000	8000	11,000	14,000	—

World War II FMC LVT4 amphibious tractor.

Model LVT 4, MK4: — The LVT 4 was a full-track amphibious vehicle used for transporting personnel and cargo from ship to shore during amphibious assaults on enemy beachheads. It was also used to move men and material inland over tough terrain, water and swampy land.

In water it drew a draft of four feet. The Army and Marine Corps used them in the Pacific and European theaters of war. They were kept in service for many years after World War II.

The body and hull of this vehicle was a one-piece unit of welded steel. The power train was from the M3 light tank and was successfully adapted for this application. The Continental seven-cylinder radial engine was at the front of the cargo compartment with large access panels for service. Entry to the driver's compartment was on the left side of the engine. A small drive shaft went forward to the controlled differential in the upper part of the bow. The tank's five-speed transmission was used with planetary final drives. This was pretty much a one-piece unit without the armored nose of the tank. Different sprockets were used as this vehicle did not use tracks. These were actually large precision chains with removable steel grousers, which helped in the soft terrain of the beaches and was the means of propulsion in the water. A torsion type rubber suspension was used with rubber tired bogie wheels. An adjustable idler was at the rear. Being a sealed unit, the large area between the tracks was for added flotation.

A crew of two to seven was used as necessary. The driver and his assistant, the bow gunner, sat in the cab in the front of the vehicle. The others manned the weapons in the cargo compartment. The rear cargo compartment was quite large and had a full-width rear ramp that lowered to the ground for an easy, sheltered exit of troops or equipment. It was capable of carrying a jeep, a three-quarter ton truck, and 75mm or 105mm howitzer carriages. Cargo capacity was 9,000 pounds. The cab had 1/2-inch armor, but the rest of the vehicle was constructed of 1/4-inch armor plate.

I.D. Data: — The serial number was located on the identification data plate inside the driver's compartment.

Suspension of LVT4.

Engine: — Continental W670-9A, seven-cyclinder, four-cycle, radial air-cooled, steel block, aluminum cylinders. Bore and stroke: 5-1/8 x 4-5/8 inches. Compression ratio: 6.1:1. Brake horsepower: 250 at 2400 rpm. Main bearings: Three. Valve lifters: Mechanical. Carburetor: Zenith updraft.

Chassis and Body: — Track on the ground: 156 inches. Overall length: 314 inches. Height: 99 inches. Width: 128 inches. Tread center of track to center of track: 114 inches. Tracks were heat-treated precision steel alloy chain with removable grousers, as track life was very short.

Technical: — Manual selective gear transmission. Speeds: 5F/1R. Single dry disc clutch. Torsional rubber mount suspension with single rubber tired bogie wheels running inside the track. Mechanically controlled differential with levers for steering and braking. Planetary final drives and steel sprockets to propel the tracks. Transmission, differential and final drives were from the M3 light tank. Twelve-volt electrical system. Top speed: 15 mph land; 7 mph water. Fuel capacity: 140 gallons. Cruising range: 150 miles land; 100 miles water.

Model No.	Body Type	Weight	GVW	Prod. Total
LVT 4	Amphibious	27,400	36,400	8348

World War II LVT4 amphibious tractor with rear ramp.

Rear idler and track of LVT4.

Standard Accessories: — Two .50 caliber and three .30 caliber machine guns, pintle assemblies, tripods; hand and vehicle tools; fire extinguisher; radio with antenna.

Historical: — The LVT 4 was developed in the mid-1930s as a rescue unit after hurricanes in the Florida Everglades. Its design was improved at the request of the U.S. Navy, and several different models were built. It was built by the Food Machinery Company of Lakeland, Florida, San Jose and Riverside, California; St. Louis Car Corporation, St. Louis, Missouri; and Graham-Paige Motor Corporation, Detroit, Michigan from 1943 to 1945.

LVT4's engine compartment with seven-cylinder radial power plant.

Model No.	6	5	4	3	2	1
			PRICE			
LVT 4	800	1700	2600	3800	5500	—

LeTourneau Westinghouse LARC V amphibious truck.

Model LARC-V: — The LARC was a large amphibious truck designed to transfer and transport cargo ships to shore in marine operations. The acronym stood for "lighter amphibious resupply cargo." It was a modern replacement for the World War II DUKW, but was much more sophisticated in many ways.

The LARC was powered by a large diesel engine at the rear of the hull and had an automatic transmission. The entire vehicle was larger in all aspects — length, width, height, weight, and cargo carrying capacity. The entire body and hull were made of aluminum and had a boat-like appearance.

The driver and passengers sat in the front behind an enclosure which housed the controls for the vehicle. A hard cab or a canvas top was provided for the crew of two. The vehicle was designed to function in a wide variety of temperatures. The controls were quite complex and very specific as to how the unit was operated. Hydraulic power steering was used. The engine sat in the rear and was mounted in reverse of what was normally used in a vehicle, with the radiator at the rear of the rear deck. A large transfer case sat in the center of the hull under the cargo deck, and transferred the power from the engine and the transmission to the four wheels by means of right-angle drives and planetary hubs.

The cargo was carried on the center deck, and side curtains could be installed to protect it from the surf. A hydraulic bilge pump was used, and a very efficient fuel filtration and water separation system was employed for the engine. The vehicle had navigational lights in the front and rear of the hull, and came equipped to use radio communication. Seat belts were provided for the crew. The load capacity was five tons.

I.D. Data: — The serial number was located on the identification data plate on the left side of the instrument panel.

Model No.	Body Type	Weight	GVW	Prod. Total
LARC-V	Amphibious	19,000	31,000	968

Engine: — Cummins V8-300, diesel, eight-cylinder, V-Type, OHV, four-cycle. Cast iron block and heads. Displacement: 785 cubic inches. Bore and Stroke: 5.5 x 4.125 inches. Compression ratio: 22:1. Brake horse-power: 300 at 2900 rpm. Five main bearings. Mechanical valve lifters. Cummins fuel injection.

Chassis and Body: — Wheelbase: 192 inches. Overall length: 420 inches. Height: 122 inches. Width: 120 inches. Tread center to center front: 92 inches. Tires: 18.00 x 25 12-ply straight-ribbed highway tread.

Technical: — Automatic transmission. Speeds: 1F/1R. Hydraulic retarder, torque converter with lock up. Two-speed transfer case. Solid suspension. Planetary final drives. Hydraulic brakes. Hydraulic power steering. Twenty-four-volt electrical system. Top speed: 30 mph land; 10 mph water. Fuel capacity: 144 gallons. Cruising range: 250 miles land, 40 miles water.

Standard Accessories: — Hand, vehicle, engine tools; anchor, mooring lines, boat hook, first aid kit, hand bilge pump; magnetic compass, bulwark curtains, cab canvas, hand lantern, trouble light, fire extinguisher; marker light buoy.

Historical: — The LARC was built by Le Tourneau and Consolidated Diesel Corporation in the late 1950s.

			PRICE			
Model No.	6	5	4	3	2	1
LARC-V	5000	7000	9000	—	—	—

Rear of LARC V amphibious truck.

Right side view of M116A1. (Jon Bircheff, Fontana, California)

Model M116: — The M116 was a small full-tracked cargo and personnel carrier. It was a very compact and light vehicle because the entire body was made of aluminum. This gave the vehicle an extremely low ground pressure of 1.9 p.s.i. when empty. The tracks were so wide that nearly half of the undercarriage was covered by track on the ground. This low ground pressure enabled it to cross almost any type of soft terrain.

The M116's performance in mud, sand, snow, and soft marsh land was excellent, and the one-piece welded hull allowed it to be fully amphibious on inland waterways. It had metal swim vanes on the sides of the body that allowed the tracks to propel and steer it in the water. The body was also insulated so it could be used and operated in all climatic conditions from tropic to desert and arctic to temperate. The vehicle's compact size and light weight allowed it to be fully air transportable and air dropped.

A militarized version of the Chevrolet 283 cubic inch V-8 engine, with GM's Hydramatic transmission, sat in the center of the body under the center passenger's seat. A small driveshaft went forward to the differential in the very front of the hull. The radiator sat on the right side of the vehicle with the fan driven remotely off the engine. Sealed ignition and carburetion systems were used. The power train components were very similar to the M114 armored personal carrier's components. There was some interchangeability of major components.

The tracks were built in sections with metal crossbars riveted to the cable-reinforced belts. Being sectioned, replacement and repair were quite easy. The road wheels were of aluminum construction. The drive sprockets in the front had rubber rings on the assembly for quieter operation and longer life.

Canvas and weathertight hard cover tops were used over the rear cargo compartment. It had a crew of one — the driver — who sat at the left front inside the cab, with room for two more passengers in the front seat. A total of 11-13 troops could be carried, or 3000 pounds of cargo. The rear cargo area had padded bench seats on each side with a fuel cell under the floor. A fold-down type tailgate was located at the rear of the body; it was used for exit and entry. One rifle was carried. The vehicle was radio equipped.

I.D. Data: — The serial number was on the identification data plate inside the driver's compartment, on the left side above the driver's seat.

Front view of M116A1. (Jon Bircheff, Fontana, California)

Model No.	Body Type	Weight	GVW	Prod. Total
M116	Welded Aluminum	7880	10,880	330

Engine: — Chevrolet, 90-degree V-8, OHV, four-cycle, cast iron block and head. Displacement: 283 cubic inches. Bore and Stroke: 3-7/8 in.x 3 inches. Compression ratio: 8:1. Brake horsepower: 160 at 4600 rpm. Five main bearings. Valve lifters: Hydraulic. Carburetor: Rochester 2V.

Chassis and Body: — Ground contact length: 103 inches. Overall length: 189 inches. Height: 79 inches. Width: 82 inches. Tread center to center of track: 58.5 inches. Tracks: 20 inches wide, rubber belts with riveted aluminum grousers, bolted together in replaceable sections.

Pacific Car & Foundry M116A1 amphibious cargo carrier. (Jon Bircheff, Fontana, California)

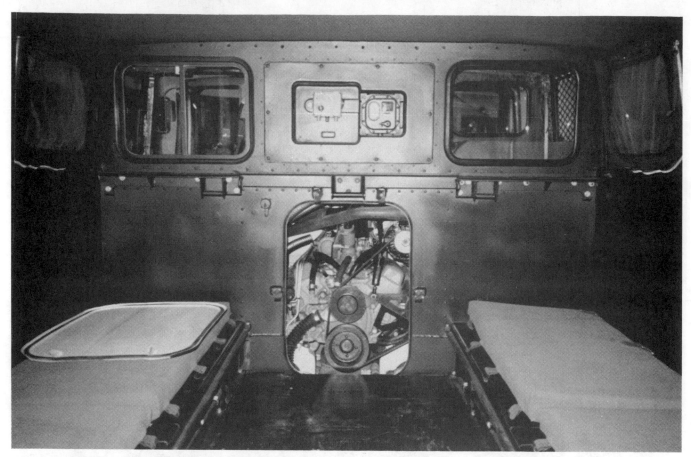

Interior shot of M116A1. (Jon Bircheff, Fontana, California)

Rear view of M116A1. (Jon Bircheff, Fontana, California)

Technical: — Automatic transmission. Speeds: 4F/1R. Torsion bar suspension, with five per side, double tired bogie wheels on each. Front drive sprocket, adjustable rear idler. Hydraulically actuated geared steer differential. Pedal-controlled brakes in differential. Twenty-four-volt electrical system. Top speed: 37 mph hard surface land, 4 mph water. Fuel capacity: 65 gallons. Cruising range: 300 miles land, 22 miles water.

Standard Accessories: — One M14 rifle, radio with antenna, hand and vehicle tools, spare parts, fire extinguisher.

Historical: — Designed in the late 1950s and early 1960s, this was the successor to the M29 Weasel and the M76 Otter. It was a very sophisticated design and a true all-season, all-terrain vehicle. A very small quantity were built by Pacific Car and Foundry Company in 1962.

PRICE

Model No.	6	5	4	3	2	1
M116	2500	7500	12,000	16,000	20,000	25,000

World War II GMC 6X6 2-1/2-ton DUKW. (Reg Hodgson, Jim Fitzgerald, Edmonton, Alberta, Canada)

Model GMC DUKW-353: — The GMC "Duck" was an amphibious six-wheel drive truck with a boat-type hull that was built on a modified GMC channel style truck frame and power train. It was very roadworthy as well as being fully amphibious. It could be easily driven in and out of the water on a good ramp.

The original design was based on the GMC AFKWX-353 long-wheelbase truck chassis. The body was made of light sheet steel with a metal framework used as reinforcement. The front of the vehicle had towing shackles at the bottom of the bow and a folding surf shield at the top. Directly behind the surf shield were two decklids, one for radiator air intake, bow stowage, air compressor access and service, and the other for engine access and service.

The cab area had a folding windshield (early models had a verticle windshield) and seating capacity for the crew of two: driver and assistant. A circular ring mount for a .50 caliber machine gun could be attached to the body using brackets located above the passenger seat on each truck. The vehicle was steered by normal truck steering gear on land, and by a cable operated rear rudder mechanism when in water. Propeller, winch, and other driving controls were all located in the cab and had a conventional operating layout. The tire air inflation gauge and controls were on the instrument panel and on the side of the passenger seat. The engine air intake was located behind the driver's compartment. Air was drawn in here and pushed forward through the radiator and exhausted out the side grilles alongside the driver and passenger. The exhaust system also exited from the right vent.

Air inflation devices were bolted in place on the wheel hubs. A tin shield covered the air hose from the center hub to the valve stem of the tire. These were part of the system that allowed the driver to raise or lower the air pressure according to ground conditions. The single wheels and tires of the DUKW followed in line of one another. These were combat wheels such as other armored vehicles used, but they were 18 inches rather than 20 inches in size. They had a different offset, and the lock rings were held on with nuts and studs rather than bolts that were screwed into the rims of the 20-inch type.

The cargo compartment had top bows for canvas, a removable plywood floor, stowage areas, bilge pump and rear drivetrain access for service. The rear deck carried the spare tire, anchor and gas cans. The winch was located on the rear of the deck and had provisions to be used front

Rear body showing propeller and winch on DUKW.

or rear. Some vehicles had an A-frame boom assembly on the rear for lifting purposes, using the winch for power. The rudder, propeller and shaft were under the rear deck and cargo compartment. Rubber boots were used to seal the hollow tubes containing the drive shafts. The powertrain was the General Motors banjo design, and most components were interchangeable with the other GMC 6x6 military trucks. The truck's cargo capacity was 5,000 pounds or 25 men with their equipment.

I.D. Data: — The serial number was on the identification data plate on the instrument panel and on the left front frame rail directly above the front axle housing.

Model No.	Body Type	Weight	GVW	Prod. Total
DUKW-353	Amphibious Cargo	14,880	20,055	21,147

Left side view of DUKW. (Reg Hodgson, Jim Fitzgerald, Edmonton, Alberta, Canada)

Rear view of DUKW. (Reg Hodgson, Jim Fitzgerald, Edmonton, Alberta, Canada)

Front deck of World War II GMC 2-1/2-ton DUKW.

Rear deck of DUKW.

Engine: — GMC Model 270, six-cylinder, in-line, OHV, four-cycle, cast iron block and head. Displacement: 270 cubic inches. Bore and Stroke: 3-25/32 x 4 inches. Compression ratio: 6.75:1. Brake horsepower: 91.5 at 2750 rpm. Five main bearings. Mechanical valve lifters.

Chassis and Body: — Wheelbase: 164 inches. Overall length: 372 inches. Height: 106 inches. Width: 99 inches. Tread center to center front and rear: 63-7/8 inches. Tires: 11.00 x 18 12-ply military non-directional.

Technical: — Manual constant mesh transmission. Speeds: 5F/1R. Two-speed transfer case. Single dry disc clutch. Semi-elliptic leaf spring suspension. General Motors banjo single reduction differentials. Gear ratio: 6.6:1. Hydraulic vacuum-assisted power brakes. Manual steering. Steel combat wheels. Six-volt electrical system. Top speed: 50 mph land, 6 mph water. Fuel capacity: 40 gallons. Cruising range: 240 miles land, 50 miles water.

Standard Accessories: — Canvas cab and cargo compartment top, anchor, hand bilge pump, pike pole, pioneer tools; rope bumpers, life preservers, hand and vehicle tools, spare parts, fire extinguisher, gas cans, spare tire and wheel assembly; circular ring mount for a .50 caliber machine gun if applicable.

Historical: — The Duck's original design began in 1940 at the request of the National Defense Research Committee by the commanding general of supply services. Prototypes were designed by Sparkman and Stephens of New York and built by Yellow Truck and Coach Division of General Motors. Quantity production was by GM in Pontiac, Michigan from 1943 to 1945.

			PRICE			
Model No.	6	5	4	3	2	1
DUKW-353	2000	4000	8000	11,000	14,000	19,000

Driver's compartment of DUKW.

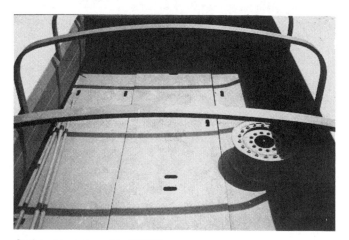

Cargo compartment in DUKW.

Rear inflation hubs on DUKW.

Mid-1960s Cadillac Gage V-100 armored car.

Model V-100: — The V-100 was a highly mobile, fully amphibious armored car used for reconnaissance, convoy escort, riot control, security and as a personnel carrier. The vehicle protected the crew from small arms fire, grenades and anti-personnel mines. All surfaces were angled for maximum deflection.

The V-100's body was an all-welded unit unitized for strength. The vehicle's light weight allowed it to be air transportable. Its armor was three-eighths to one-quarter inch thick, depending on the area. Three doors and three hatches were used for entry and exit. Three top, one rear, and two side doors were used. The body, being unitized, was sealed for amphibious operations without any preparation. The driveline was fully enclosed in the body for protection.

The open-topped hull was a modular feature. Several different weapons configurations could be installed. Three different turrets were offered: a twin .30 caliber, twin .30 caliber NATO machine guns, and a .30 and .50 caliber combination. The turret traversed 360 degrees. A double hatch configuration allowed three machine guns on pintle mounts to be fired simultaneously. A mortar baseplate could be installed in the center of the vehicle, allowing a mortar to be fired through the roof. There were 11 gun ports from which the troops fired when inside the vehicle, whether or not the vehicle was moving.

The unit was designed with four-wheel drive, high ground clearance and high angles of approach and departure for use in rough terrain, but power steering, locking differentials and conventional driving controls made the vehicle easy to drive in all types of terrain.

A series of 12 vision blocks gave the crew a 360-degree field of vision around the entire vehicle. A roof extension with additional vision blocks increased headroom inside when the vehicle was used for riot control. A hydraulically operated winch at the front of the vehicle was used for self recovery. The hydraulic pump was PTO-driven off the transmission. Special "run flat" tires were designed for the vehicle, and when punctured, these tires could be driven far enough to permit retreat or allow the vehi-

cle to continue to operate. A wide variety of radios and intercom equipment could be installed.

I.D. Data: — The serial number was located on the data plate in the driver's compartment.

Model No.	Armored Body Type	Weight	GVW	Prod. Total
V-100	Body Type	13,500	16,250	—

Engine: — Chrysler 75M, V-8, eight-cylinder, 90-degree, OHV, four-cycle. Cast iron heads and block. Displacement: 361 cubic inches. Bore and Stroke: 4.125 x 3.375 inches. Compression ratio: 7.8:1. Brake horsepower: 215 at 4000 rpm. Five main bearings. Hydraulic valve lifters. Carburetor: Military designed all-terrain four-barrel built by Holley.

Chassis and Body: — Wheelbase: 105 inches. Overall length: 224 inches. Width: 89 inches. Height: 96 inches. Tread center to center: 73 inches. Tires: 14.00 x 20 20-ply "run flat" grader tread or military non-directional.

Technical: — Manual synchromesh transmission. Speeds: 5F/1R. Dry disc clutch, single-speed transfer case. Semi-elliptic leaf spring suspension front and rear with shock absorbers. Rockwell double reduction axles. Overall ratio: 6.7:1. Vacuum-assisted hydraulic brakes. Variable ratio power steering. Twenty-four-volt electrical system. Top speed: 62 mph. Fuel capacity: 80 gallons. Cruising range: 550 miles.

Standard Accessories: — Hand, vehicle, pioneer tools; radios, fire extinguishers; first aid kits; small arms, machine guns, ammunition; spare vision blocks; snatch block for winch.

Historical: — Designed and built by Cadillac Gage of Warren, Michigan in the mid-to-late 1960s. Some were used by the military police in the U.S. Army; many were sold to foreign countries.

PRICE

Model No.	6	5	4	3	2	1
V-100	10,000	15,000	25,000	30,000	—	—

AMBULANCES

Early 1950s M170 quarter-ton jeep ambulance.

Model M170: — The M170 was a small four-wheel drive quarter-ton truck based on the M38A1 Jeep chassis, which had the body and frame lengthened by 20 inches and had suspension modifications for use as an ambulance.

It required a crew of two, one to drive and one to attend to the injured personnel being transported. The vehicle could carry three litter patients or six sitting ambulatory patients.

A canvas cab enclosure was used; it was mounted on a metal framework, which also served as a support system for the stretchers, with straps and hangers. An emergency light was provided, and the interior of the body had crash pads for safety. Additional brackets for the stretchers were in the floor, and the folding tailgate had holes in it so the bottom stretcher handles could protrude.

The spare tire was carried in the body next to the passenger seat. A larger fuel tank was used. The vehicle was not equipped with a pintle hitch or front mounted winch.

I.D. Data: — The serial number was located on the identification data plate on the instrument panel.

Model No.	Body Type	Weight	GVW	Prod. Total
M170	Ambulance	2963	3763	4155

Engine: — Willys MD, four-cylinder, in-line, F-head, four-cycle. Cast iron block and head. Displacement: 134 cubic inches. Bore and Stroke: 3.125 x 4.375 inches. Compression ratio: 6.9:1. Brake horsepower: 68 at 4000 rpm. Three main bearings. Mechanical valve lifters. Carburetor: Carter YS950S.

Chassis and Body: — Wheelbase: 101 inches. Overall length: 155 inches. Height: 80 inches. Width: 60.5 inches. Tread center to center front: 49 inches. Tires: 7.00 x 16 six-ply military non-directional.

Technical: — Manual synchromesh transmission. Speeds: 3F/1R. Two-speed transfer case. Single dry disc clutch. Leaf spring suspension front and rear. Dana hypoid gear full floating differentials. Gear ratio: 5.38:1. Hydraulic brakes. Manual steering. Twenty-four-volt electrical system. Top speed: 55 mph. Fuel capacity: 20 gallons. Cruising range: 300 miles.

Standard Accessories: — Hand, vehicle tools; spare parts; canvas top, bows, doors; three stretchers with brackets and support straps.

Rear view of the M170 jeep ambulance.

Historical: — Designed and built by Kaiser Jeep of Toledo, Ohio, from the mid-1950s to the early 1960s. The body of this vehicle was based on the civilian Jeep CJ6 model.

Model No.	6	5	4	3	2	1
			PRICE			
M170	500	1500	3000	4500	5500	6500

World War II Dodge WC18 half-ton ambulance.

Model WC 9, WC 18, WC 27: — The half-ton Dodge ambulances were built on the basic half-ton four-wheel drive chassis used in this series of trucks.

The ambulance had a longer wheelbase and different front and rear springs, required by the all-steel panel body and the need for a smoother ride as needed by the injured personnel carried. The body was fully insulated with an unusual "honeycomb"-style cardboard insulation fitted between the inner and outer steel panels of the body. The interior paneling was a type of masonite on the sides and metal panels on the ceiling. Inside were folding bench seats for six sitting patients and brackets so four litter patients could be carried.

The rear of the body had a pair of double panel doors with windows. Below the rear doors was a folding step to assist entering the unit from the rear. A dome light and powered roof ventilator were in the roof of the vehicle. The front bucket seats folded forward, and there was no partition to separate the front and rear compartments.

The driving controls were the same as the other trucks in the half-ton series. The front doors were slightly different in that the top rear corner had a right angle to it, differing from the pickup cab which had rounded corners. The panel truck and carryall used the ambulance-style door as well. The spare tire was carried on a bracket on the left side of the body, with a large recess in the side panel. The trucks were fitted with a spotlight on the driver's windshield post. A large water heater was mounted on the cowl inside the vehicle. It used two blower fans for heat, and a third fan for defrosting the windshield. The floor of the truck was all metal with a linoleum covering. This ambulance was not fitted with a front winch.

I.D. Data: — The serial number was located on the identification data plate on the glove compartment door, and on the left front frame rail above the left front spring.

Model No.	Body Type	Weight	GVW	Prod. Total
WC 9,18,27	Ambulance	5640	6640	6422

Engine: — Dodge T215, six-cylinder, in-line, L-head, four-cycle. Cast iron block and head. Displacement: 230 cubic inches. Bore and Stroke: 3.25 x 4.625 inches. Compression ratio: 6.7:1. Brake horsepower: 76 at 3200 rpm. Four main bearings. Mechanical valve lifters. Carburetor: Carter DTA-1.

Chassis and Body: — Wheelbase: 123 inches. Overall length: 195 inches. Height: 90 inches. Width: 76 inches. Tread center to center front: 59-3/8 inches. Tires: 7.50 x 16 6-ply military non-directional.

Technical: — Manual sliding gear transmission. Speeds: 4F/1R. Single speed transfer case. Single dry disc clutch. Leaf spring suspension front and rear. Dodge banjo hypoid gear differentials. Gear ratio: 4.89:1. Hydraulic brakes. Manual steering. Six-volt electrical system. Top speed: 55 mph. Fuel capacity: 25 gallons. Cruising range: 300 miles.

Standard Accessories: — Hand, vehicle tools; spare parts; four stretchers and related medical equipment.

Historical: — Designed and built by the Dodge Division of Chrysler Corporation in Mound Park, Michigan from 1940 to 1942. This is the ambulance seen in the opening scenes of the TV show, "M*A*S*H."

PRICE

Model No.	6	5	4	3	2	1
WC 9, 18, 27	1000	3000	6000	9000	12,000	15,000

Left side view of WC18.

Front view of WC54.

Model WC 54: — The three-quarter-ton Dodge ambulance of World War II had a much stronger chassis than its predecessor, the half-ton truck. This included a heavier frame, springs and axle assemblies.

The engine, transmission and transfer case were basically the same, but the axles had a much lower gear ratio to improve offroad performance. The truck was wider and had much better ground clearance. This unit was similar to the half-ton in that the chassis was the same as the other trucks in the three-quarter-ton series, as were the half-tons. The bodies and equipment were nearly the same in both trucks. The WC 54 used the longer wheelbase and different springs also.

The masonite interior side paneling, metal roof paneling and honeycomb insulation were retained. The folding rear bench seats, stretcher brackets and storage compartments were in the rear. The wheel wells in the rear of the body were much larger, due to the larger tires. Four litter patients and six sitting patients could be carried. The double rear doors and folding rear step were used. The dome light and roof ventilator were on the top of the vehicle. The folding front bucket seats, driver's spotlight and large water heater under the dash panel were still there.

This vehicle used combat wheels and was built without the front mounted winch. The driving controls were the same as the other three-quarter-ton trucks. No partition was used between the front and rear compartments inside. The spare tire was also carried on the left outside of the body, in the recessed panel just behind the driver's door. The rear body floor was metal with linoleum covering. The rear springs also were changed for a smoother ride. Although the three-quarter-ton trucks look nearly the same as the half-tons, they were were really completely different with some interchangeable parts.

I.D. Data: — The serial number is located on the identification data plate on the glove compartment door, and on the left front frame rail above the left front spring.

Model No.	Body Type	Weight	GVW	Prod. Total
WC 54	Ambulance	5920	7720	—

Engine: — Dodge T214, six-cylinder, in-line, L-head, four-cycle. Cast iron block and head. Displacement: 230 cubic inches. Bore and Stroke: 3.25 x 4.625 inches. Compression ratio: 6.7:1. Brake horsepower: 76 at 3200 rpm. Four main bearings. Mechanical valve lifters. Carburetor: Zenith Model 29.

Chassis and Body: — Wheelbase: 121 inches. Overall length: 194.5 inches. Height: 90 inches. Width: 77.75 inches. Tread center to center front: 64.75 inches. Tires: 9.00 x 16 8-ply military non-directional.

Technical: — Manual sliding gear transmission. Speeds: 4F/1R. Single-speed transfer case. Single dry disc clutch. Leaf spring suspension front and rear. Dodge banjo hypoid gear differentials. Gear ratio: 5.83:1. Hydraulic brakes. Manual steering. Six-volt electrical system. Top speed: 54 mph. Fuel capacity: 30 gallons. Cruising range: 240 miles.

Standard Accessories: — Hand, vehicle tools; spare parts; four stretchers and related medical equipment; fire extinguisher.

Historical: — Designed and built by the Dodge Division of Chrysler Corporation in Mound Park, Michigan from 1942 to 1945.

			PRICE			
Model No.	6	5	4	3	2	1
WC 54	1000	3000	6000	9000	12,000	15,000

World War II Dodge WC54 three-quarter-ton ambulance.

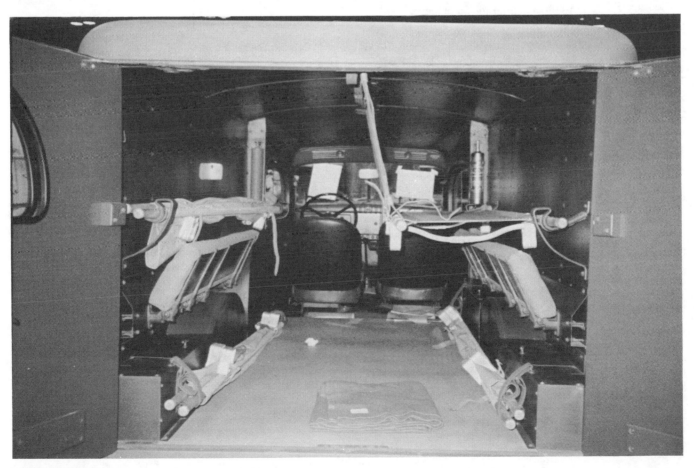

Interior of WC54.

Early 1950s Dodge M43 three-quarter-ton ambulance.

Model M43: — The M43 three-quarter-ton ambulance was built on a slightly modified M37 frame and power train. Again, like its predecessors, it had a longer frame and wheelbase with different rear springs. This vehicle also had a large frame reinforcement in between the front and rear springs.

More modern tubular-style shock absorbers were added to this chassis. The interior was updated from the earlier models. There was a sliding door between the driver's compartment and the patient area in the rear. The rear floor was metal over plywood. The interior panels were all metal with updated insulation.

A forced air ventilation system was located in the rear with two fan blowers, one in each upper rear corner of the patient area. A surgical and dome light were mounted in the ceiling of the rear compartment. Stretcher brackets were on the walls with safety straps from the ceiling. Stowage compartments were under the folding seat cushions, with the metal seat tops doubling as litter racks that could be raised up and supported by a folding metal leg directly above the rear seats. The rear folding step was changed; it folded up inside the body and also acted as a seat for the medical attendant in the rear. A spotlight was in the ceiling of the driver's compartment.

A gasoline fired heater was located under the right rear bench to warm the vehicle. The batteries were under the left rear bench seat. The windows in the double rear panel doors had shades for blackout purposes. Four litter patients and six sitting patients could be carried.

The spare tire was carried on a swinging frame attached to the driver's door hinges, and could be swung open with the door. This truck was not equipped with a pintle hitch, but some M43s were equipped with PTO-driven front-mounted winches. Controls for the lights, ventilation equipment and heater were in the front ceiling area of the rear compartment. An additional gas can bracket was on the left rear door. Outside stowage compartments were on the sides behind the doors, near the bottom of the body.

I.D. Data: — The serial number was located on the identification data plate on the instrument panel, and on the left front frame rail above the left spring.

Model No.	Body Type	Weight	GVW	Prod. Total
M43	Ambulance	5687	7687	—

Engine: — Dodge T245, six-cylinder, in-line, L-head, four-cycle. Cast iron block and head. Displacement: 230 cubic inches. Bore and Stroke: 3.25 x 4.625 inches. Compression ratio: 6.7:1. Brake horsepower: 78 at 3200 rpm. Four main bearings. Mechanical valve lifters. Carburetor: Carter ETW-1.

Chassis and Body: — Wheelbase: 126 inches. Overall length: 198.75 inches. Height: 92 inches. Width: 73 inches. Tread center to center front: 62 inches. Tires: 9.00 x 16 8-ply military non-directional.

Technical: — Manual synchromesh transmission. Speeds: 4F/1R. Single dry disc clutch. Two-speed transfer case. Leaf spring suspension front and rear. Dodge banjo hypoid gear full floating differentials. Gear ratio: 5.83:1. Hydraulic brakes. Manual steering. Twenty-four-volt electrical system. Top speed: 55 mph. Fuel capacity: 24 gallons. Cruising range: 225 miles.

Standard Accessories: — Hand, vehicle tools; spare parts; four stretchers and related medical equipment; fire extinguisher.

Historical: — Designed and built by the Dodge Division of Chrysler Corporation in Mound Park, Michigan from 1950 to 1954.

PRICE

Model No.	6	5	4	3	2	1
M43	300	1200	2500	4000	6500	9500
M43B1	300	1200	2500	4000	6500	9500

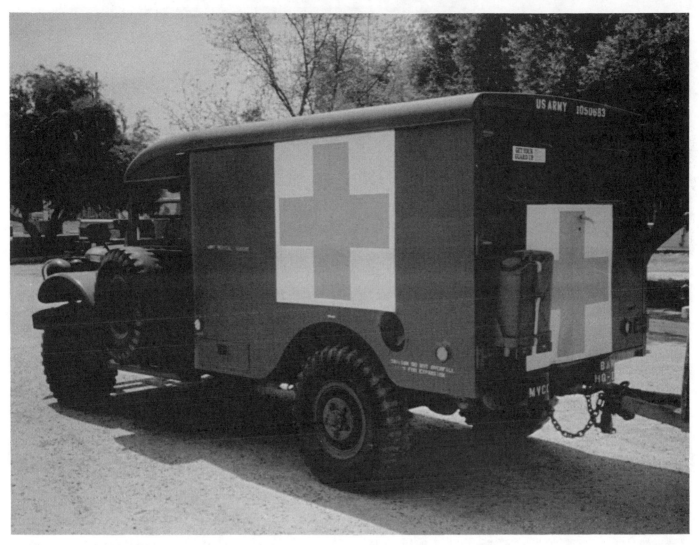

Early 1960s Dodge M43B1 three-quarter-ton ambulance.

Late 1960s Jeep M725 1-1/4-ton ambulance.

Model M725: — The M725 1-1/4-ton ambulance was a companion vehicle to the M715 1-1/4 ton cargo truck. This ambulance used the same power train and frame that the cargo vehicle used; it had the same wheelbase as well. The all-metal steel body was very similar to that of the M43 ambulance.

This series of trucks was an interim successor to the long-running series that Dodge produced. Consequently, the specifications and performances were nearly the same. Needless to say, the rear bodies were almost the same as well.

This truck did not have different rear springs, and the few other differences were probably due to the fact that it was built in later years. The driving controls were the same as the cargo truck. A water heater was located in the front to warm the driver's area. A gasoline-fired heater was in the rear compartment on the left rear bench seat. The batteries were under the right rear bench seat.

A sliding door partition was provided to separate the compartments. The vehicle could carry four litter patients and six ambulatory patients sitting on the bench seats. The same style litter racks and seat combination was used for the stretchers. The folding rear step had two steps; it went inside this vehicle and doubled as a seat for the medical attendant. The rear double doors had larger windows with shades for blackout use.

The gas can carrier was on the left rear door. The lower outside storage compartments were a little larger. The spare tire was carried on the rack under the rear body. The spotlight was on the roof of the driver's compartment. The sliding door inside contained a window. The controls for the dome and surgical lights and personnel heater were in the upper front area of the rear compartment. Double ventilation fans were used in the rear corners of the patient area. The M725 came equipped without a front-mounted winch and did not have pintle hooks.

I.D. Data: — The serial number was located on the identification data plate on the instrument panel.

Model No.	Body Type	Weight	GVW	Prod. Total
M725	Ambulance	6400	8800	—

Engine: — Jeep Tornado 230, six-cylinder, in-line, OHV, OHC, four-cycle, cast iron head and block. Displacement: 230 cubic inches. Bore and Stroke: 3.34 x 4.375 inches. Compression ratio: 7.5:1. Brake horsepower: 132 at 4000 rpm. Four main bearings. Hydraulic valve lifters.

Chassis and Body: — Wheelbase: 126 inches. Overall length: 210 inches. Height: 95 inches. Width: 85 inches. Tires: 9.00 x 16 8-ply military non-directional.

Technical: — Manual synchromesh transmission. Speeds: 4F/1R. Two-speed transfer case. Single dry disc clutch. Leaf spring suspension front and rear. Dana 60 front, Dana 70 rear hypoid differentials. Gear ratio: 5.83:1. Hydraulic brakes. Manual steering. Twenty-four-volt electrical system. Top speed: 60 mph. Fuel capacity: 28 gallons. Cruising range: 225 miles.

Standard Accessories: — Hand, vehicle tools; spare parts; four stretchers and related medical equipment.

Historical: — Designed and built by Kaiser Jeep of Toledo, Ohio from 1967 to 1969. This vehicle saw some use in Vietnam.

PRICE

Model No.	6	5	4	3	2	1
M725	300	1200	2000	3500	5500	—

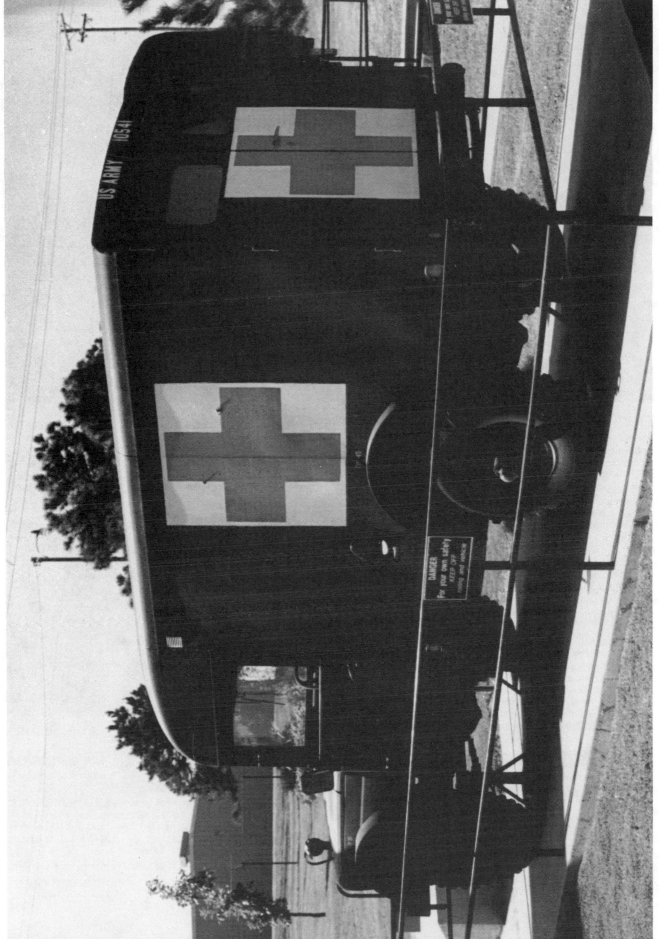

Left rear view of Jeep M725.

Right rear view of 1940 Chevrolet ambulance. (Ralph Doubek, Wild Rose, Wisconsin)

Model Chevrolet WA 1-1/2-ton Field Ambulance: This ambulance was really a civilian truck that was a prewar model. It was built in 1940 on a civilian panel truck chassis with necessary modifications for use as an ambulance.

The entire truck was covered with a coat of semigloss paint even over the chrome items in the front. The red crosses appeared on the front sides and rear with the Army Medical Corps insignia on the sides just behind the doors. A brush guard for the headlights and grille was fitted, and a modified front bumper was installed. Tow hooks were a must. A roof vent was added above the windshield and running lights. A tool box was provided on the left running board, just ahead of the left rear fender.

The rear bumper was modified with two outer halves and a retracting wooden step for entry in the center. Being a 1-1/2-ton model, dual rear wheels were used, and the spare was carried on the right side just behind the door.

The rear interior had a standard wood floor and masonite paneling on the sides and the ceiling. Wooden bench seats that folded were provided for eight ambulatory patients. Stretchers and mounting brackets suspended from the ceiling were used for two litter patients. A third could be carried on the floor. Two jump seats were located towards the front of the rear compartment for attendants. Two standard front seats were used in the driver's area with the right seat folding up for rear entry. No bulkhead or partition was used between the front and rear compartments.

The power train and mechanical aspects of the truck were bascially all civilian as the unit was a rear wheel drive for stateside use only. Vacuum-assisted power brakes were provided, and an auxiliary heater drew heat from the exhaust pipe under the truck and forced it into the rear compartment by means of a metal duct. A crew of two people operated the unit.

I.D. Data: The serial number was located on the identification data plate on the instrument panel.

Model No.	Body Type	Weight	GVW	Prod. Total
W.A	Ambulance	5485	7885	462

Engine: Chevrolet BQ1001, six-cylinder, in-line, overhead valve, four-cycle. Cast iron head and block. Displacement: 216 cubic inches. Bore and Stroke: 3-1/2 x 3-3/4 inches. Compression ratio: 6.5:1. Four main bearings. Mechanical valve lifters. Carburetor: Carter W1 downdraft.

Chassis: Wheelbase: 134.5 inches. Overall length: 288 inches. Width:

Interior view of 1940 Chevrolet ambulance. (Ralph Doubek, Wild Rose, Wisconsin)

81 inches. Height: 84 inches. Tread center to center front: 66 inches. Tires: 6.50 x 20 six-ply highway tread.

Technical: Manual nonsynchromesh transmission. Speeds: 4F/1R. Single dry disc clutch. Semi-elliptic leaf spring suspension front and rear. Chevrolet hypoid gear rear differential. Gear ratio: 6.17:1. Hydraulic vacuum assisted brakes. Manual steering. Top speed: 45 mph. Fuel capacity: 18 gallons. Cruising range: 144 miles.

Standard Accessories: Hand, vehicle tools; fire extinguisher; two litters.

Historical: Built by Chevrolet for government use by various agencies. Stateside use only, built in 1940.

PRICE

Model No.	6	5	4	3	2	1
WA	2000	4000	7000	10,000	13,000	—

1940 Chevrolet 1-1/2-ton ambulance. (Ralph Doubek, Wild Rose, Wisconsin)

FULL TRACKED VEHICLES

Right rear view of M7 snow tractor. (James Welty, Ohio Military Museum Inc., Fairborn, Ohio)

Model M7: — The M7 snow tractor was a small, high-speed vehicle with skis on the front and tracks on the rear for use in deep snow.

The skis could be removed and replaced with wheels and tires that were carried on the sides of the engine compartment when not needed. The M7 used a crew of two, and one sat one behind the other. The payload was 500 pounds, including the crew. The M7 was capable of towing a trailer (weighing 2,000 pounds) on skis also.

The large skis and long wide tracks gave the M7 a very low ground pressure of 0.75 pounds per square inch. The power train was from a Willys MB, using the four-cylinder engine, transmission and differential with some modifications. The vehicle had standard driving controls with the exception of the brakes. There were two pedals: Each one could be used individually to brake one track at a time to assist in steering, or both could be applied at once to stop the vehicle.

The track frame assemblies pivoted in the center on the differential hubs. From here a chain drove the sprocket in the front, and a spring idler in the rear kept the track tensioned. The rear suspension was unsprung, and the track rode on bogie rollers similar to the Weasel. The front axle was of the small farm tractor design with the adaptations for

Front view of M7 snow tractor. (James Welty, Ohio Military Museum Inc., Fairborn, Ohio)

World War II Allis Chalmers M7 snow tractor. (James Welty, Ohio Military Museum Inc., Fairborn, Ohio)

Tracks on M7 snow tractor. (James Welty, Ohio Military Museum Inc., Fairborn, Ohio)

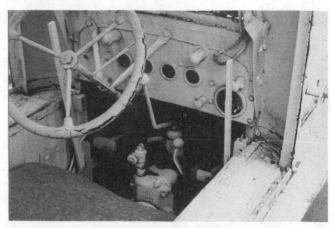

Interior of M7 snow tractor. (James Welty, Ohio Military Museum Inc., Fairborn, Ohio)

the skis. The body was made of sheet metal and plywood. A spotlight was provided along with the standard military lighting system. Top bows, canvas cover and side curtains enclosed the passenger compartment. The vehicle was used mainly for search and rescue of downed pilots in far northern climates.

I.D. Data: — The serial number was located on the identification data plate on the inside of the body to the right of the driver's seat.

Model No.	Body Type	Weight	GVW	Prod. Total
M7	Passenger	2549	3049	291

Engine: — Willys MB, four-cylinder, L-head, in-line, four-cycle, cast iron head and block. Displacement: 134 cubic inches. Bore and Stroke: 3-1/8 x 4-3/8 inches. Compression ratio: 6.48:1. Brake horsepower: 54 at 4000 rpm. Three main bearings. Mechanical valve lifters. Carburetor: Carter Model WO.

Chassis and Body: — Ground contact length: skis 45 inches, tracks 60 inches. Overall length: 136 inches. Height: 64 inches. Width: 63 inches. Tread center to center: 45 inches. Tires: 4.00 x 15 implement

tread. Skis: wood, 9 inches wide, 70 inches long. Tracks: endless rubber band with cable reinforcements in bands attached to metal shoes, 18 inches wide.

Technical: — Manual transmission. Speeds: 3F/1R. Auxiliary two-speed transmission. Single dry disc clutch. Solid front suspension. Unsprung walking beam rear suspension. Spicer rear differential with mechanical brakes, chain drive to sprockets. Manual steering. Six-volt electrical system. Top speed: 40 mph. Fuel capacity: 10.5 gallons. Cruising range: 160 miles.

Standard Accessories: — Canvas top and bows, side curtains; hand and vehicle tools; tow chain, two spare skis; cold weather starting equipment for the engine.

Historical: — Built by the Allis Chalmers Company from 1943 to 1945.

PRICE

Model No.	6	5	4	3	2	1
M7	800	1600	2400	4500	—	—

Right front view of M2 Cletrac. (David Wright, Wright Museum, Shrewsbury, Massachusetts)

Model M2: — The M2 Cletrac was a full-tracked, seven-ton high-speed tractor designed for towing heavy bombers. Specialty equipment was adapted to a commercial tractor by the U.S. Ordnance Department.

This tractor was built on an assembled steel channel frame with all replaceable components. The controlled differential and drive sprockets were at the rear, putting the large adjustable idler at the front. The design of the unit was very much like the commercial tractors of the period, but the suspension of the vehicle was quite different from a civilian model. Vertical volute springs were mounted on top of small bogie clusters using four wheels per cluster; there were two clusters per side. Two top rollers supported the track. The tracks were just about the same construction as the half-tracks, however, they were longer and had crossbars that protruded from the sides. This allowed removable rubber pads to be used and conveniently changed when needed. This would have been a great advantage for the half-track had they used it.

The unit was built with several uses in mind. With the windshield folded, the vehicle had such a low profile it could be driven under the wings of a plane. This low profile also allowed it to be used as a service platform for working on the aircraft. Its the short length and turning radius made it very easy to maneuver.

The vehicle had a unique hitch that went from the rear forward, under the power train, so that when it began to pull on a plane, the chassis was pulled down onto the tracks evenly for better traction on all surfaces. This feature enabled it to pull the much heavier weight of the bombers. The ends of the crossbars protruded far enough from the track so a detachable rubber pad could be bolted on and replaced when needed.

Full fenders were over the tracks, and many accessories were mounted on them. A heavy wire mesh brush guard, with headlight guards as well, was mounted in front of the radiator. The front bumper had replaceable wooden inserts. Three men could sit in the vehicle with the driver in the center. A metal bow was used to support the canvas top, which was attached to the windshield frame when needed.

Left front view of M2 Cletrac. (David Wright, Wright Museum, Shrewsbury, Massachusetts)

The vehicle was able to operate on soft grass runways, hard pavement and other types of terrain. The controls, power train and general design made it possible to tow and turn on all types of landing areas without damaging the aircraft. The tractor was equipped with a large rear air compressor used to pump up landing gear shock struts, at pressures as high as 2000 psi. A belt-driven generator provided 100-volt DC power with 3 KW capacity. A 10,000-pound capacity, PTO-driven winch was mounted in front of the radiator.

I.D. Data: — The serial number was located on the identification data plate on the instrument panel.

World War II M2 Cletrac seven-ton high-speed tractor. (David Wright, Wright Museum, Shrewsbury, Massachusetts)

Model No.	Body Type	Weight	GVW	Prod. Total
M2	Personnel	14,700	14,700	8510

Engine: — Hercules WXLC3, six-cylinder, in-line, L-head, four-cycle. Cast iron block and bead. Displacement: 404 cubic inches. Bore and Stroke: 4-1/4 x 4-3/4 inches. Compression ratio: 6.5:1. Brake horsepower: 150 at 3,000 rpm. Seven main bearings. Mechanical valve lifters.

Chassis and Body: — Length of track on the ground: 63 inches. Overall length: 166 inches. Height: 68 inches. Width: 70 inches. Tread center to center of track: 52 inches. Tracks: endless rubber band with detachable rubber grousers. Width: 13.5 inches.

Technical: — Manual constant mesh transmission. Speeds: 4F/1R. Single dry disc clutch. Vertical volute spring suspension. Cletrac mechanically controlled differential. Overall ratio: 23.1:1. Hand lever-operated steering and braking. Twelve-volt electrical system. Top speed: 22 mph. Fuel capacity: 33 gallons. Cruising range: 100 miles.

Standard Accessories: — Hand, vehicle, pioneer tools; air hoses and electrical cables or compressor and generator; spotlight; three-stage rear-mounted air compressor; belt-driven fender-mounted D.C. generator; fire extinguishers; spare parts and rubber track pads; canvas top.

Historical: — Designed and built by the Cleveland Tractor Company and by John Deere from 1941 to 1945.

	PRICE					
Model No.	6	5	4	3	2	1
M2	1000	2000	5000	8000	10,000	—

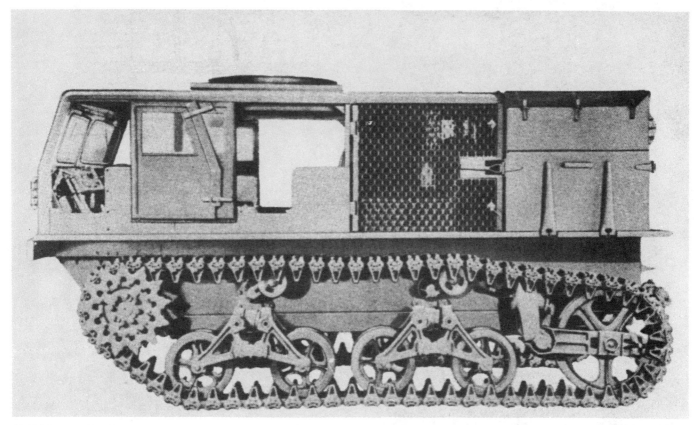

M4 high-speed tractor.

Model M4: — The M4 high-speed tractor was a full-track vehicle originally designed for use as a prime mover for heavy artillery. The five guns it towed were: three-inch antiaircraft, 90mm antiaircraft, 155mm gun carriage, eight-inch howitzer carriage and 240mm howitzer carriage.

The M4 tractor was built on a welded steel chassis, similar to a tank. The front section was bolted onto the front of the chassis. This allowed the differential and transmission assembly to be separated when service or repair was required. Access panels were located on the bottom of the hull for service of components. The fuel tank sat on the bottom of the hull towards the rear.

Four different tread designs were used on the tracks: steel chevron, rubber chevron, steel bar cleat and smooth rubber block. These were the same tracks used on the M3 and M4 medium tanks. Drive sprockets and bogie wheels were also interchangeable as well. However, the suspension was a different type with a large trailing idler wheel at the rear. The springs themselves were a horizontal volute type. The high-speed tractors of World War II used this type of idler exclusively; it was also used on light tanks. Its appearance was quite noticeable and easily distinguished these vehicles from other tracked vehicles. The medium tanks that used the same track, sprockets, bogie tires, etc. had the idler at the rear of the hull, but it was mounted higher. Keeping as many moving parts as possible off the ground and out of the dirt dramatically increased track life.

The M4 was steered by two levers actuating oil-bathed bands inside the differential. This principal was used on most tracked vehicles in World War II. The engine was mounted in the center of the vehicle with the clutch and torque converter attached at the rear of the unit. A drive shaft went to the transmission, which was bolted directly to the differential. The radiator was mounted on the side of the engine, on the right side of the vehicle. Belt-driven fans were used and were run remotely from the engine.

A 40,000-pound PTO-driven winch was mounted inside the hull at the rear under the ammunition cabinets. This winch was used for gun emplacement and self-recovery work. A large pintle hitch, designed for towing artillery, was located at the rear. Electrical and air trailer connections were used for trailer or gun control when towing.

The gun crew, section equipment and a small quantity of ammunition were carried on board. The tractor was unarmored and carried a crew of 11 men. The driver and two others sat in the front compartment, and eight crew members faced each other in the center compartment directly

Engine being removed from M4 high-speed tractor. (Chet Krause, Iola, Wisconsin)

behind them. The engine and ammunition were in the rear.

Small cranes with trolley style chain hoists at the rear loaded and unloaded ammunition into the stowage cabinets. A machine gun in a circular ring mount in the roof of the cab was used to defend the vehicle.

M4A1: — This was the same basic vehicle as the M4, but it used extended end connectors on the inside and outside of the track, widening it considerably. Consequently, the suspension was spaced out from the hull. The ammunition stowage was rearranged also. The M4C and M4A1C were also the same tractors but had different ammunition arrangements.

I.D. Data: — The serial number was on the identification data plate on the instrument panel of the vehicle.

Model No.	Body Type	Weight	GVW	Prod. Total
M4	Personnel	28,000	31,400	5552
M4A1	Personnel	31,500	33,900	259

Left side view of M4 being repaired. (Chet Krause, Iola, Wisconsin)

Right side view of M4. (Chet Krause, Iola, Wisconsin)

Rear view of M4. (Chet Krause, Iola, Wisconsin)

Engine: Waukesha, six-cylinder, 145GZ, in-line, OHV, cast iron block and head. Displacement: 817 cubic inches. Bore and stroke: 5-3/8 x 6 inches. Compression ratio: 5.95:1. Brake horsepower: 190 at 2,100 rpm. Seven main bearings. Valve lifters: solid. Carburetor: Two Zenith Model 29s.

Chassis: — Track on ground: 124 inches. Overall length: 210 inches. Height: 108 inches. Width: 97 inches. Tread center of track to center of track: 80 inches. Tracks: 16-9/16 inches wide, steel or rubber block, steel pin with rubber bushings.

Technical: — Manual selective gear transmission. Speeds: 3F/1R with torque converter. Single dry disc clutch. Horizontal volute spring suspension with large diameter trailing idler wheel. Mechanically controlled differential with lever steering and braking. Planetary final drives and sprockets to propel the tracks. Bogie tires, sprockets, and tracks from the M3/M4 medium tank family. Twelve-volt electrical system. Forty-thousand-pound winch at rear of vehicle with 300 feet of cable. Top speed: 35 mph. Fuel capacity: 125 gallons. Cruising range: 100 miles.

Standard Accessories: — Canvas roof cover for gun mount, canvas doors, pioneer tools; one 50 caliber machine gun with circular ring mount, tripod, carriage, and cradle assembly; artillery section equipment, hand and vehicle tools, fire extinguisher; ammunition (quantity carried depended on the gun towed).

Historical: — The artillery's experiences in various weather and battlefield conditions during World War I dictated that large artillery pieces were best moved by tracked vehicles able to negotiate the most difficult terrain in all seasons. The trained ability to move quickly from position to position created the need for a series of high-speed tractors to be built in the early 1940s. They were built by Allis-Chalmers Company in Rock Island, Illinois.

PRICE

Model No.	6	5	4	3	2	1
M4	600	1900	2700	4000	7000	10,000
M4A1	600	1900	2700	4000	7000	10,000

World War II I.H.C. M5 13-ton high-speed tractor.

Model M5: — The M5 high-speed tractor was used to tow 105mm, 155mm or 4.5 inch guns. It was similar to the other high-speed tractors but was an entirely different model.

The M5 had a cargo capacity of 16,000 pounds and a towing capacity of 20,000 pounds. It used the track, sprockets, bogie tires and idler wheel from the M3-M5 light tanks. The suspension was slightly different because this vehicle was built on a steel channel frame with cross members rather than an armored hull of a tank. Sheet steel panels bolted to the bottom of the vehicle allowed access to the mechanical components.

The engine and clutch were at the rear, with radiators alongside them. The fuel tanks were on each side of the drive shaft in the bottom of the unit. The transmission and differential were at the front, with the driver operating the controls in the center above them.

The bogies and suspension on this tractor were mounted on a long frame inside the track. This in turn was bolted to the frame of the tractor. Vertical volute spring suspension, similar to the M3 and M5 tanks, was used. Some of the parts were interchangeable: tracks, drive sprockets, bogie tires, idler wheels, top return rollers, etc. This suspension had to be disassembled from the frame to which it was attached, where the tank had it in clusters, and these whole assemblies could be removed from the hull of the tank very quickly.

The transmission, differential and final drivers were all bolted together on this vehicle and were removed from the front by unbolting them from the frame. First the winch had to be removed.

The eight crew members sat on the sides of the center compartment with the ammunition boxes in the middle above the drive shaft. A 20,000-pound winch was mounted at the front, below the driver's windshield. Top bows and canvas were used to cover the crew and ammunition compartment. The large boxes at the rear corners of the vehicle were used to carry and store powder and fuses for the appropriate gun being towed. Front and rear pintle hitches were provided for towing and gun emplacement.

Model M5A1: — This was the same basic vehicle as the M5, but it had a different cab and seating arrangement. The front winch was inside a heavy steel housing under the front bumper. It was the same model and in the same position as the M5, but was enclosed. Entry was from the side through removable canvas doors. The seating arrangement was in three rows from side to side as was in the M4 tractor. The M5A1 had a full front with two windshields. The driver's seat and controls were slightly moved to the left side of the vehicle. (The M5's controls and driver's seat were in the center with two small doors for the front entry.) The .50 caliber ring mount was in the center of the roof of the cab. Ammunition stowage was changed as well.

Model M5A4: — This was the same basic vehicle as the M5, but was the last one of the series. The vehicle was wider because the suspension was spaced out from the frame to accommodate wider tracks. They were widened by adding extended end connectors to each of the tracks. The rest of the suspension was the same. The dual range air-operated clutch was dropped, and a simple two-auxiliary transmission was installed in front by the main transmission. Ammunition stowage was again changed with the boxes alongside the full length of the vehicle above the tracks. The interior was pretty much the same as the original M5.

I.D. Data: — The serial number was located on the identification data plate on the front of the driver's cowl just below the windshield, and on the end of the left front frame rail.

Model No.	Body Type	Weight	GVW	Prod. Total
M5	Prime Mover	23,300	28,600	—

Engine: — Continental R6572, six-cylinder, in-line, OHV, four-cycle, cast iron block and head. Displacement: 572 cubic inches. Bore and Stroke: 4-3/4 x 5-3/8 inches. Compression ratio: 6.5:1. Brake horsepower: 235 at 2900 rpm. Seven main bearings. Mechanical valve lifters. Carburetors: Zenith 0-10087 and 0-10088.

Right front view of I.H.C. M5.

World War II I.H.C. M5A1 high-speed tractor. (Chet Krause, Iola, Wisconsin)

Post-World War II M5A4 13-ton high-speed tractor. (James Welty, Ohio Military Museum Inc., Fairborn, Ohio)

Right side of M5A4. (James Welty, Ohio Military Museum Inc., Fairborn, Ohio)

Front view of M5A4. (James Welty, Ohio Military Museum Inc., Fairborn, Ohio)

Rear view of M5A4. (James Welty, Ohio Military Museum Inc., Fairborn, Ohio)

Technical: — Manual constant mesh transmission. Speeds: 4F/1R. Dual range air-operated single dry disc clutch. Mechanically controlled differential. Overall ratio: 56:1. Hand lever-operated steering and brakes. Air and electric trailer brake controls. Top speed: 35 mph. Fuel capacity: 100 gallons. Cruising range: 125 miles.

Chassis and Body: — Length of track on ground: 138 inches. Overall length: 191 inches. Height: 104 inches. Width: 101 inches. Tread center to center of tracks: 83 inches. Track: Steel or rubber block, steel pins with end connectors. Width: 12 inches.

Standard Accessories: — Hand, vehicle, pioneer, track tools; canvas top and bows; .30 caliber rifles or carbines for crew members; ammuni-

tion and section equipment for towed guns; fire extinguisher, seat cushions; ring mount for .50 caliber machine gun.

Historical: — Built by International Harvester Corporation from 1942 to 1945. Used in many combat theaters in World War II and the Korean conflict.

			PRICE			
Model No.	6	5	4	3	2	1
M5	800	1800	3500	5500	7500	—

M6 high speed tractor. (Frank Buck, Mountainhome, Pennsylvania)

Model M6: — The M6 38-ton high-speed tractor was the largest of this type vehicle used and designed in World War II. It was used as a prime mover for towing the largest artillery the Army had at the time, which was the 240mm howitzer, the eight-inch gun and the 120mm antiaircraft gun. Towing capacity was 50,000 pounds.

The rear engine layout was common to the other tractors in this series. The compartment for the driver and crew, with two rows of seats for 11 men, was located in the front of the vehicle above the differential and transmission. The engine compartment, with two engines and clutches that were tied together for synchronization by a common clutch housing, was located in the center of the vehicle. Radiators were located on the sides above the tracks. The fuel tank was behind the engine in the bottom of the hull, and the 60,000-pound winch was at the rear. The ammunition and cargo compartments were above the fuel tank and winch. There were large shell racks on each side of these compartments; a large collapsible crane and chain hoist assembly for loading and unloading shells, powder and equipment was in the center.

The size of the vehicle required an additional set of bogie wheels on each side. Horizontal volute suspension was used, but it was different from that used on the later M4 series medium tank. A ring mount for a .50 caliber machine gun was located in the roof, and a rifle was carried.

I.D. Data: — The serial number was located on the identification data plate on the instrument panel.

Model No.	Body Type	Weight	GVW	Prod. Total
M6	Prime Mover	67,000	75,000	1130

Engines: — (2) Waukesha 145GZ, six-cylinder, in-line, OHV, four-cycle, cast iron block and heads. Displacement: 817 cubic inches. Bore and Stroke: 5-3/8 x 6 inches. Compression ratio: 5.95:1. Brake horsepower: 190 at 2100 rpm. Seven main bearings. Mechanical valve lifters. Carburetors: Zenith 29BW-14 and 29BBW-14.

Chassis and Body: — Length of track on ground: 177 inches. Overall length: 258 inches. Height: 103 inches. Width: 121 inches. Tread center to center of track: 98.5 inches. Track: steel or rubber shoe, rubber bushed double pin with center guides. Width: 23 inches.

Technical: — Manual transmission with two torque converters. Speeds: 2F/1R. Two single dry disc clutches. Horizontal volute spring suspension with four rubber tired bogie wheels per cluster. Mechanically controlled differential. Overall ratio: 83.4:1. Hand lever-operated steering and brakes. Air and electric trailer brake controls. Twelve-volt electrical system. Top speed: 21 mph. Fuel capacity: 300 gallons. Cruising range: 110 miles.

Standard Accessories: — Hand, vehicle, pioneer, track tools; spare parts and track blocks; fire extinguishers; water and oil storage containers; ammunition and gun section equipment; one .50 caliber machine gun with ring mount, one .30 caliber rifle; canvas tarps for crew, cargo, ammunition compartments.

Historical: — Built by Allis-Chalmers from 1943 to 1944. Small quantity produced.

Model No.	6	5	4	3	2	1
				PRICE		
M6	1500	3000	6000	—	—	—

Model M8A1: — The M8A1 was a full-tracked vehicle used for general cargo transportation and as an artillery prime mover.

This high-speed vehicle had a large removable deck on the rear with side racks and top bows for carrying cargo. It had a payload capacity of 17,500 pounds and towing capability of 39,000 pounds. When the vehicle was used as a prime mover, it had ammunition boxes on the bed and a large hydraulic hoist on the rear to raise and lower the generator set used with the towed artillery piece. Some vehicles were equipped with a removable hydraulic dozer blade attachment in front. A hydraulically driven Garwood 45,000-pound winch was provided in the rear under the bed with a small access door in the rear just above the pintle hitch. The fuel tank, compressed air system, and power take-off-driven hydraulic system were located in the hull under the cargo deck.

The engine and cross drive transmission were in the front and were serviced by lowering the large front access door and sliding out the assembly on rails. The engine compartment was equipped with quick disconnect features for engine removal and had a fixed fire extinguisher system.

The engine was air-cooled with the air intake in the front just above the front access door; the exhaust was at the top behind the operator's compartments. The body was an all-welded steel unit. The vehicle was designed for use in all climatic conditions. Radio installation was possible in all models.

The chassis of the M8A1 was made of components from the M41 tank family of vehicles. The Continental flat-opposed six-cylinder engine and Allison cross drive transmission were all the same basic units. The tractor had the asemblies mounted in the front.

The torsion bar suspension, tracks, road wheels, sprockets and rear idlers were interchangeable with other vehicles in the family. This tractor replaced the M4, M5, M6 high-speed tractors of World War II.

The hull was longer, requiring an additional road wheel and torsion bar assembly on each side. This was a very heavy vehicle as well.

The driver and assistant sat in separate compartments with the engine in between. There was a small area near the personnel heater where they could see each other and communicate. The assistant did have some control of the vehicle, and he operated the machine gun ring mount which was above him.

I.D. Data: — The serial number was located on the identification data plate inside the vehicle in the driver's compartment on the right wall.

Model No.	Body Type	Weight	GVW	Prod. Total
M8A1	Cargo	37,500	55,000	—

Engine: — Continental AOS-895-3, six-cylinder, opposed, air-cooled, four-cycle, OHV, OHC. Aluminum alloy block and heads. Displacement: 895 cubic inches. Bore and Stroke: 5-3/4 x 5-3/4 inches. Compression ratio: 5.5:1 with supercharger. Brake horsepower: 363 at 2800 rpm. Mechanical valve lifters. Seven main bearings. Carburetor: Stromberg NA-Y5G-3.

Chassis and Body: — Ground contact length: 157 inches. Overall length: 265 inches. Height: 120 inches. Width: 130 inches. Tracks: Steel shoe with replaceable rubber pads, steel pins. Width: 21 inches.

Technical: — Allison CD-500-3 cross transmission differential with torque converter. Speeds: 2F/1R. Overall ratio: 5.34:1. Torsion bar suspension with dual rubber tired road wheels. Hand lever-operated hydraulic steering in differential. Pedal operated as service brakes. Twenty-four-volt electrical system. Top speed: 40 mph. Fuel capacity: 225 gallons. Cruising range: 180 miles.

Standard Accessories: — Canvas intake, exhaust grille covers, rear cargo tarp, top bows; hand, vehicle, pioneer tools; tow cable; spot and trouble lights; radios; machine gun mount for .50 caliber gun; fixed and portable fire extinguishers; spare track sections.

Historical: — Originally designed by Buick Division of General Motors in the mid-1940s. Production by Allis-Chalmers from the late 1940s to the late 1950s.

Model No.	6	5	4	3	2	1
				PRICE		
M8A1	1500	3000	4500	6500	8500	—

MOTORCYCLES

World War II Harley-Davidson WLA motorcycle. (Ralph Doubek, Wild Rose, Wisconsin)

Model WLA: — The WLA was Harley-Davidson's best-selling motorcycle purchased by the military in World War II. It was basically a standard model with military requirements added to it.

The front end of the bike used a double coil spring suspension with a damper just behind it near the handlebars. A headlight was mounted on top of the front fender with a blackout light sitting just ahead of it. A large leather scabbard or holster for a submachine gun was attached to a bracket on the right side of the front suspension. A small ammunition box was located on the left side. A military horn and blackout drive light were mounted above the headlight. The handlebars had a right-hand throttle and a left-hand spark advance, with a left-hand brake for the front wheel. A horn button and rearview mirror were near the hand brake on the left side.

The fuel tank above the engine had gasoline on the left side and the engine oil reservoir on the right side. The speedometer and light switches were located in the center. The transmission shift lever was on the left side of the fuel tank. Leg guards and shields were mounted to the frame just in front of the engine. The motorcycle's frame was built from tubular steel; the leather covered seat was on a tubular shaft with the spring inside of it.

View of speedometer and handles of Harley-Davidson WLA. (Ralph Doubek, Wild Rose, Wisconsin)

Rear of Harley-Davidson WLA. (Ralph Doubek, Wild Rose, Wisconsin)

Engine area on Harley-Davidson WLA. (Ralph Doubek, Wild Rose, Wisconsin)

Light on Harley-Davidson WLA. (Ralph Doubek, Wild Rose, Wisconsin)

The 45-degree V-twin air-cooled engine sat below the tank with the transmission just behind it. The clutch mechanism and pedal were on the left side of the engine, and the chain drive system was on the right. Left and right footrests were provided near the left clutch and right brake pedals. The right brake pedal operated the rear wheel brakes. The distributor was on the right side of the engine in between the cylinders. A small metal cover was placed over the distributor, and a cable extended to the handlebars for spark advance. The carburetor was between the cylinders, and the remote oil bath air cleaner with a rubber hose to the carburetor connected the two.

A small metal toolbox was just under the right side of the seat. The exhaust system was on the right side beneath the chain, with a muffler and baffle near the rear sprocket. A chain guard kept oil and dirt away from the operator. A kickstand was located at the left front near the footrest, and a larger wheel stand at the rear of the rear fender held the bike upright for service.

A double taillight assembly sat on the rear fender side-by-side with a left taillight and stop light and a right blackout marker light. A large rear platform or parcel shelf for carrying small items was on top of the rear fender. The foot kickstarter was on the right just below the toolbox. The front and rear fenders had a much more military design and appearance to them. The fenders were spaced a little farther away from the tires for additional wheel travel when off-road.

Front and rear mud flaps were not used. Some models had sidecars attached to the right side. Leather saddlebags were fastened to the rear parcel shelf on each side for carrying items that needed to be enclosed.

I.D. Data: — The serial number was stamped on the engine block and served as the identification number for the vehicle.

Model No.	Body Type	Weight	GVW	Prod. Total
WLA	Motorcycle	583	763	60,486

Engine: — Harley-Davidson WLA. V-2 cylinder, 45-degree. L-head, air-cooled, four-cycle. Cast iron block and cylinders, aluminum heads. Displacement: 45 cubic inches. Bore and Stroke: 2.75 x 3.8125 inches. Compression ratio: 4.32:1. Brake horsepower: 23 at 4600 rpm. Two roller main bearings. Mechanical valve lifters. Carburetor: Linkert M series.

Chassis: — Wheelbase: 57.5 inches. Overall length: 88 inches. Width: 36 inches. Height: 41 inches. Tires: 4.00 x 18 4-ply civilian highway tread.

Technical: — Manual constant mesh transmission. Speeds: 3F/1R. Dual disc dry clutch. Coil spring front suspension. Chain drive to rear wheel. Gear ratio: 4.74:1. Mechanical front hand and rear foot brakes. Six-volt electrical system. Top speed: 70 mph. Fuel capacity: 3.375 gallons. Cruising range: 124 miles.

Standard Accessories: — Leather saddlebags, leg shields, windshield, ammunition box; leather scabbard for .45 caliber submachine gun; hand, vehicle tools, spare parts, rearview mirror.

Historical: — Built by Harley-Davidson Company of Milwaukee, Wisconsin from 1940 to 1945.

	PRICE					
Model No.	6	5	4	3	2	1
WLA	1500	3000	4000	5000	6000	7500

World War II Indian 741B motorcycle. (Ralph Doubek, Wild Rose, Wisconsin)

Model 741B: — The 741B was one of Indian's models used mostly overseas. The 741B was similar in design and appearance to other motorcycles but was a completely different machine.

The same basic mechanical principles were used in each motorcycle. The front suspension used a single coil spring and a slightly different damper control. The handlebars and controls were laid out in a similar manner as the Harley-Davidson. The speedometer was mounted above the headlight, which was just above the front fender on the suspension, and the blackout drive light was next to the headlight. The blackout marker light was on top of the front fender.

The fenders on the Indian had a little more civilian design in them. Both this bike and the Harley-Davidson WLA used the same scabbard, ammunition box, brackets and submachine gun. An amp meter and light switch were at the front of the fuel tank. The Indian fuel tank had gasoline on the left side; the right side contained the engine oil reservoir with a small gasoline reserve tank inside it. A data plate was on top of the fuel tank.

The front of the seat was hinged just behind the data plate. The leather-covered driver's seat was on two exposed coil springs for suspension. The coil springs were secured to the tubular steel frame. The Indian's horn was mounted below the gas tank on the frame, just behind the front fender on the left side. Leg or crash guards were used with left and right footrests. The 741B and WLA footrests were different in shape and color.

The transmission shift lever was mounted at the rear of the gas tank and could be switched to either the left or right side of the bike. The V-twin air-cooled engine was similar to the WLA with a right side distributor and carburetor between the cylinders. The remote oil bath air cleaner was the same unit on both cycles, and was mounted in the same location on both bikes as well.

The clutch and clutch pedal were mounted on the left side of the 741B with the transmission behind and bolted to the engine crankcase. The drive chain, chain guard, and rear sprocket were on the right side. The foot kick starter and exhaust system were also on the right side. No toolbox was used on the Indian. The exhaust pipe with muffler were

Handlebars of Indian 741B. (Ralph Doubek, Wild Rose, Wisconsin)

quite different in appearance from the WLA. The rear wheel stand on the Indian operated in the same way as the WLA but was constructed differently, with several pieces of metal rather than the WLA's one-piece unit.

The double taillight system was used, but the Indian's lights were mounted one above the other. The stop lamp was on top and the blackout marker lamp was on the bottom. The rear fender platform on the Indian was more open on the top and smaller in overall size than the WLA. The generator was mounted at the front of the engine crankcase.

I.D. Data: — The serial number was located on the left side of the frame near the rear axle.

Model No.	Body Type	Weight	GVW	Prod. Total
741B	Motorcycle	460	635	40,000

Right front view of Indian 741B. (Ralph Doubek, Wild Rose, Wisconsin)

Engine area of Indian 741B. (Ralph Doubek, Wisconsin)

Left side closeup of Indian 741B. (Ralph Doubek, Wild Rose, Wisconsin)

Engine: — Indian GDA-101 V-2 cylinder, 90-degree. L-head, air-cooled, four-cycle. Cast iron head and cylinders, aluminum heads. Displacement: 30.5 cubic inches. Bore and Stroke: 2.5 x 3.0625 inches. Compression ratio: 7.5:1. Brake horsepower: 15 at 4200 rpm. Two roller main bearings. Mechanical valve lifters. Carburetor: Schebler side draft.

Chassis: — Wheelbase: 57 inches. Overall length: 88 inches. Width: 34 inches. Height: 40 inches. Tires: 3.50 x 18 4-ply civilian highway tread.

Technical: — Manual constant mesh transmission. Speeds: 3F. Dual dry disc clutch. Coil spring front suspension. Chain drive. Gear ratio

5.46:1. Mechanical front and rear brakes. Six-volt electrical system. Top speed: 65 mph. Fuel capacity: three gallons. Cruising range: 90 miles.

Standard Accessories: — Leather saddlebags, ammunition box; leather scabbard for .45 caliber submachine gun; hand, vehicle tools, spare parts, rearview mirror.

Historical: — Designed and built by the Indian Motorcycle Company of Springfield, Massachusetts from 1942 to 1945.

			PRICE			
Model No.	6	5	4	3	2	1
741B	1500	3000	4000	5000	6000	7500

Left front area of Indian 741B. (Ralph Doubek, Wild Rose, Wisconsin)

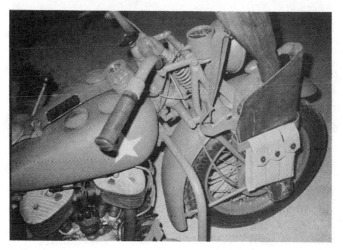

Storage area for gun on Indian 741B. (Ralph Doubek, Wild Rose, Wisconsin)

Rear view of Indian 741B. (Ralph Doubek, Wild Rose, Wisconsin)

BIBLIOGRAPHY

Books

AFV Weapons Profiles, Numbers 4, 11, 16, 26, 32, 41, 46, 52, 64. Chamberlain, Duncan, Ellis, Icks. Profile Publications Ltd., Coburg House, Sheet St., Windsor, Berkshire, England. 1972-1974.

Allied Combat Tanks, Chamberlain and Milsom. Arco Publishing Company Inc., New York, New York. 1978.

Allied Tank Destroyers. Perret. Osprey Publishing Ltd., London, England. 1979.

American Armoured Cars. Ellis and Chamberlain. Almarks Publishing Company, Edgeware, Middlesex, England. 1969.

American Half-Tracks of World War Two. Ellis and Chamberlain. Bellona Publications, Watford, Herts, England. 1978.

American Tanks and Tank Destroyers. Conger. Henry Holt and Company, New York New York. 1944.

Amtracs: US Amphibious Assault Vehicles. Zaloga. Osprey Publishing Ltd., London, England. 1987.

Armored Fighting Vehicles of the World. Foss. Charles Scribner, New York, New York. 1977.

Army Vehicle Manuals. Spence. Portrayal Press, Bloomfield, New Jersey. 1989.

Artillery Materiel and Associated Equipment TM9-2300. Department of the Army. Washington, D.C. 1949.

Automotive Assembly, Automotive Series, Engineering Design Handbook AMCP 706-355. Headquarters, U.S. Army Materiel Command, Washington, D.C. 1965.

Bantam Model BRC. Post. Post-Era Motorbooks. Arcadia, California. 1971.

Continental! Its Motors and Its People. Wagner. Aero Publishers, Inc., Fallbrook, California. 1983.

Dodge Military Vehicles 1940-1945. Collection No.1. Richards. Brooklands Book Distribution Ltd., Cobham, Surrey, England. 1984.

Encyclopedia of Armoured Cars. Crow and Icks. Chartwell Books Inc., Secaucus, New Jersey. 1976.

Equipment Data Sheets for TARCOM Equipment. TM 43-0001-31. Headquarters, Department of the Army, Washington, D.C. 1978.

Firepower: A History of the American Heavy Tank. Hunnicutt. Presidio Press, Novato, California. 1988.

Ford Model GP. Post. Post-Era Motorbooks, Arcadia, California. 1971.

Ford Machinery Corporation. Procurement and Engineering Division. San Jose, California. 1945.

Fundamentals of Artillery Weapons. TM9-2305. War Department, Washington, D.C. 1948.

GMC 6x6 and DUKW, A Universal Truck. Boniface and Jeudy. Motorbooks International, Osceola, Wisconsin. 1978.

Hail to the Jeep. Wells. EMS Publications, North Point, Hong Kong. 1946.

Half-Tracks. Olyslager Organization and Vanderveen. Frederick Warne and Company Ltd., London, England.

Handbook of Ordnance Materiel. U.S. Army Ordnance Center and School, ST9-159 Aberdeen Proving Ground, Maryland. 1968.

Historic Military Vehicles Directory. Vanderveen. Battle of Britain Prints International Ltd., London, England. 1989.

Illustrated Encyclopedia of Artillery. Hogg. Chartwell Books Inc., Secaucus, New Jersey. 1988.

Illustrated Encyclopedia of Military Vehicles. Hogg and Weeks. Prentice Hall Inc., Englewood Cliffs, New Jersey. 1980.

Inspection Handbook for Ordnance Vehicles. Tank Automotive Center, Engineering-Manufacturing Branch, Detroit, Michigan. 1943.

Inside Harley-Davidson. Hatfield. Motorbooks International, Osceola, Wisconsin. 1990.

Jeep. Olyslager Organization and Vanderveen. Frederick Warne and Company Ltd., London, England.

Mechanized Infantry. Perrett. Osprey Publishing Ltd., London, England. 1984.

Military Motor Transportation. Bookshop. The Coast Artillery Journal, Fort Monroe, Virginia. 1927.

Military Motorcycles of World War Two. Bacon. Osprey Publishing Ltd., London, England. 1985.

Military Vehicles, Gun Carriers, Mechanical Mules, Ducks and Super Ducks. Colby. Coward-McCann, New York, New York. 1956.

Military Vehicles. TM9-2800. Department of the Army, Washington, D.C. 1947.

Military Vehicles. TM9-2800-1. Department of the Army, Washington, D.C. 1953.

Military Vehicles of the World. Foss. Charles Scribner, New York, New York. 1976.

Observer's Army Vehicles Directory to 1940. Vanderveen. Frederick Warne and Company Ltd., London, England. 1974.

Observer's Fighting Vehicles Directory World War Two. Vanderveen. Frederick Warne and Company Ltd., London, England. 1972.

Observer's Military Vehicles Directory from 1945. Vanderveen. Frederick Warne and Company Ltd., London, England. 1972.

M24 Chaffee in Action. Mesko. Squadron Signal Publications, Inc., Carrollton, Texas. 1988.

Patton, A History of the American Main Battle Tank. Hunnicutt. Presidio Press, Novato, California. 1984.

Pershing, A History of the Medium Tank M20 Series. Hunnicutt. Feist Publications, Berkeley, California. 1971.

Pictorial History of Tanks of the World 1915-1945. Chamberlain and Ellis. Arms and Armor Press, London, England. 1972.

Portrait of Power. Jarret and Icks. Normount Technical Publications, Forest Grove, Oregon. 1971.

Principles of Automotive Vehicles, TM9-8000. Departments of the Army and the Air Force, Washington, D.C. 1956.

Scout-Cars and Half-Tracks. Boniface and Jeudy. Editions Presse Audiovisuel, Paris, France. 1989.

Self-Propelled Anti-Tank and Anti-Aircraft Guns. Chamberlain and Milsom. Arco Publishing Company Inc., New York, New York. 1975.

Sherman. Chamberlain and Ellis. Arco Publishing Company Inc., New York, New York. 1969.

Sherman, A History of the American Medium Tank. Hunnicutt. Taurus Enterprises. Belmont, California. 1978.

Sherman in Action. Culver. Squadron Signal Publications Inc., Warren, Michigan. 1977.

Standard Military Motor Vehicles. TM9-2800. War Department, Washington, D.C. 1943.

Stuart Light Tank Series. Perrett. Osprey Publishing Ltd., London, England. 1980.

Stuart U.S. Light Tanks in Action. Zaloga. Squadron Signal Publications Inc., Warren, Michigan. 1979.

Summary Report of Acceptances Tank and Automotive Materiel 1940-1945. Chief of Ordnance, Detroit Production Division, Requirements and Progress Branch. 1945.

Tank, A History of the Armoured Fighting Vehicle. Macksey and Batchelor. Random House Inc., New York, New York. 1971.

Tank Data 2. Hoffschmidt and Tantum. WE Inc., Old Greenwich, Connecticut. 1969.

Tank Data 3. Johnson. WE Inc., Old Greenwich, Connecticut. 1972.

Tanks, An Illustrated History of Fighting Vehicles. Halle. Crescent Books, New York, New York. 1971.

Tanks and Armored Vehicles 1900-1945. Icks. WE Inc., Old Greenwich, Connecticut.

Tanks Are Mighty Fine Things. Stout. Chrysler Corporation, Detroit, Michigan. 1946.

Tanks and Other A.F.V.'s 1942-1945. White. MacMillan Publishing Company Inc., New York, New York. 1976.

Tanks and Other Tracked Vehicles in Service. White. Blanford Press Ltd., Poole, Dorset, England. 1978.

U.S. Half-Tracks of World War II. Zaloga. Osprey Publishing Ltd., London, England. 1983.

U.S. Military Tracked Vehicles. Crismon. Motorbooks International, Osceola, Wisconsin. 1992.

U.S. Military Wheeled Vehicles. Crismon. Crestline Publishing, Sarasota, Florida. 1983.

U.S. Army Vehicles of World War Two. Boniface and Jeudy. Haynes Publishing Group, Somerset, England. 1991.

U.S. Army Military Vehicles WW2. Brooklands Book Distribution Ltd., Cobham, Surrey, England.

U.S. Military Vehicles World War 2. Hoffschmidt and Tantum. WE Inc., Old Greenwich, Connecticut. 1970.

United States Military Vehicles 1941-1945. Bryson. EMS Publications, Hong Kong.

V for Victory, America's Homefront During World War Two. Cohen. Pictorial Histories Publishing Company Inc., Missoula, Montana. 1991.

Vehicle Characteristics. The Armored School, Victory Memorial Museum, Belgium.

Wheels and Tracks. (All issues used for reference.) Battle of Britain Prints International Ltd., London, England.

Wheels of Time. (All issues used for reference.) American Truck Historical Society, Birmingham, Alabama.

World Directory of Modern Military Vehicles. Vanderveen. Arco Publishing Inc., New York, New York. 1984.

World War II U.S. Army Regulations for the Service and Field Uniforms. War Department, Washington, D.C. 1941.

Periodicals

Hemmings Motor News. Bennington, Vermont. 1985-1992.

Military Vehicles. (All issues used for reference.) Eagle Press, Union, New Jersey.

Army Motors and Supply Line. (All issues used for reference.) Military Vehicle Preservation Association, Independence, Missouri. 1976-1992.

Military TM's and Ord 7, 8, 9, as well as operator's manuals, were used on all vehicles.

ABOUT THE AUTHOR

"If it was green, buy it; if it has a star on it, own it!"

Tom Berndt's interest in military vehicles started when he was six years old. His first experience was with small Matchbox toys of the period. He began to collect them and quickly acquired the entire group of military items, which included American and British vehicles.

Next, Tom collected comic books for many years. Comic books led to modeling. Modeling developed a spatial aptitude for Tom. It was an invaluable tool in reading military manuals and identifying parts and vehicles in later years.

Tom graduated from high school in 1968 and then attended college. About a year later he joined the National Guard as an artilleryman in the 151st Field Artillery at the Minneapolis Armory.

Each month, as he went to National Guard meetings, he drove past the local military surplus company. His favorite vehicle was always the half-track, and, of course, they always had one in the front row. Tom ended up purchasing a very rare International Harvester half-track with 41.9 actual miles on it, and about two years later he restored it to its original condition. This was the beginning of extensive restorations, ownership and sales of military vehicles for Tom.

Tom attended his first military show and swap meet in 1975. His interests quickly spread to all types of vehicles. His research for vehicles led to friendships around the United States as well as tremendous parts accessibility. Each year, in addition to attending the shows, Tom made

sure he visited many surplus and salvage yards. He contacted individual collectors, interviewing them and examining their collections. Since 1974, he has seen most of the standard surplus in the United States. Many of these surplus companies are no longer in business.

In 1981, Tom began selling military vehicles and civilian trucks on a full-time basis. By this time he had owned, reconditioned and sold numerous vehicles of all types. This also included purchasing and reselling GSA surplus vehicles from western states.

From 1973 to the present, Tom has been almost constantly involved with some type of military vehicle. This constant exposure made book collecting a must. To date, he has about 2,500 books on vehicles. These include actual military vehicle manuals as well as numerous civilian reference books, of which many are out of print. The extensive traveling also gave him a tremendous opportunity to photograph endless types of vehicles.

Collecting, searching, parts sourcing, reconditioning and reselling -- combined with traveling, reading, manual collecting and photography -- have allowed Tom to write this book to help collectors and to spur interest in the hobby for all the people out there who have always wondered what a military vehicle is and how to get more information on it.

* * *

Tom, a native of Minneapolis, lives in Rogers, Minnesota with his wife of 20 years and two children.

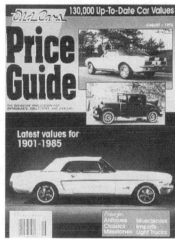